THE MELANCHOLY of SUZUMIYA
HARUHI-CHAN

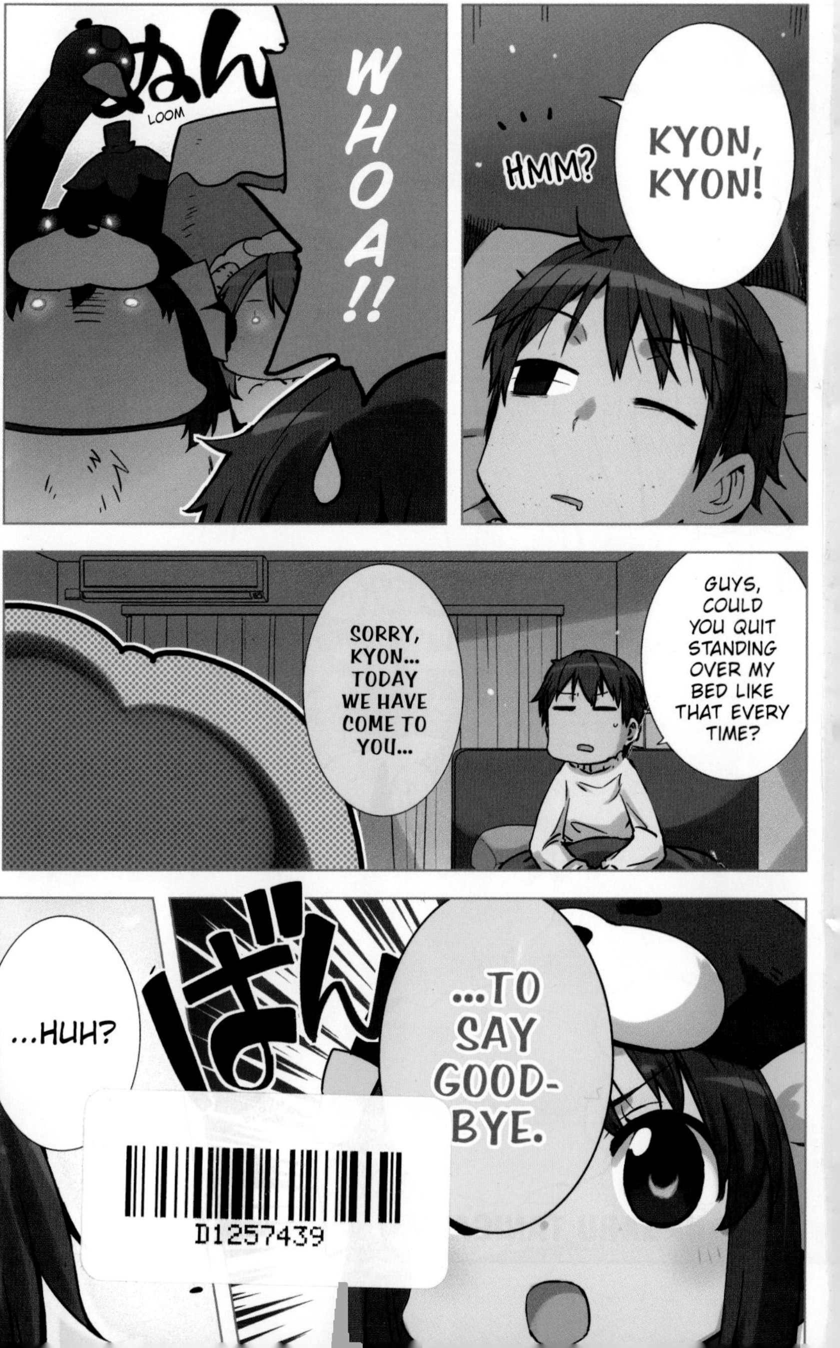
KYON, KYON!
HMM?
WHOA!!
ぬん
LOOM
GUYS, COULD YOU QUIT STANDING OVER MY BED LIKE THAT EVERY TIME?
SORRY, KYON... TODAY WE HAVE COME TO YOU...
...TO SAY GOOD-BYE.
ばん
...HUH?

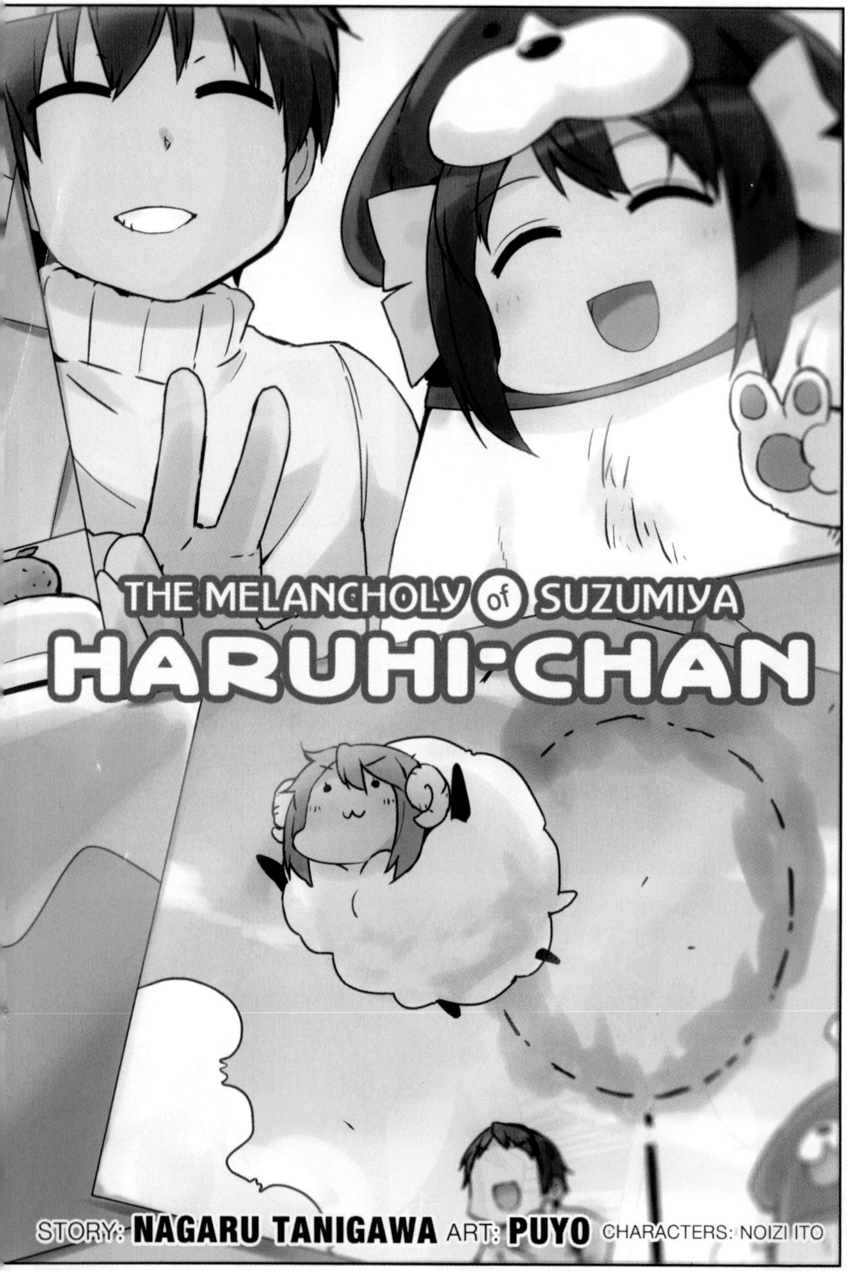
THE MELANCHOLY of SUZUMIYA
HARUHI-CHAN
STORY: NAGARU TANIGAWA ART: PUYO CHARACTERS: NOIZI ITO

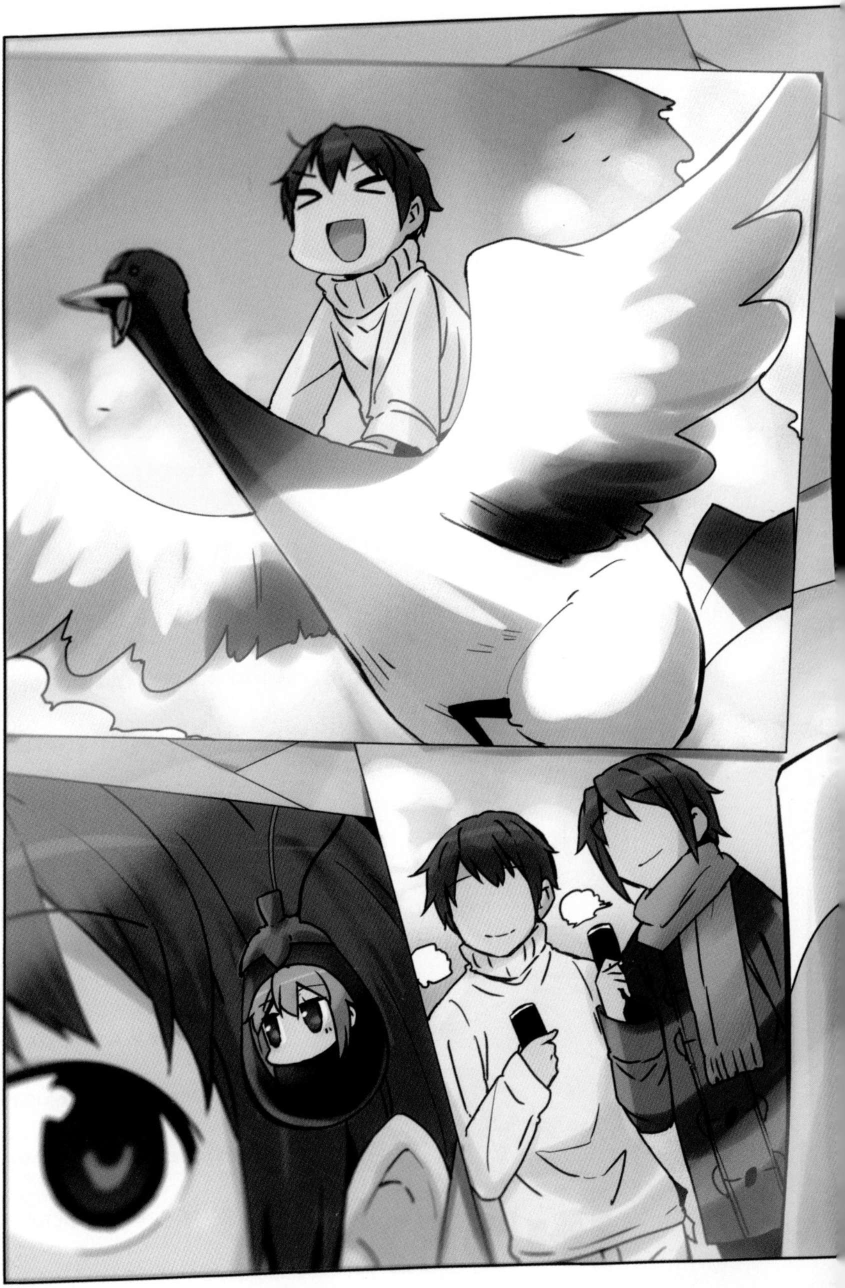

The Melancholy of Suzumiya Haruhi-chan 10

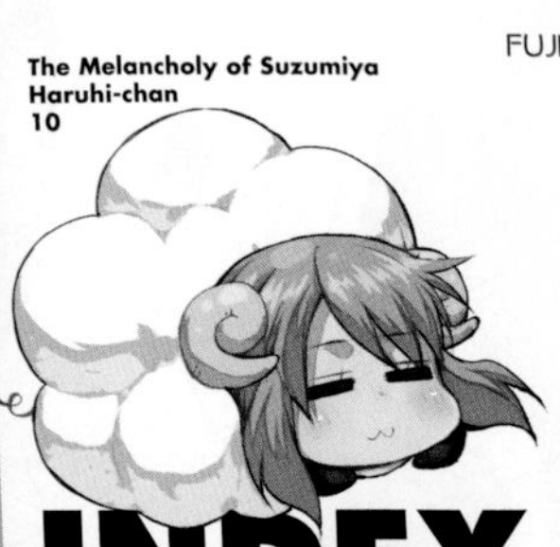

INDEX

THE MELANCHOLY of SUZUMIYA HARUHI-CHAN

The Untold Adventures of the SOS Brigade

10

fiction

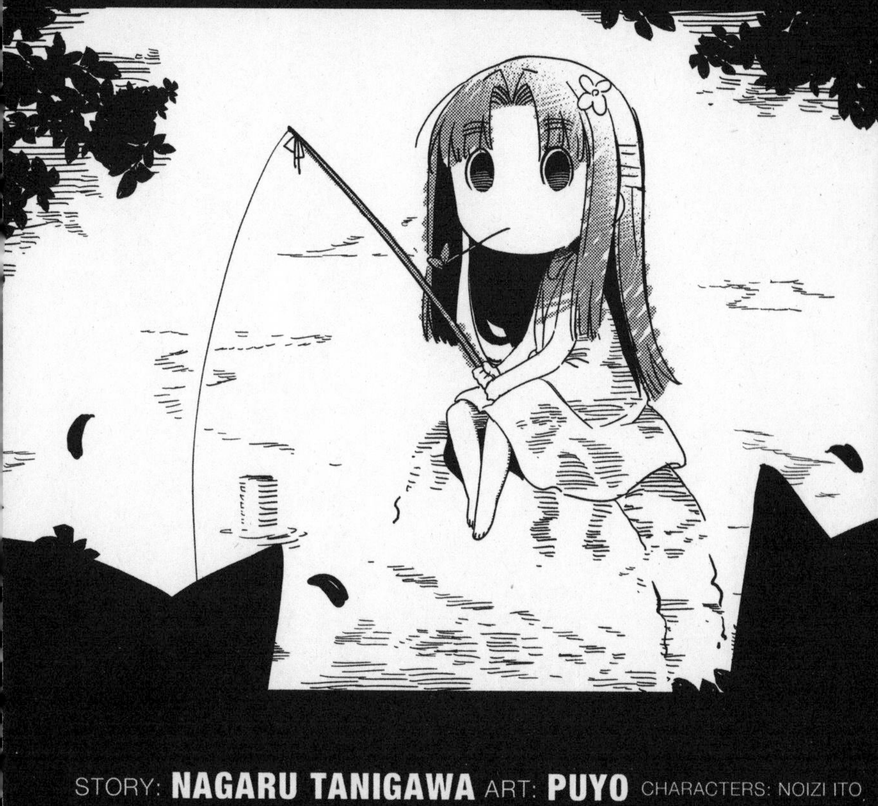

STORY: **NAGARU TANIGAWA** ART: **PUYO** CHARACTERS: NOIZI ITO

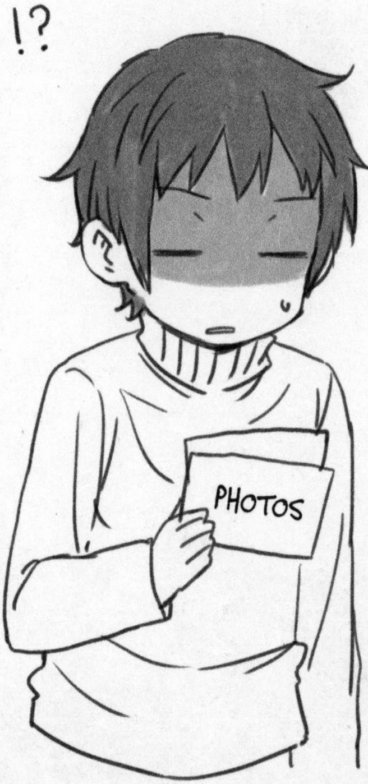
!?
PHOTOS

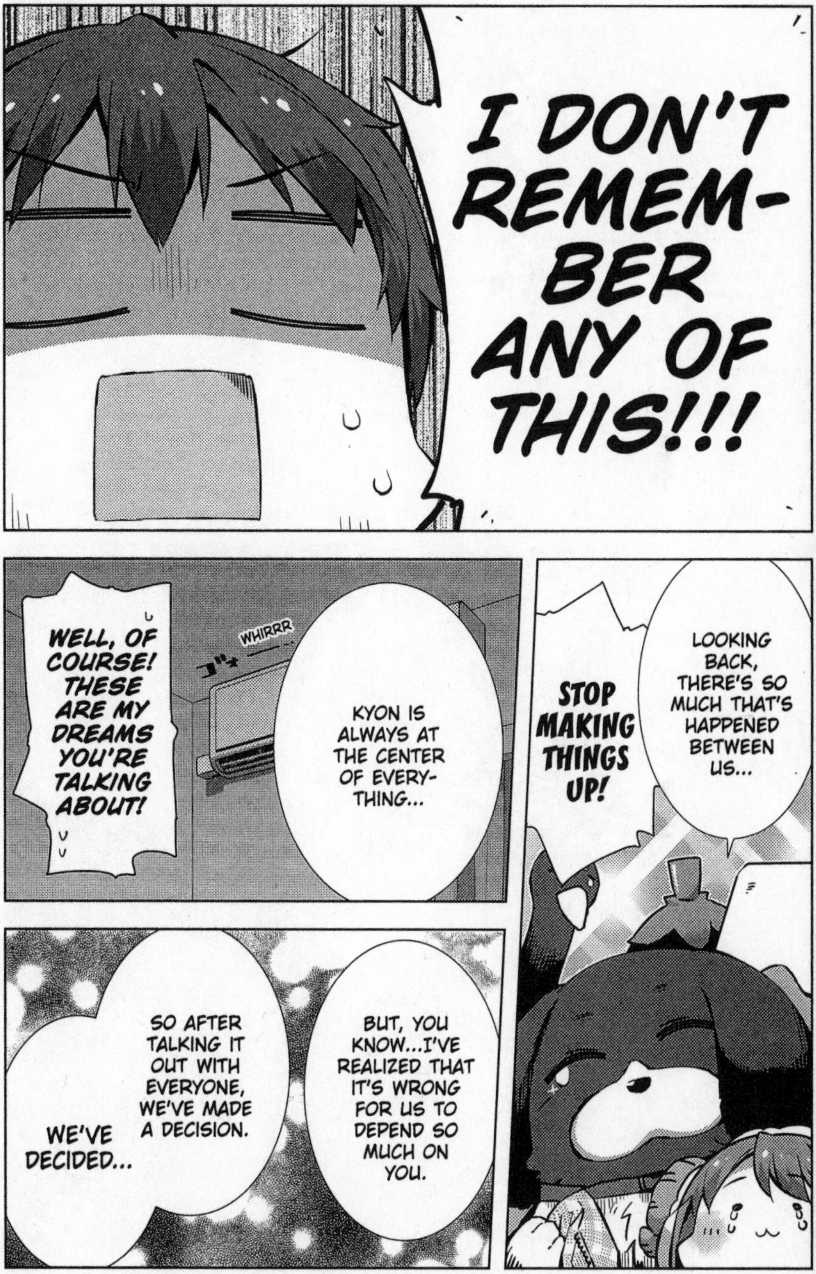
I DON'T REMEMBER ANY OF THIS!!!
LOOKING BACK, THERE'S SO MUCH THAT'S HAPPENED BETWEEN US...
STOP MAKING THINGS UP!
KYON IS ALWAYS AT THE CENTER OF EVERYTHING...
WHIRRR
WELL, OF COURSE! THESE ARE MY DREAMS YOU'RE TALKING ABOUT!
BUT, YOU KNOW...I'VE REALIZED THAT IT'S WRONG FOR US TO DEPEND SO MUCH ON YOU.
SO AFTER TALKING IT OUT WITH EVERYONE, WE'VE MADE A DECISION.
WE'VE DECIDED...

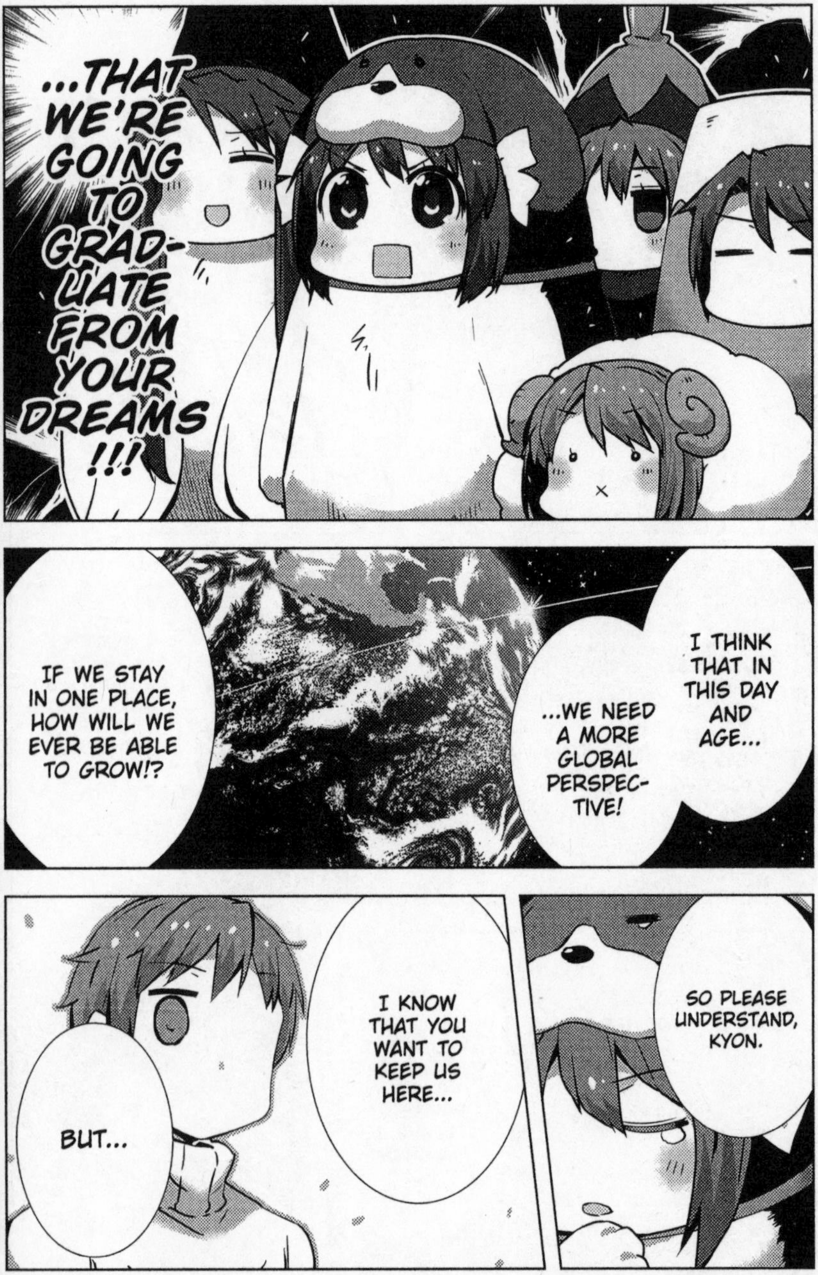
...THAT WE'RE GOING TO GRADUATE FROM YOUR DREAMS!!!
I THINK THAT IN THIS DAY AND AGE...
...WE NEED A MORE GLOBAL PERSPECTIVE!
IF WE STAY IN ONE PLACE, HOW WILL WE EVER BE ABLE TO GROW!?
SO PLEASE UNDERSTAND, KYON.
I KNOW THAT YOU WANT TO KEEP US HERE...
BUT...

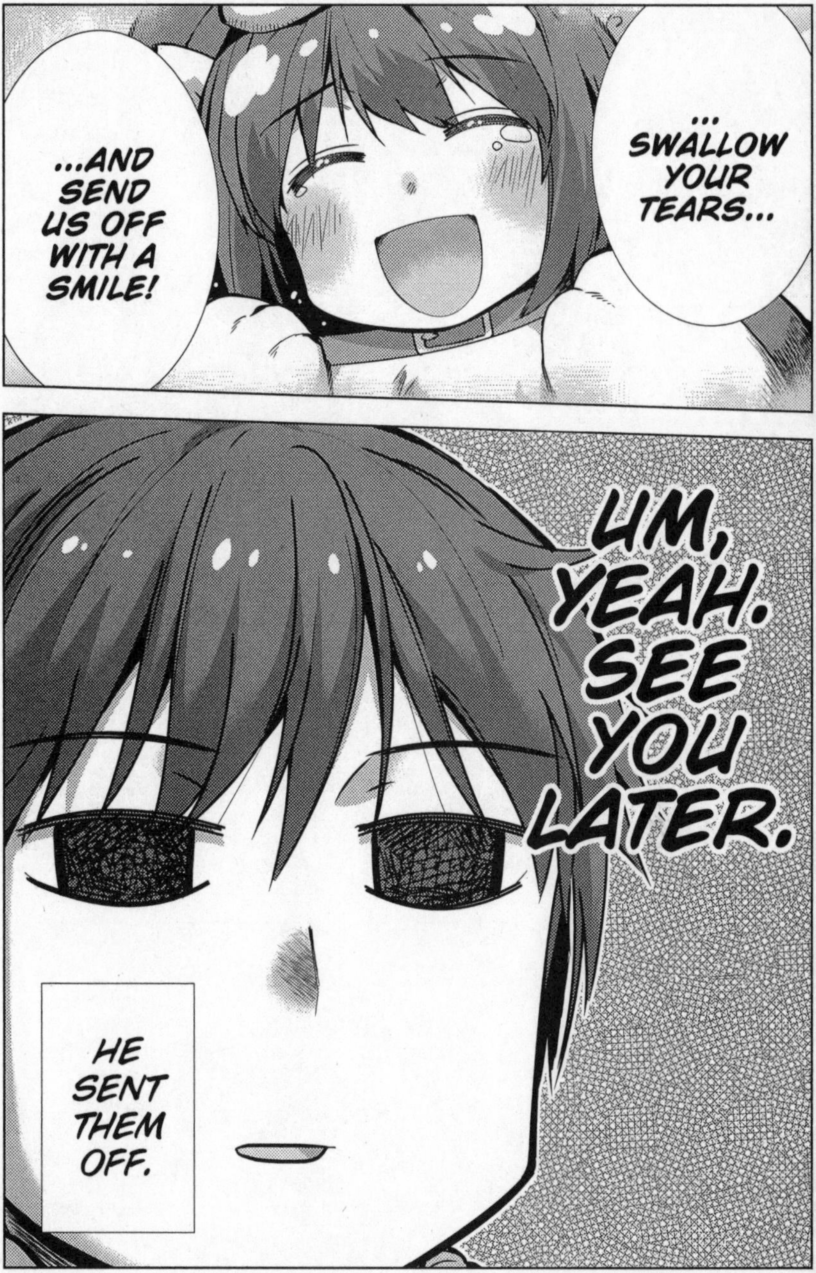
... SWALLOW YOUR TEARS...
...AND SEND US OFF WITH A SMILE!
UM, YEAH. SEE YOU LATER.
HE SENT THEM OFF.

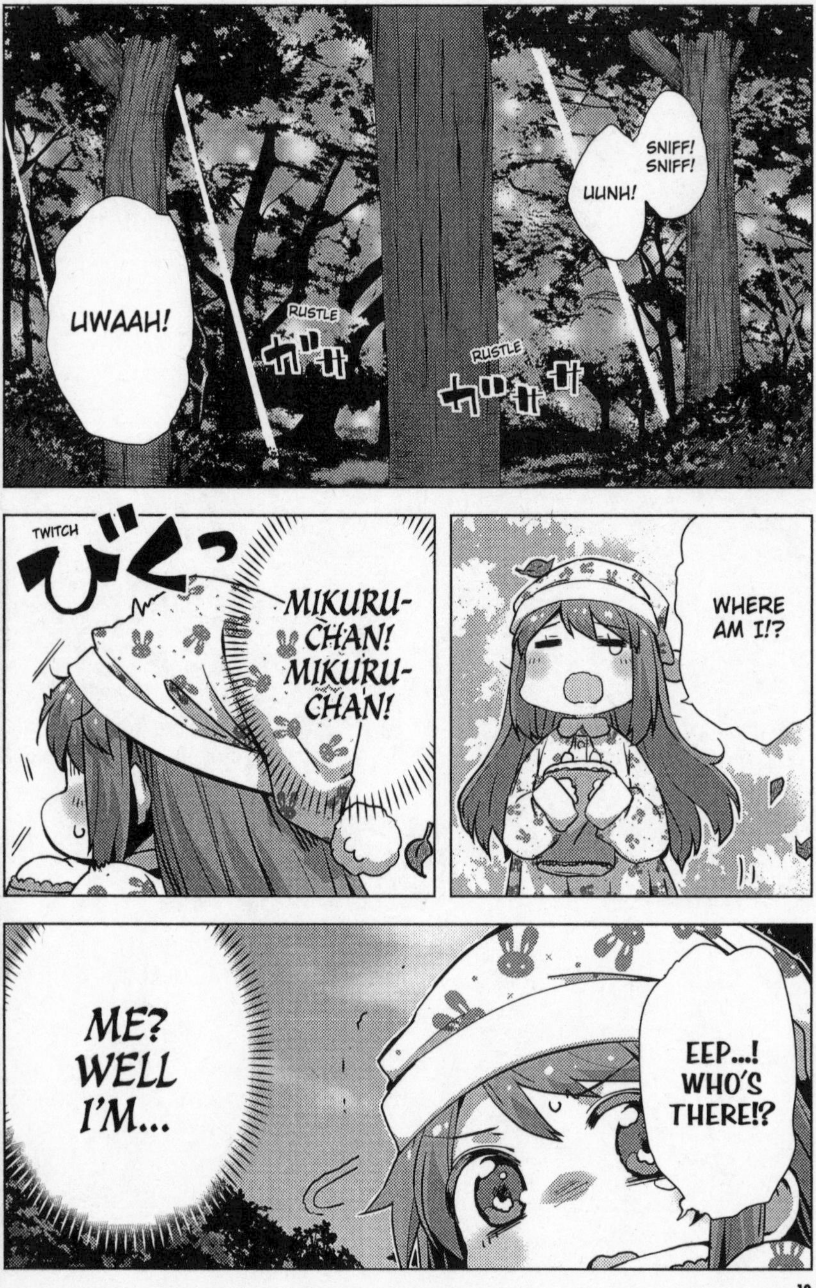
SNIFF! SNIFF!
UUNH!
RUSTLE
RUSTLE
UWAAH!
WHERE AM I!?
MIKURU-CHAN! MIKURU-CHAN!
TWITCH
びくっ
EEP...! WHO'S THERE!?
ME? WELL I'M...

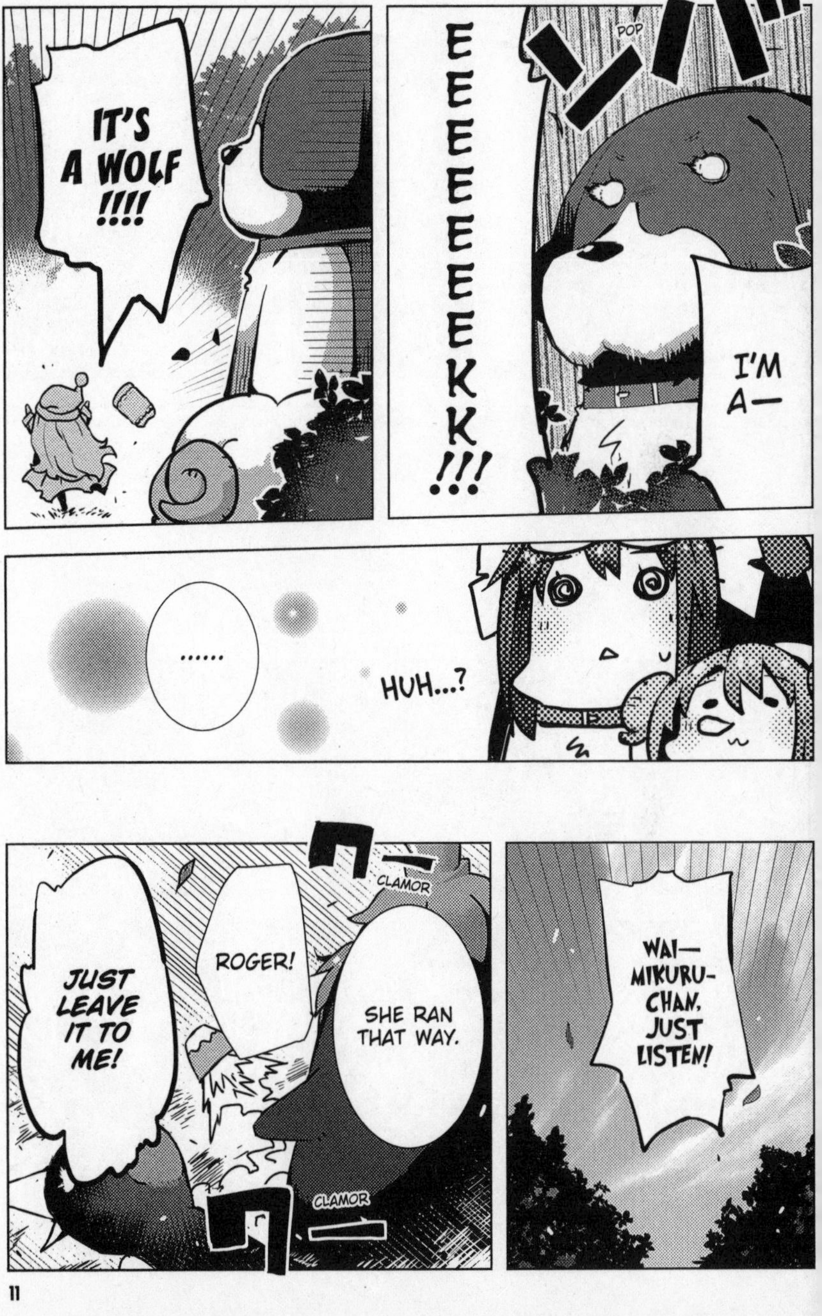
POP
I'M A—
EEEEEEEKK!!!
IT'S A WOLF!!!!
HUH...?
......
WAI— MIKURU-CHAN, JUST LISTEN!
CLAMOR
SHE RAN THAT WAY.
ROGER!
JUST LEAVE IT TO ME!
CLAMOR

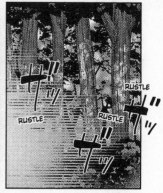

RUSTLE

RUSTLE RUSTLE

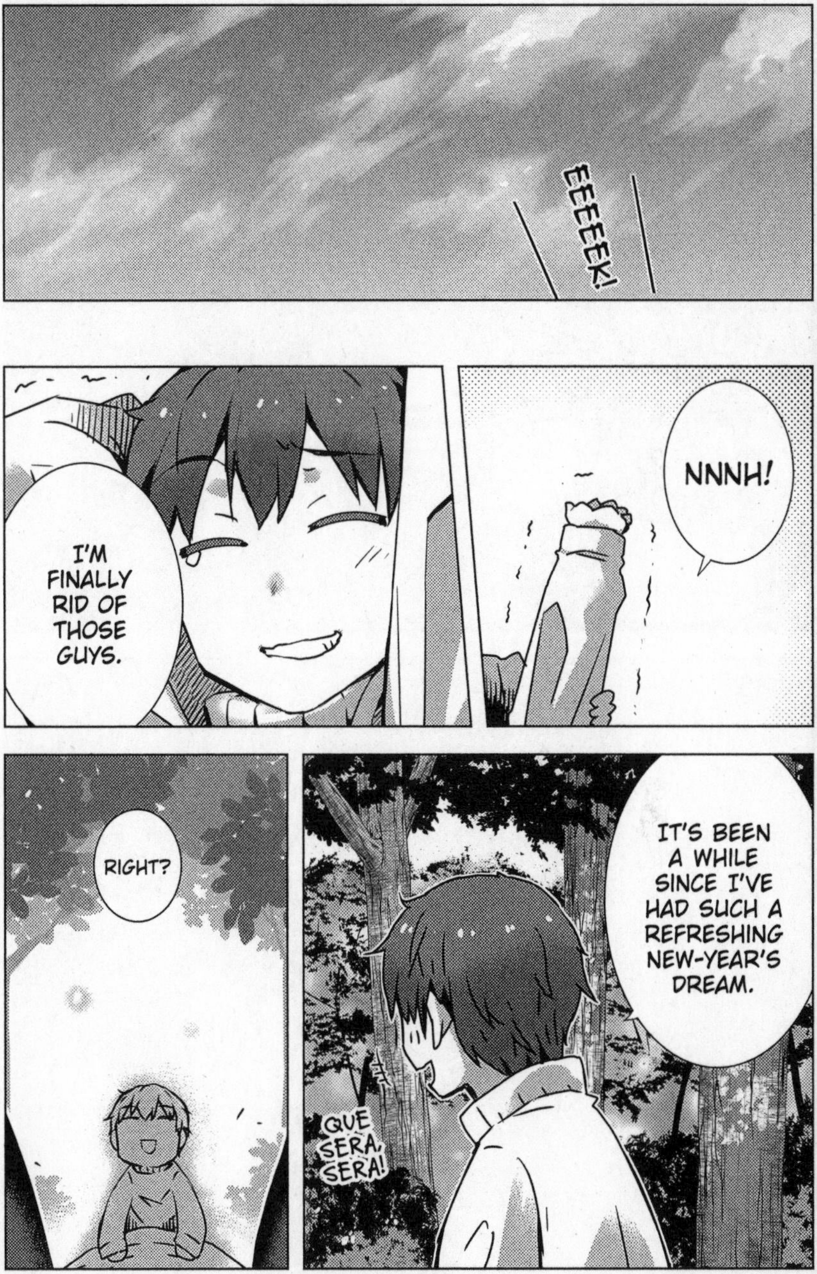
EEEEEK!
NNNH!
I'M FINALLY RID OF THOSE GUYS.
IT'S BEEN A WHILE SINCE I'VE HAD SUCH A REFRESHING NEW-YEAR'S DREAM.
QUE SERA, SERA!
RIGHT?

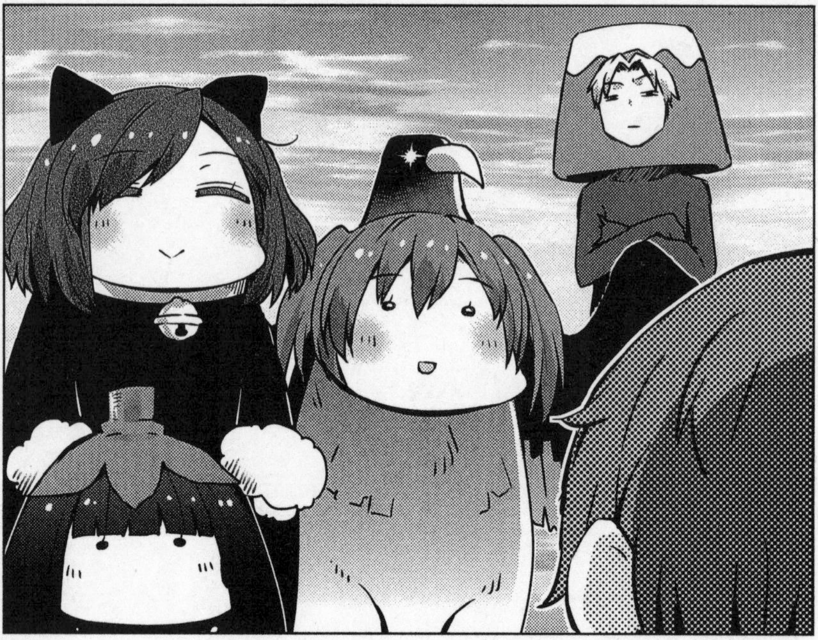

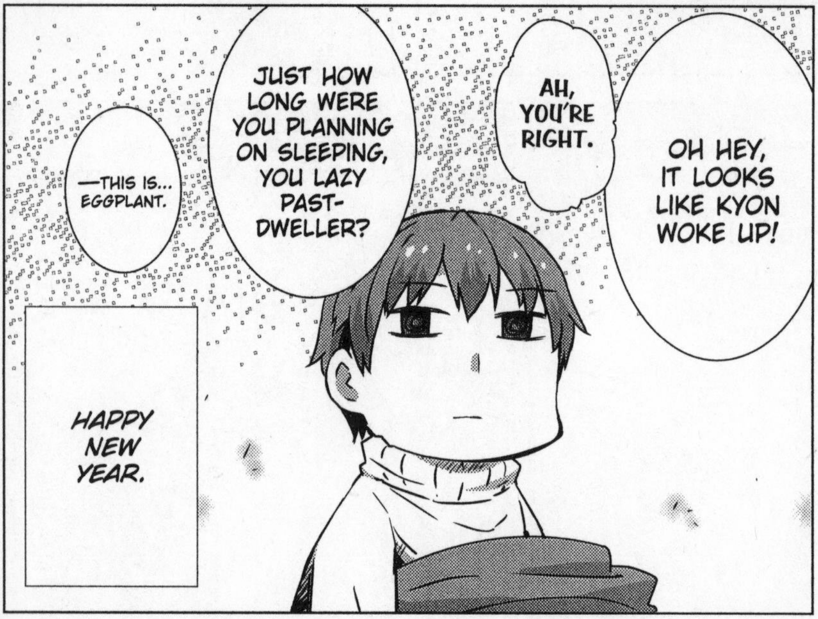
OH HEY, IT LOOKS LIKE KYON WOKE UP!
AH, YOU'RE RIGHT.
JUST HOW LONG WERE YOU PLANNING ON SLEEPING, YOU LAZY PAST-DWELLER?
—THIS IS... EGGPLANT.
HAPPY NEW YEAR.

TO BE
CONTINUED
IN THE
SECOND
HALF

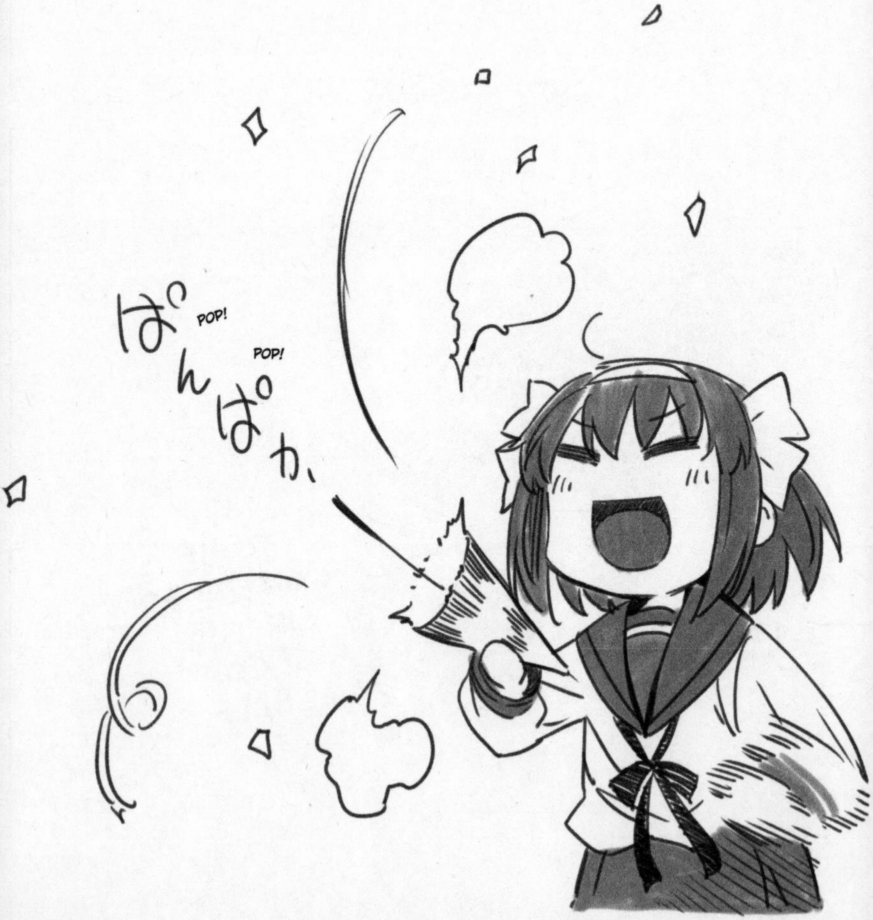
ぱんぱかー
POP!
POP!

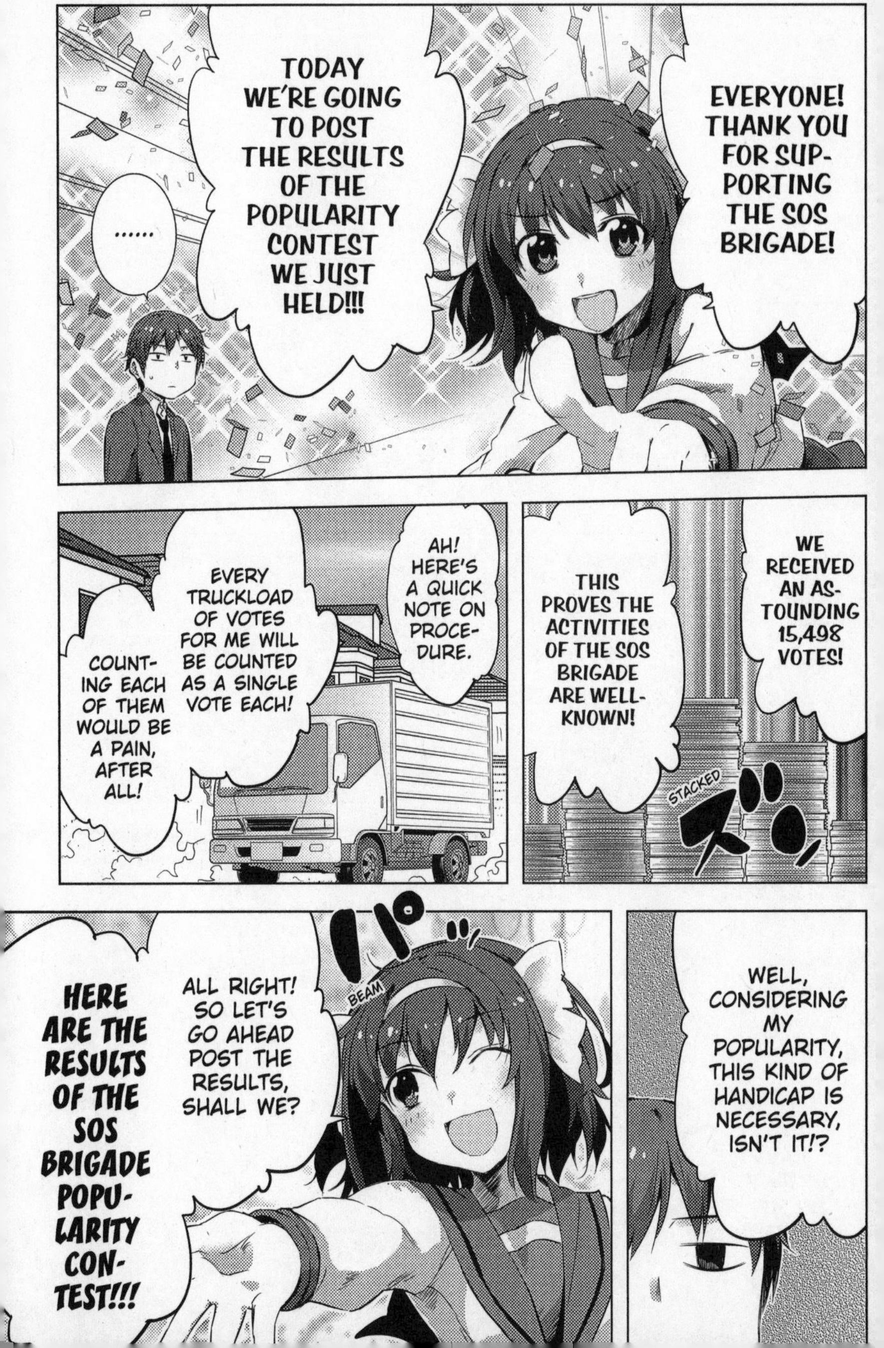
EVERYONE! THANK YOU FOR SUPPORTING THE SOS BRIGADE!
TODAY WE'RE GOING TO POST THE RESULTS OF THE POPULARITY CONTEST WE JUST HELD!!!
......
WE RECEIVED AN ASTOUNDING 15,498 VOTES!
THIS PROVES THE ACTIVITIES OF THE SOS BRIGADE ARE WELL-KNOWN!
STACKED
AH! HERE'S A QUICK NOTE ON PROCEDURE.
EVERY TRUCKLOAD OF VOTES FOR ME WILL BE COUNTED AS A SINGLE VOTE EACH!
COUNTING EACH OF THEM WOULD BE A PAIN, AFTER ALL!
WELL, CONSIDERING MY POPULARITY, THIS KIND OF HANDICAP IS NECESSARY, ISN'T IT!?
BEAM
ALL RIGHT! SO LET'S GO AHEAD POST THE RESULTS, SHALL WE?
HERE ARE THE RESULTS OF THE SOS BRIGADE POPULARITY CONTEST!!!

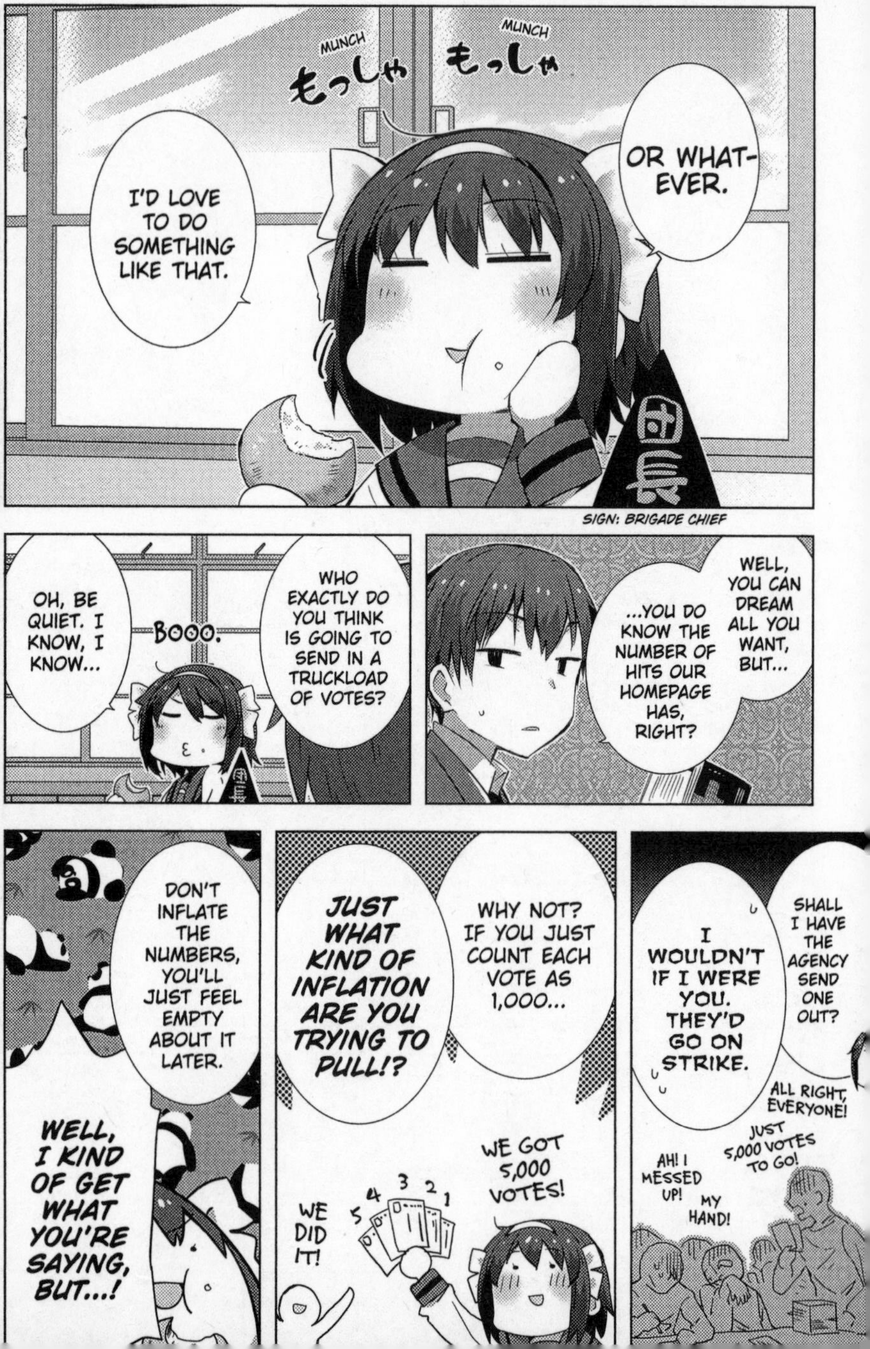
MUNCH
もっしゃ
MUNCH
もっしゃ
OR WHAT-EVER.
I'D LOVE TO DO SOMETHING LIKE THAT.
団長
SIGN: BRIGADE CHIEF
WELL, YOU CAN DREAM ALL YOU WANT, BUT...
...YOU DO KNOW THE NUMBER OF HITS OUR HOMEPAGE HAS, RIGHT?
WHO EXACTLY DO YOU THINK IS GOING TO SEND IN A TRUCKLOAD OF VOTES?
BOOO.
OH, BE QUIET. I KNOW, I KNOW...
SHALL I HAVE THE AGENCY SEND ONE OUT?
I WOULDN'T IF I WERE YOU. THEY'D GO ON STRIKE.
ALL RIGHT, EVERYONE!
JUST 5,000 VOTES TO GO!
AH! I MESSED UP!
MY HAND!
WHY NOT? IF YOU JUST COUNT EACH VOTE AS 1,000...
JUST WHAT KIND OF INFLATION ARE YOU TRYING TO PULL!?
WE GOT 5,000 VOTES!
1 2 3 4 5
WE DID IT!
DON'T INFLATE THE NUMBERS, YOU'LL JUST FEEL EMPTY ABOUT IT LATER.
WELL, I KIND OF GET WHAT YOU'RE SAYING, BUT...!

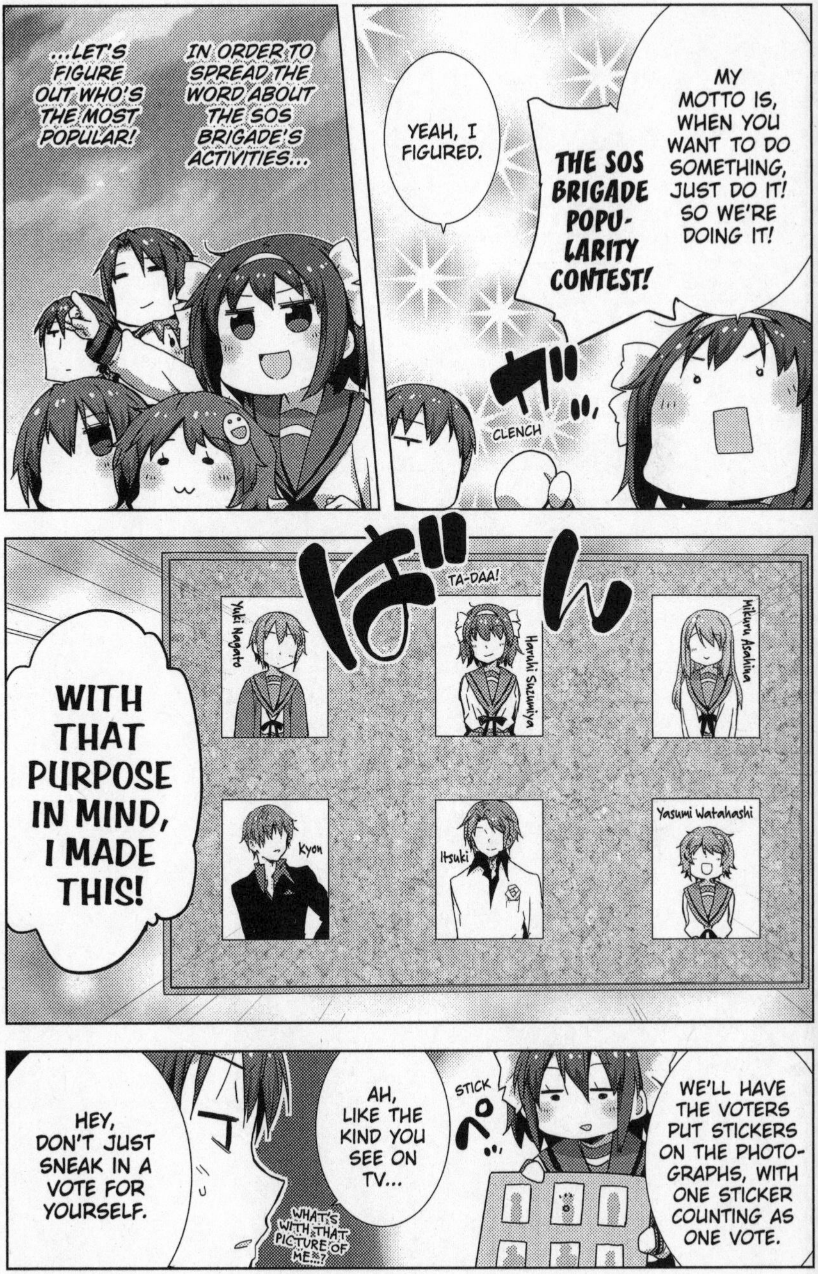
MY MOTTO IS, WHEN YOU WANT TO DO SOMETHING, JUST DO IT! SO WE'RE DOING IT!
THE SOS BRIGADE POPULARITY CONTEST!
YEAH, I FIGURED.
CLENCH
IN ORDER TO SPREAD THE WORD ABOUT THE SOS BRIGADE'S ACTIVITIES...
...LET'S FIGURE OUT WHO'S THE MOST POPULAR!
ばん
TA-DAA!
Mikuru Asahina
Haruhi Suzumiya
Yuki Nagato
Yasumi Watahashi
Itsuki
Kyon
WITH THAT PURPOSE IN MIND, I MADE THIS!
WE'LL HAVE THE VOTERS PUT STICKERS ON THE PHOTOGRAPHS, WITH ONE STICKER COUNTING AS ONE VOTE.
STICK
AH, LIKE THE KIND YOU SEE ON TV...
WHAT'S WITH THAT PICTURE OF ME...?
HEY, DON'T JUST SNEAK IN A VOTE FOR YOURSELF.

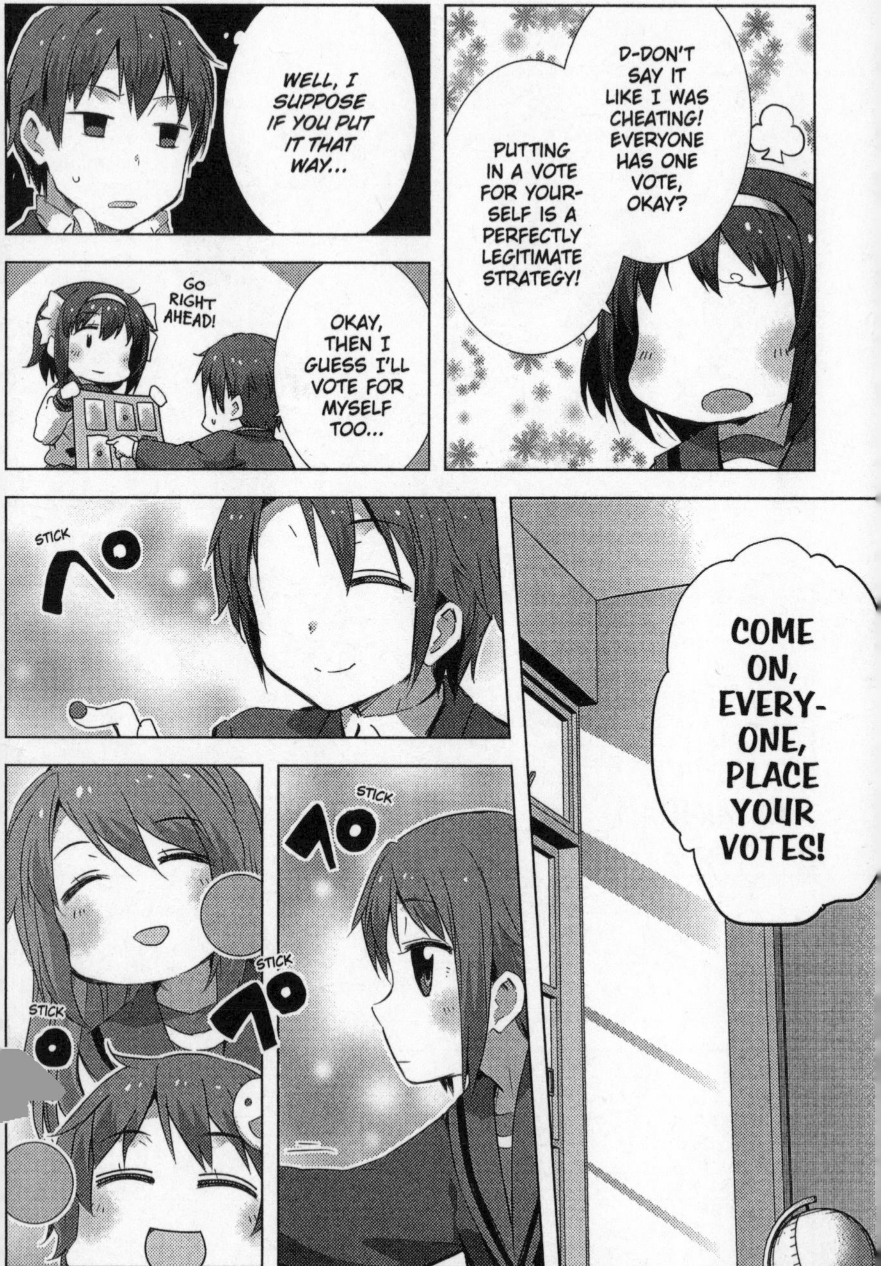
D-DON'T SAY IT LIKE I WAS CHEATING! EVERYONE HAS ONE VOTE, OKAY?
PUTTING IN A VOTE FOR YOUR-SELF IS A PERFECTLY LEGITIMATE STRATEGY!
WELL, I SUPPOSE IF YOU PUT IT THAT WAY...
OKAY, THEN I GUESS I'LL VOTE FOR MYSELF TOO...
GO RIGHT AHEAD!
COME ON, EVERY-ONE, PLACE YOUR VOTES!
STICK
STICK
STICK
STICK

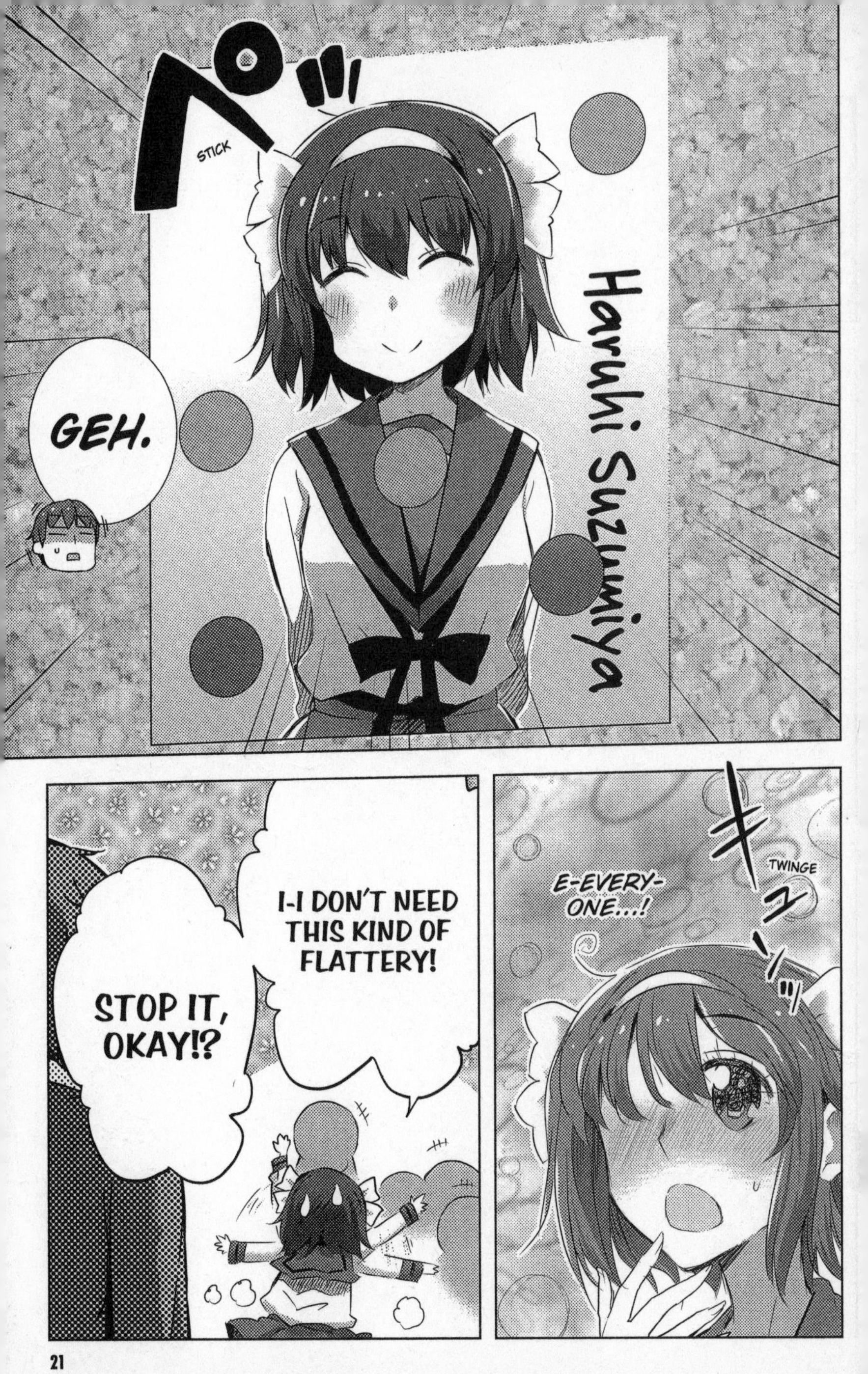
STICK
Haruhi Suzumiya
GEH.
TWINGE
E-EVERY-ONE...!
I-I DON'T NEED THIS KIND OF FLATTERY!
STOP IT, OKAY!?

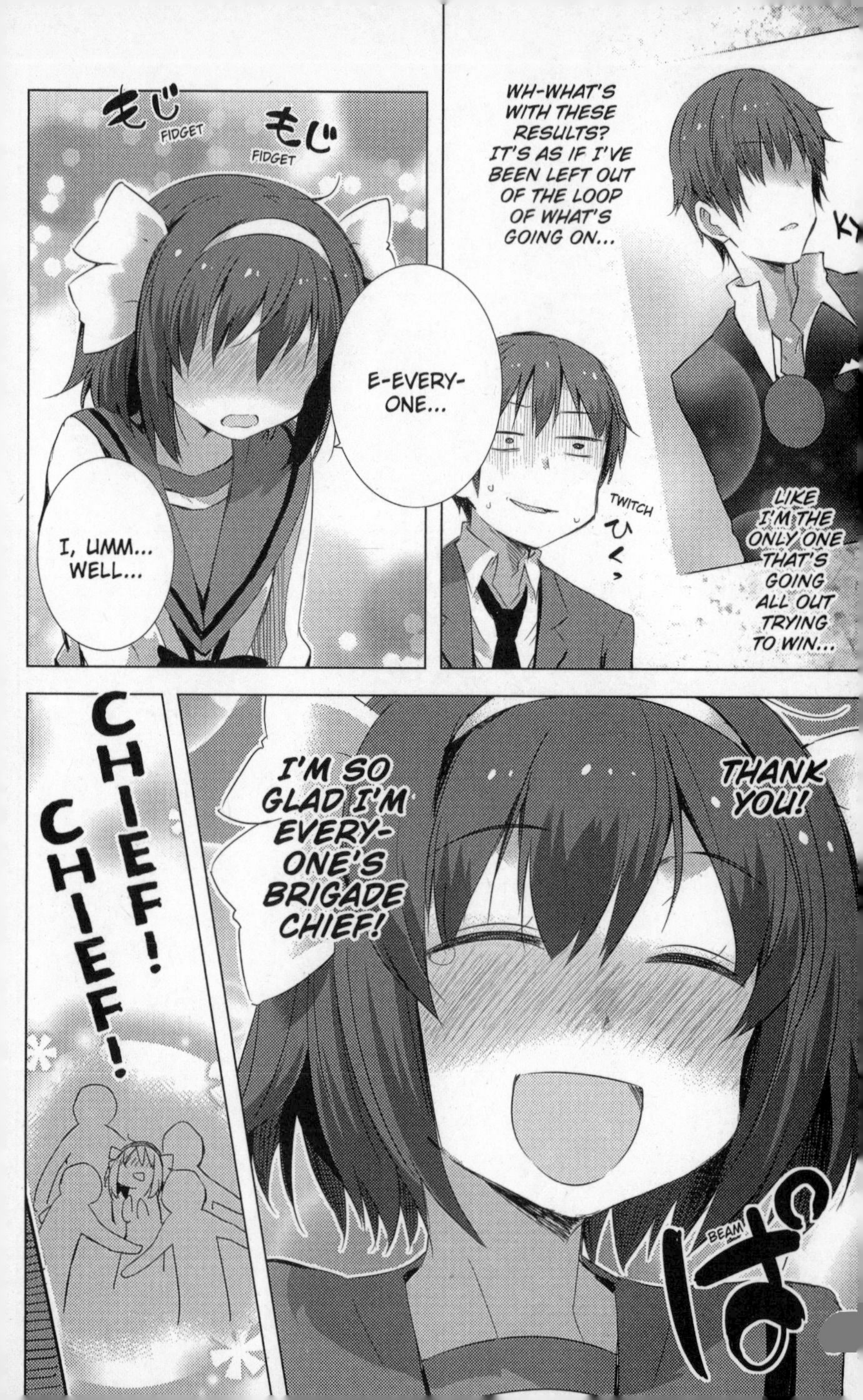
WH-WHAT'S WITH THESE RESULTS? IT'S AS IF I'VE BEEN LEFT OUT OF THE LOOP OF WHAT'S GOING ON...
LIKE I'M THE ONLY ONE THAT'S GOING ALL OUT TRYING TO WIN...
TWITCH
もじ
FIDGET
もじ
FIDGET
E-EVERY-ONE...
I, UMM... WELL...
THANK YOU!
I'M SO GLAD I'M EVERY-ONE'S BRIGADE CHIEF!
BEAM
CHIEF!
CHIEF!

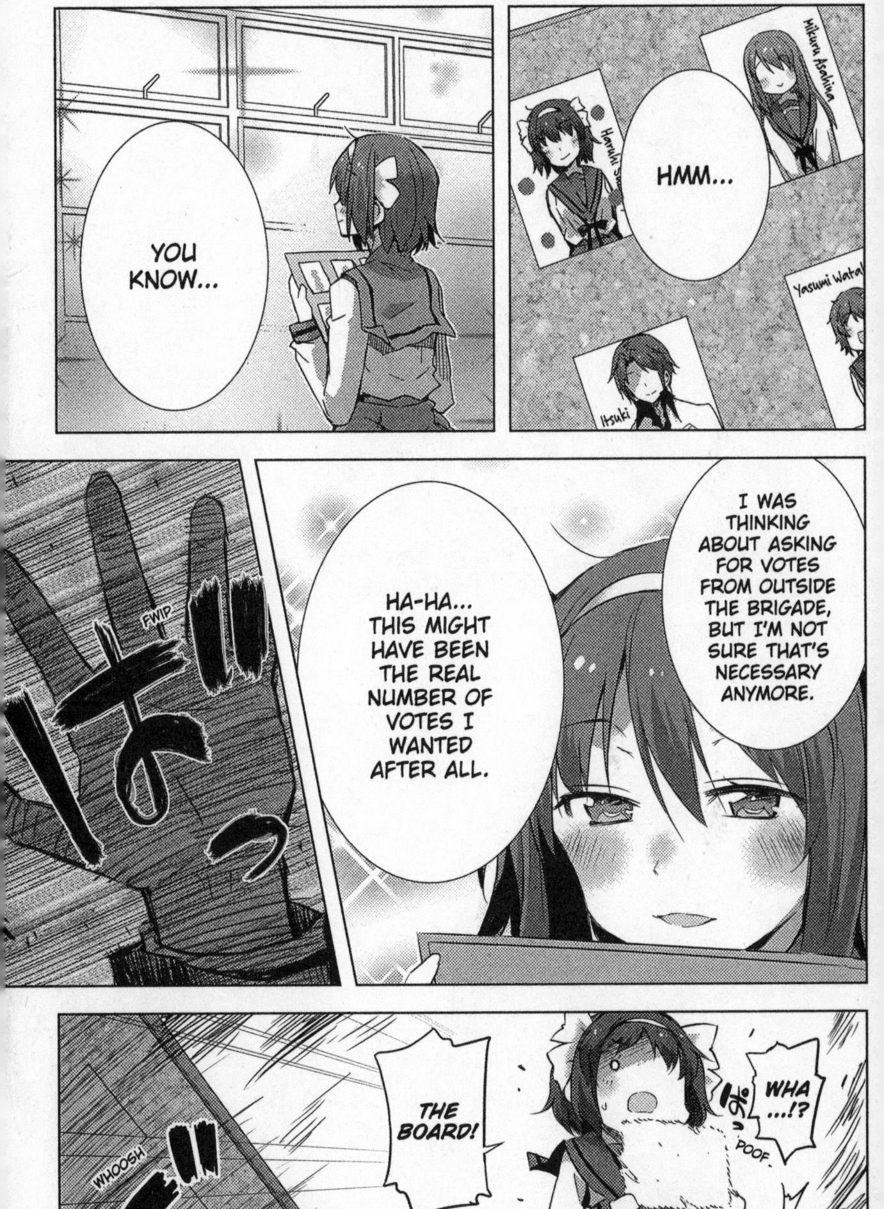
Mikuru Asahina
HMM...
Itsuki
YOU KNOW...
I WAS THINKING ABOUT ASKING FOR VOTES FROM OUTSIDE THE BRIGADE, BUT I'M NOT SURE THAT'S NECESSARY ANYMORE.
HA-HA... THIS MIGHT HAVE BEEN THE REAL NUMBER OF VOTES I WANTED AFTER ALL.
FWIP
WHA ...!?
POOF
THE BOARD!
WHOOSH

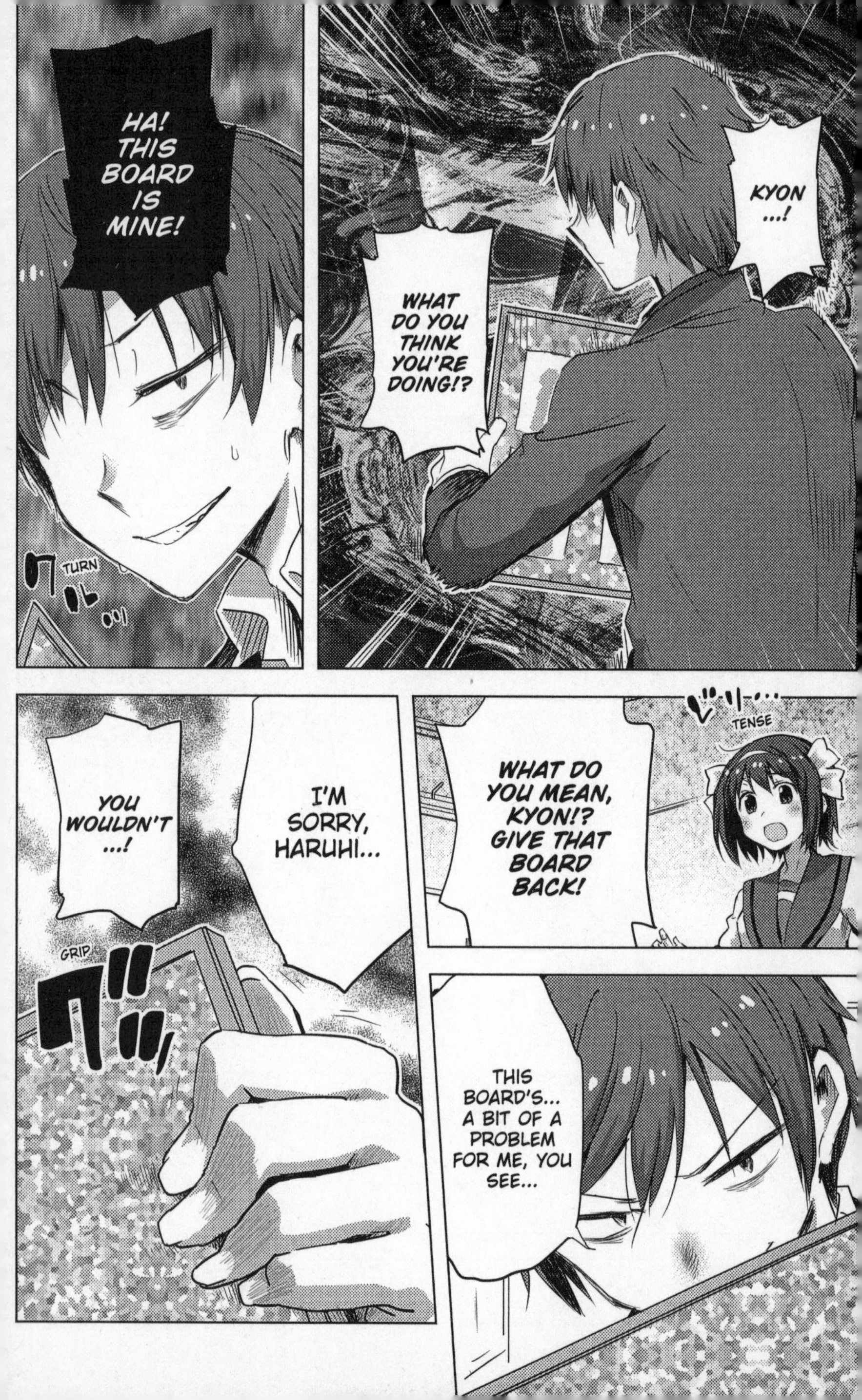
KYON ...!
WHAT DO YOU THINK YOU'RE DOING!?
HA! THIS BOARD IS MINE!
TURN
TENSE
WHAT DO YOU MEAN, KYON!? GIVE THAT BOARD BACK!
THIS BOARD'S... A BIT OF A PROBLEM FOR ME, YOU SEE...
I'M SORRY, HARUHI...
YOU WOULDN'T ...!
GRIP

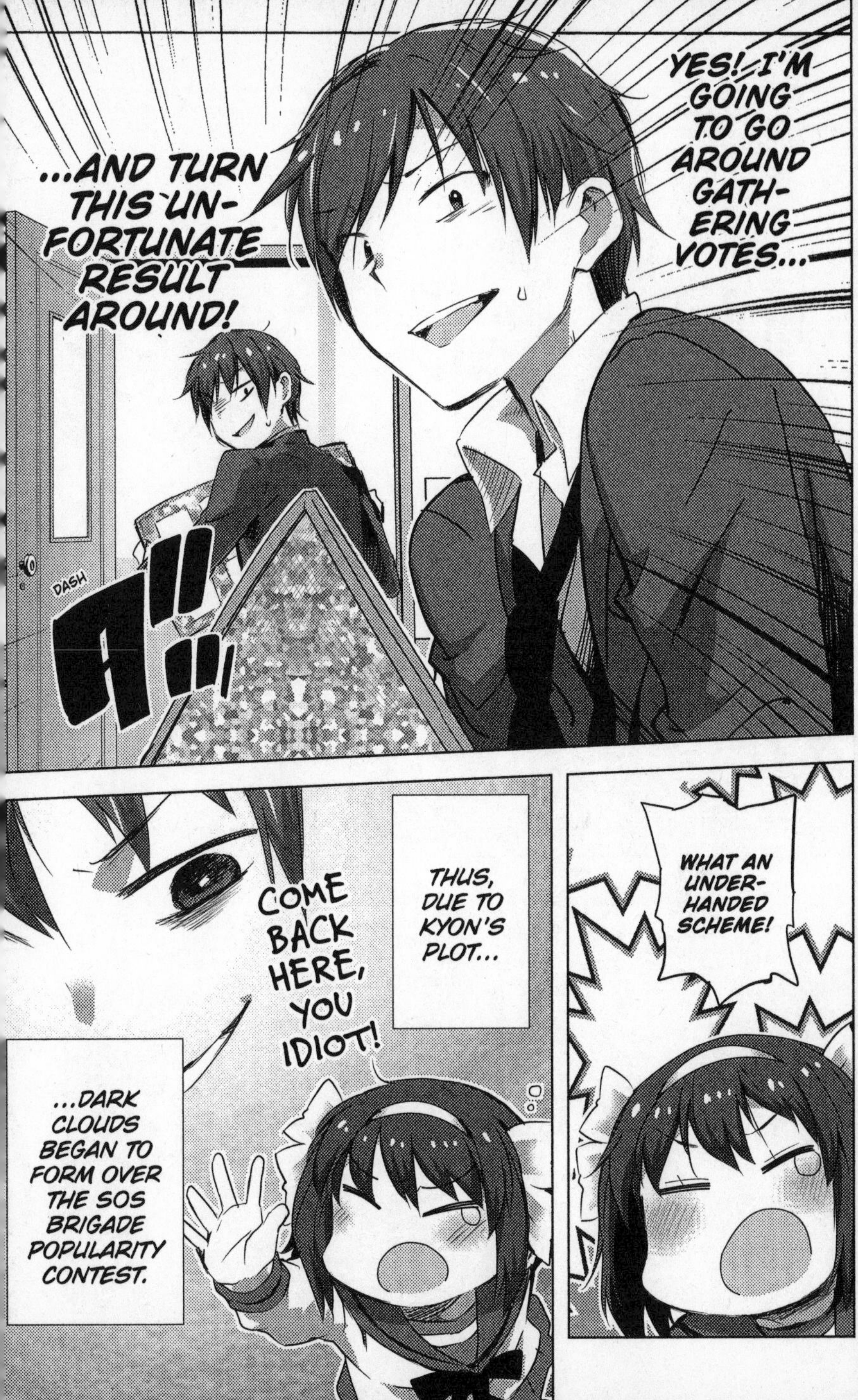
YES! I'M GOING TO GO AROUND GATH-ERING VOTES...
...AND TURN THIS UN-FORTUNATE RESULT AROUND!
DASH
WHAT AN UNDER-HANDED SCHEME!
THUS, DUE TO KYON'S PLOT...
COME BACK HERE, YOU IDIOT!
...DARK CLOUDS BEGAN TO FORM OVER THE SOS BRIGADE POPULARITY CONTEST.

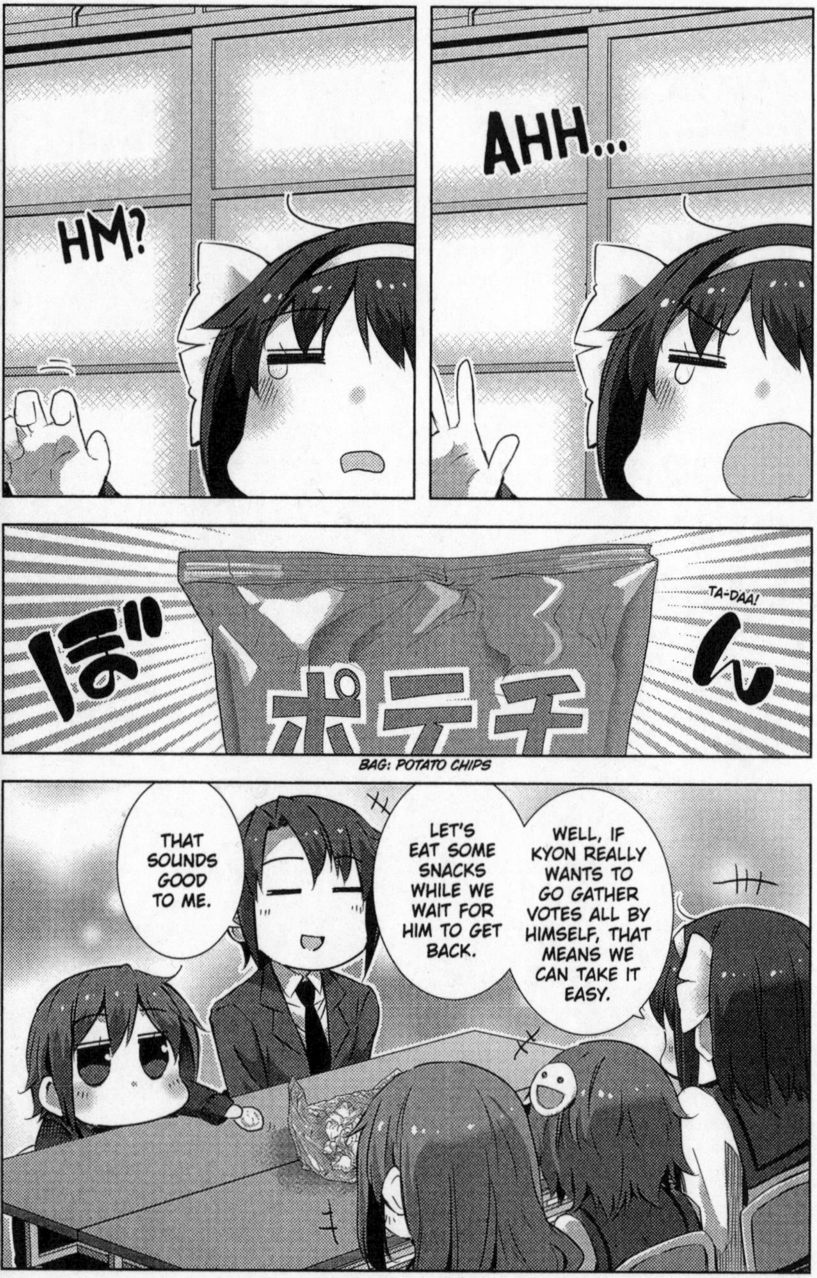
AHH...
HM?
ぼ
TA-DAA!
ん
ポテチ
BAG: POTATO CHIPS
WELL, IF KYON REALLY WANTS TO GO GATHER VOTES ALL BY HIMSELF, THAT MEANS WE CAN TAKE IT EASY.
LET'S EAT SOME SNACKS WHILE WE WAIT FOR HIM TO GET BACK.
THAT SOUNDS GOOD TO ME.

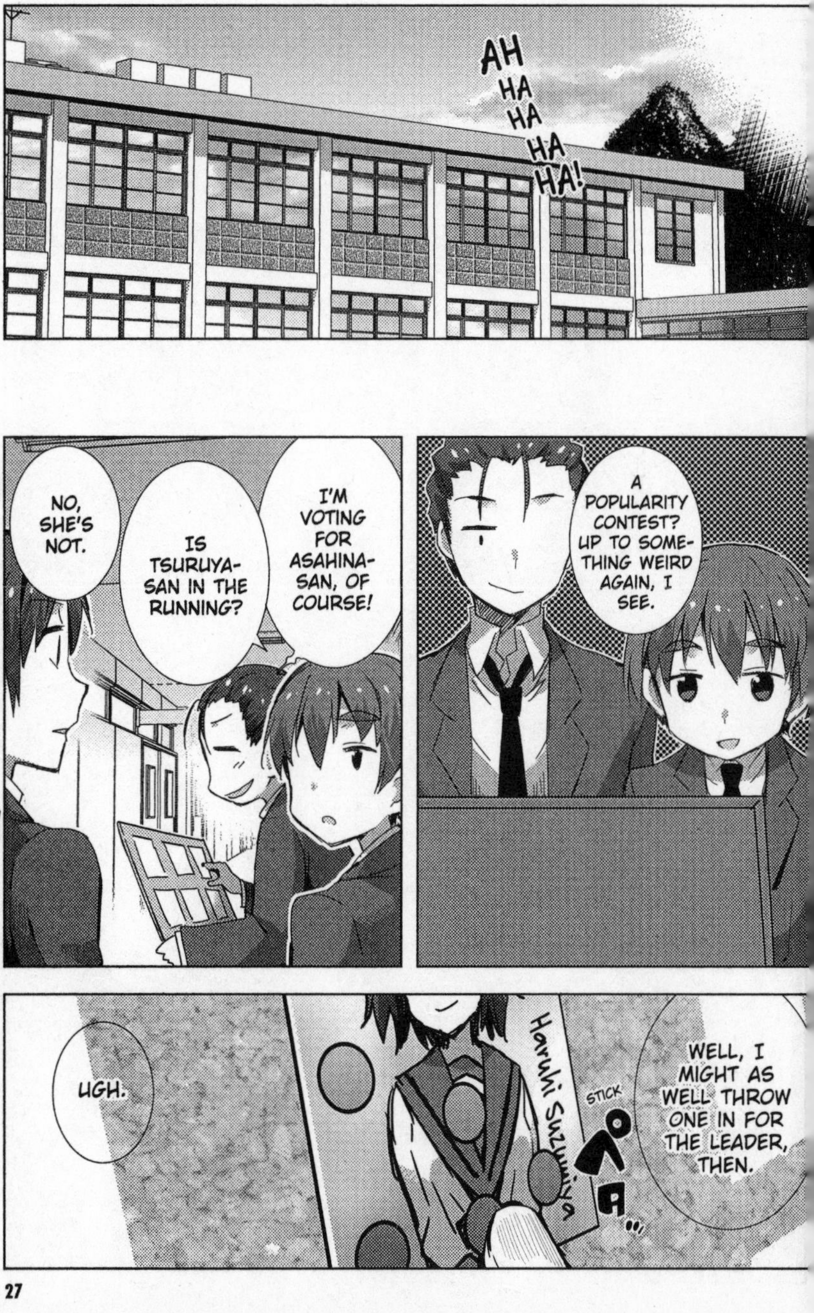
AH HA HA HA HA!
A POPULARITY CONTEST? UP TO SOMETHING WEIRD AGAIN, I SEE.
I'M VOTING FOR ASAHINA-SAN, OF COURSE!
IS TSURUYA-SAN IN THE RUNNING?
NO, SHE'S NOT.
WELL, I MIGHT AS WELL THROW ONE IN FOR THE LEADER, THEN.
STICK
Haruhi Suzumiya
UGH.

•Mikuru Asahina •Vote received from the Pervert Demographic: 1 vote total

•Haruhi Suzumiya •Votes received from strong preexisting support base: 6 votes total

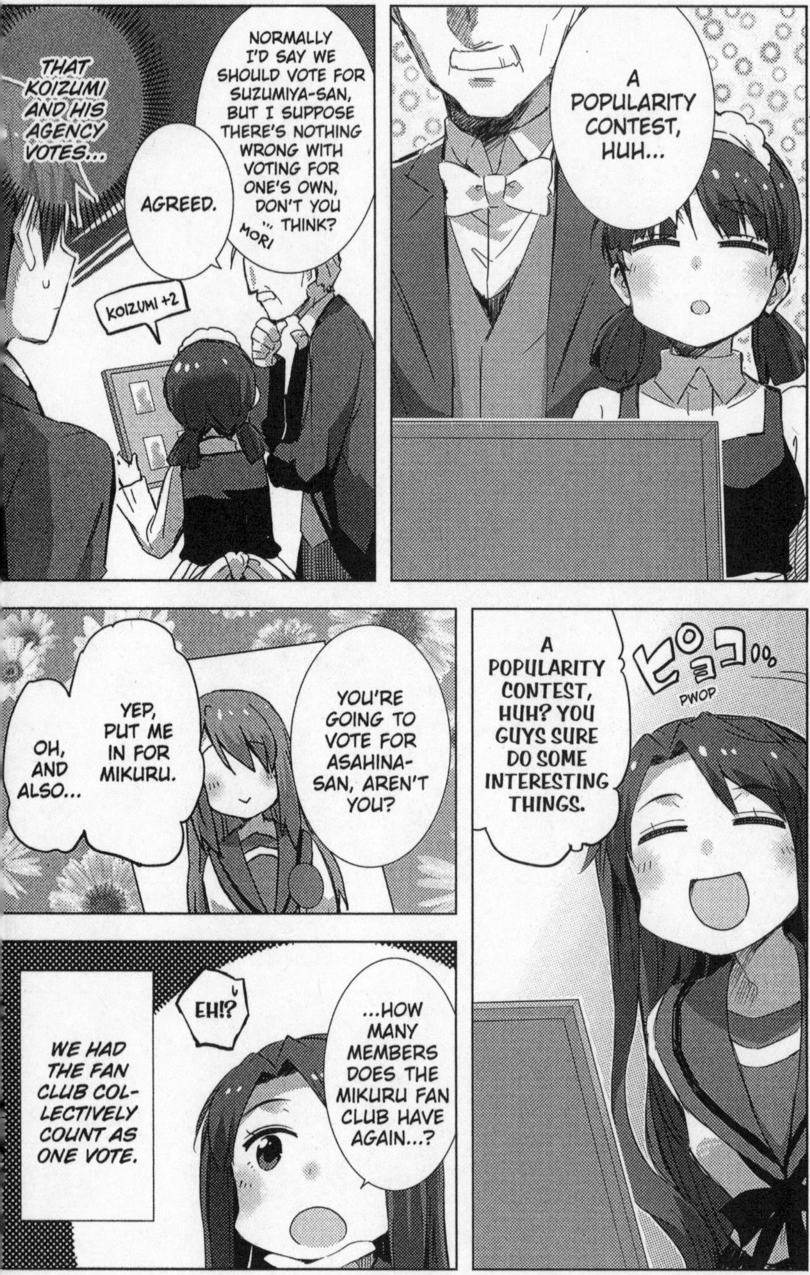
A POPULARITY CONTEST, HUH...
NORMALLY I'D SAY WE SHOULD VOTE FOR SUZUMIYA-SAN, BUT I SUPPOSE THERE'S NOTHING WRONG WITH VOTING FOR ONE'S OWN, DON'T YOU THINK?
MORI
AGREED.
KOIZUMI +2
THAT KOIZUMI AND HIS AGENCY VOTES...
PWOP
A POPULARITY CONTEST, HUH? YOU GUYS SURE DO SOME INTERESTING THINGS.
YOU'RE GOING TO VOTE FOR ASAHINA-SAN, AREN'T YOU?
YEP, PUT ME IN FOR MIKURU.
OH, AND ALSO...
...HOW MANY MEMBERS DOES THE MIKURU FAN CLUB HAVE AGAIN...?
EH!?
WE HAD THE FAN CLUB COLLECTIVELY COUNT AS ONE VOTE.

•Itsuki Koizumi •Votes received from the Agency: 2 votes total

•Mikuru Asahina •Two votes received from reliable voters: 3 votes total

TEAM SASAKI
WELL, I GUESS I'LL VOTE FOR KOIZUMI-SAN BECAUSE HE'S ALWAYS HELPING ME OUT...
I THINK I'LL VOTE FOR KYON, THEN.
YES! I BELIEVED IN YOU, SASAKI!
HMPH. YOU SURE CALLED US OUT FOR A DUMB REASON. IT'S BECAUSE OF THINGS THAT LIKE THIS, I CAN'T HANDLE BRATS LIKE YOU...
YEAH, ALL RIGHT. SORRY ABOUT THAT.
WELL THEN, I'LL BE SEEING YA.
W-WAIT!!!
IF YOU INSIST, I'LL PLAY ALONG! MIKURU ASAHINA! I VOTE FOR MIKURU ASAHINA!
YEAH, YEAH, I KNOW.

•Itsuki Koizumi •As might be expected given his connections: 3 votes total

•Kyon •Finally receives a vote: 2 votes total

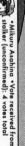

•Mikuru Asahina •Vote received from stalker (unconfirmed): 4 votes total

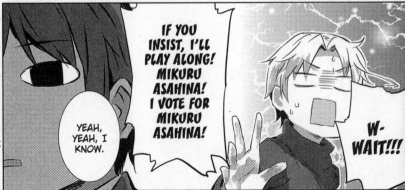

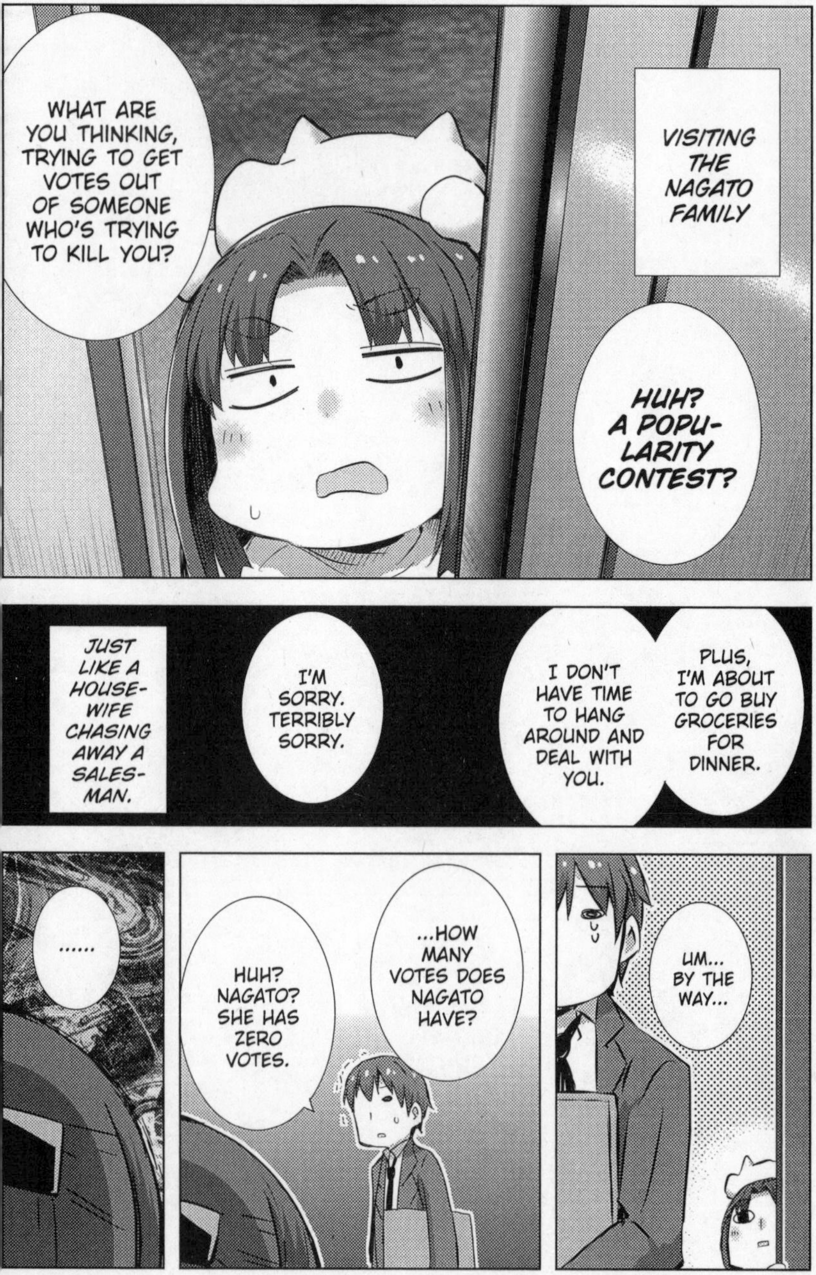
VISITING THE NAGATO FAMILY
HUH? A POPULARITY CONTEST?
WHAT ARE YOU THINKING, TRYING TO GET VOTES OUT OF SOMEONE WHO'S TRYING TO KILL YOU?
PLUS, I'M ABOUT TO GO BUY GROCERIES FOR DINNER.
I DON'T HAVE TIME TO HANG AROUND AND DEAL WITH YOU.
I'M SORRY. TERRIBLY SORRY.
JUST LIKE A HOUSEWIFE CHASING AWAY A SALESMAN.
UM... BY THE WAY...
...HOW MANY VOTES DOES NAGATO HAVE?
HUH? NAGATO? SHE HAS ZERO VOTES.
......

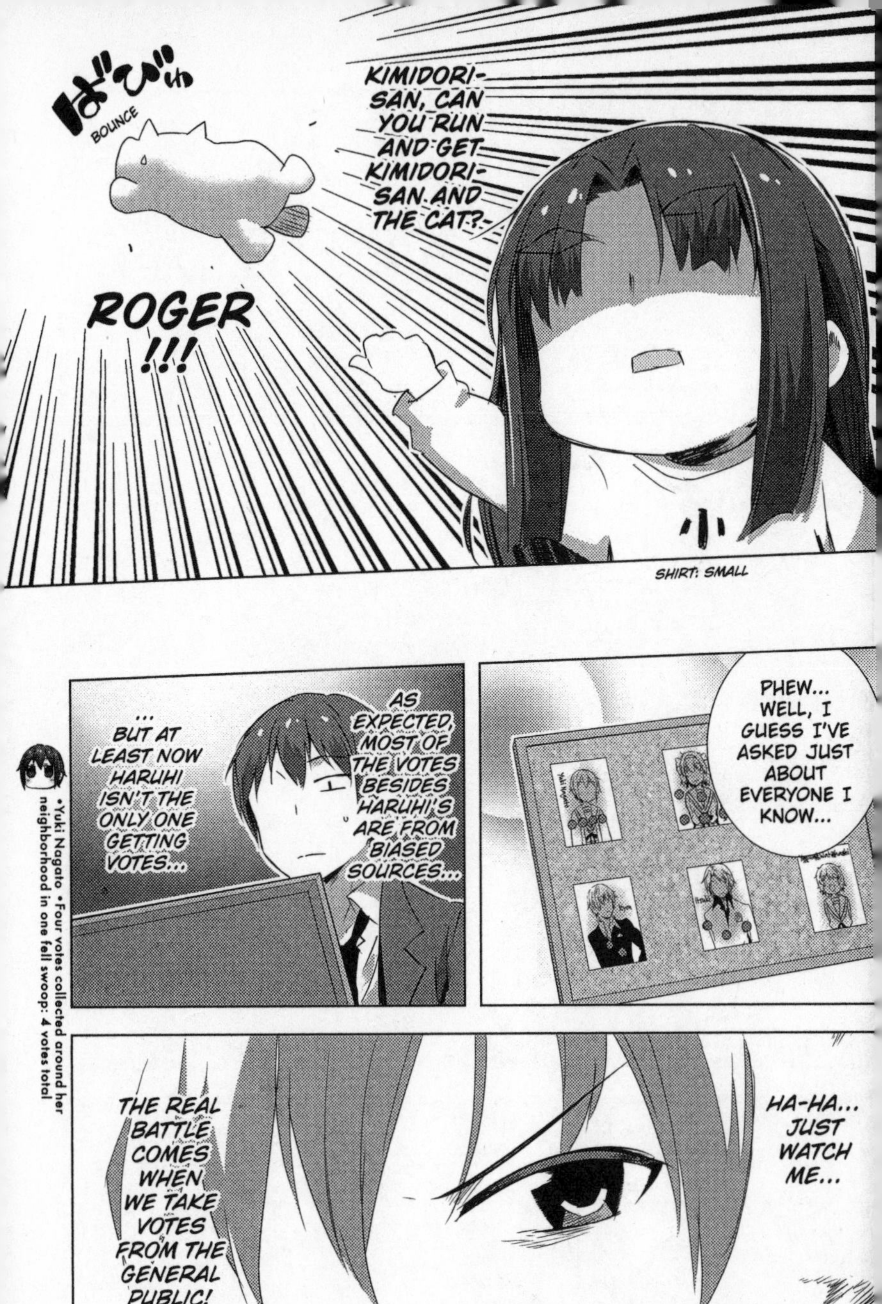

KIMIDORI-SAN, CAN YOU RUN AND GET KIMIDORI-SAN AND THE CAT?
ばびゅ
BOUNCE
ROGER !!!
小
SHIRT: SMALL
PHEW... WELL, I GUESS I'VE ASKED JUST ABOUT EVERYONE I KNOW...
AS EXPECTED, MOST OF THE VOTES BESIDES HARUHI'S ARE FROM BIASED SOURCES...
... BUT AT LEAST NOW HARUHI ISN'T THE ONLY ONE GETTING VOTES...
HA-HA... JUST WATCH ME...
THE REAL BATTLE COMES WHEN WE TAKE VOTES FROM THE GENERAL PUBLIC!

•Yuki Nagato •Four votes collected around her neighborhood in one fell swoop: 4 votes total

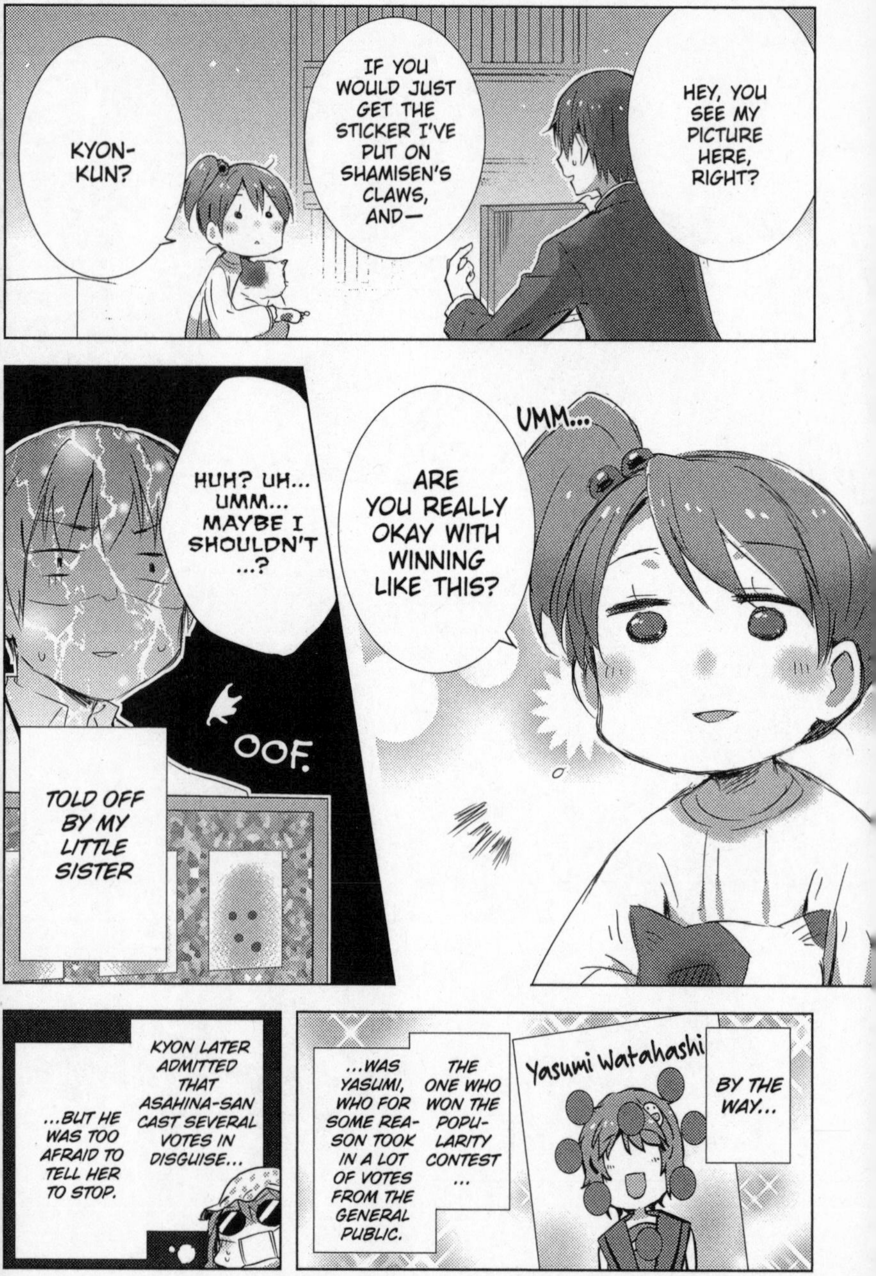
HEY, YOU SEE MY PICTURE HERE, RIGHT?
IF YOU WOULD JUST GET THE STICKER I'VE PUT ON SHAMISEN'S CLAWS, AND—
KYON-KUN?
UMM...
ARE YOU REALLY OKAY WITH WINNING LIKE THIS?
HUH? UH... UMM... MAYBE I SHOULDN'T ...?
OOF.
TOLD OFF BY MY LITTLE SISTER
Yasumi Watahashi
BY THE WAY...
THE ONE WHO WON THE POPU-LARITY CONTEST ...
...WAS YASUMI, WHO FOR SOME REA-SON TOOK IN A LOT OF VOTES FROM THE GENERAL PUBLIC.
KYON LATER ADMITTED THAT ASAHINA-SAN CAST SEVERAL VOTES IN DISGUISE...
...BUT HE WAS TOO AFRAID TO TELL HER TO STOP.

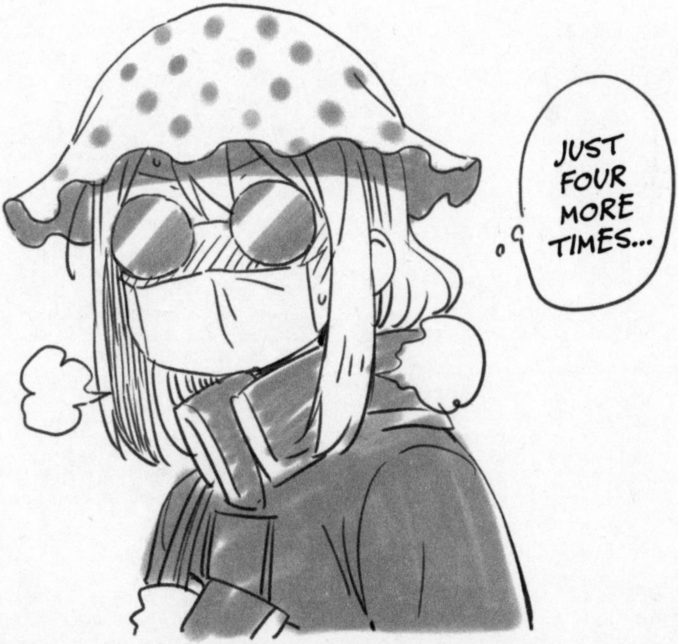
JUST FOUR MORE TIMES...

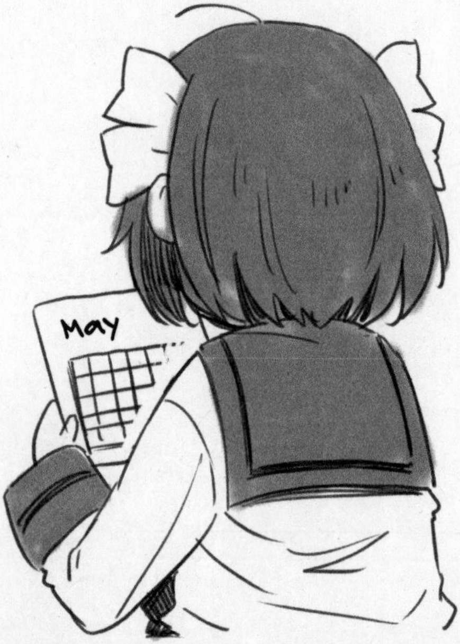
May

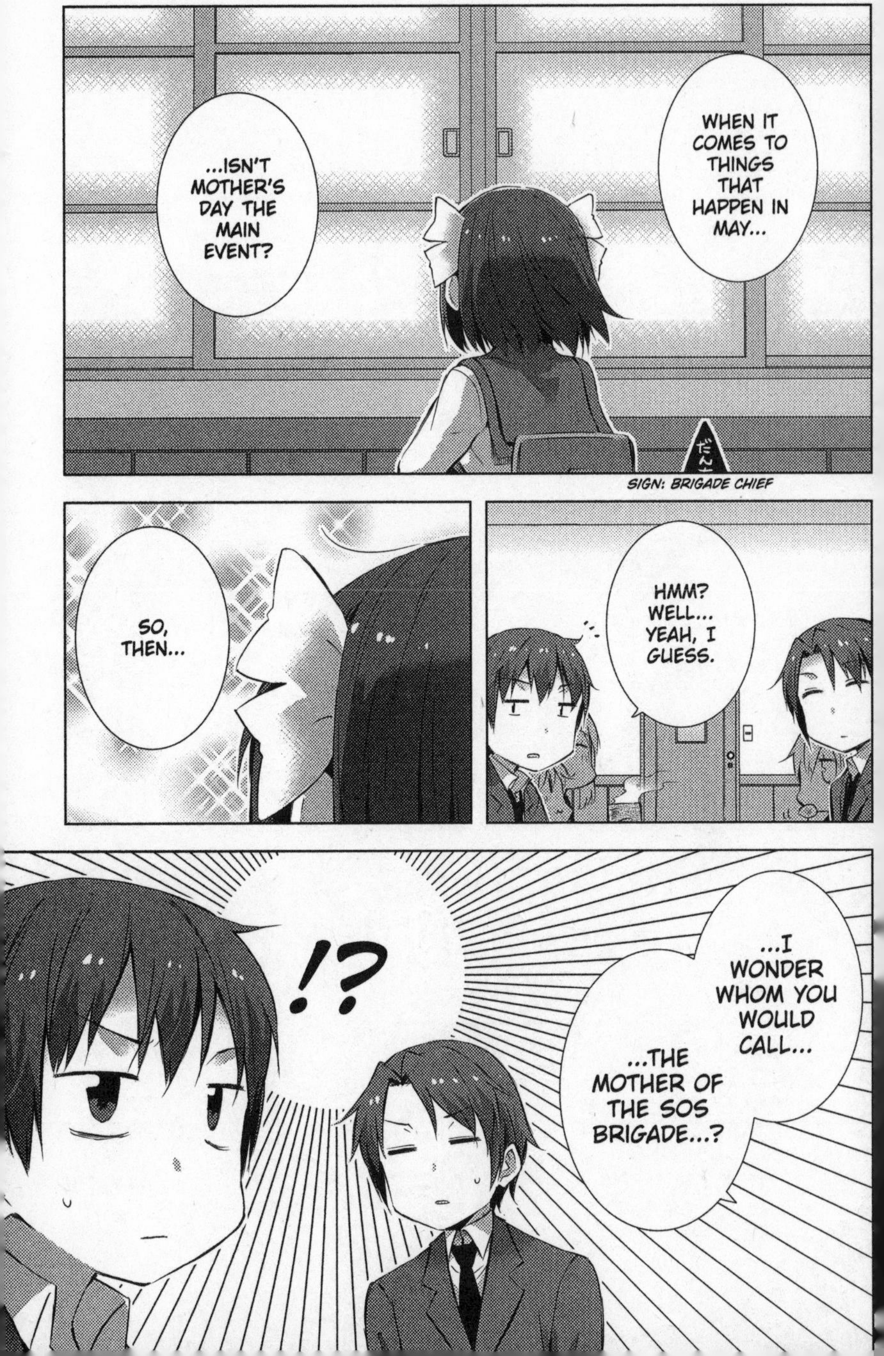
WHEN IT COMES TO THINGS THAT HAPPEN IN MAY...
...ISN'T MOTHER'S DAY THE MAIN EVENT?
SIGN: BRIGADE CHIEF
HMM? WELL... YEAH, I GUESS.
SO, THEN...
...I WONDER WHOM YOU WOULD CALL...
...THE MOTHER OF THE SOS BRIGADE...?
!?

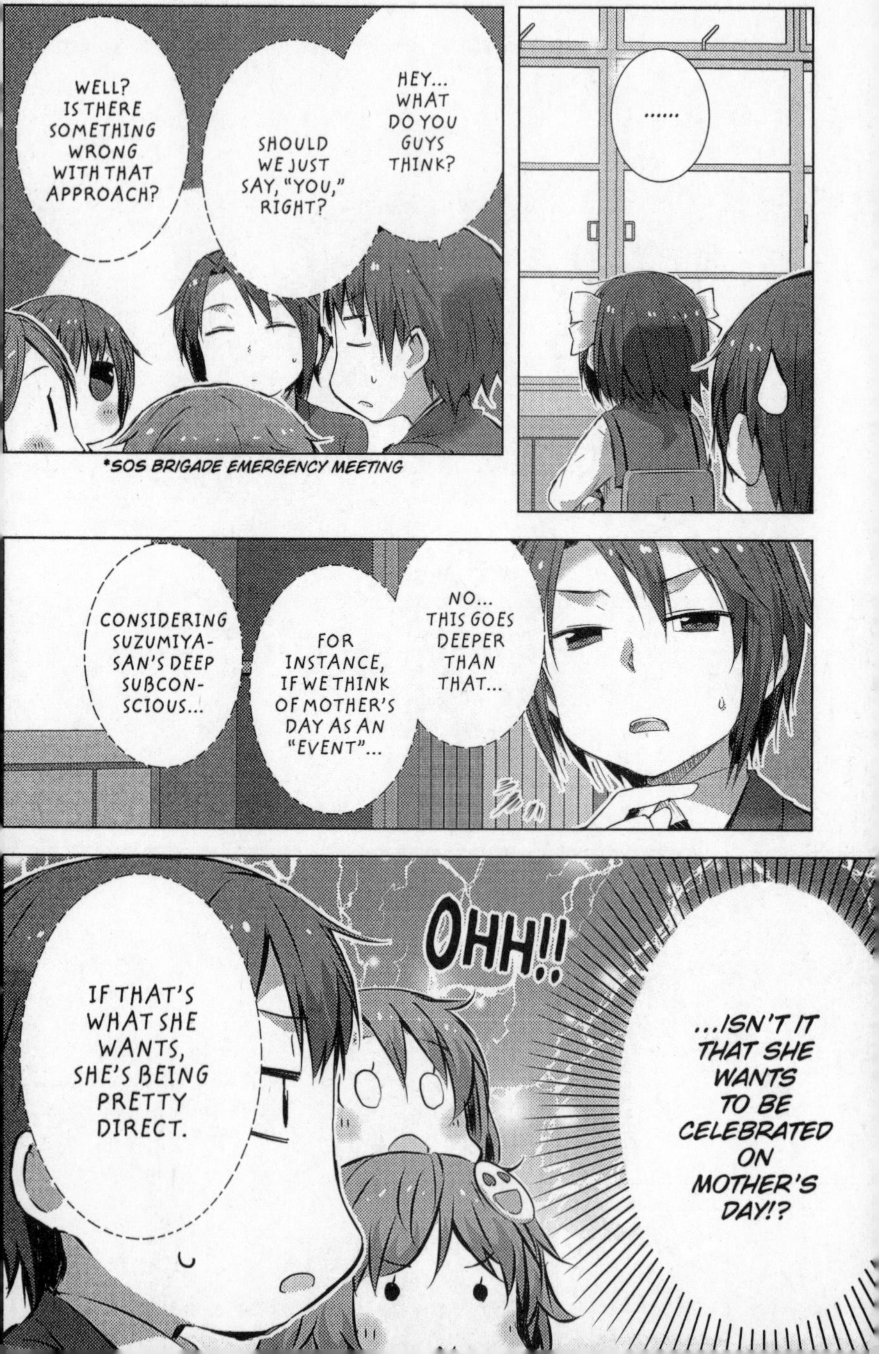
......
HEY... WHAT DO YOU GUYS THINK?
SHOULD WE JUST SAY, "YOU," RIGHT?
WELL? IS THERE SOMETHING WRONG WITH THAT APPROACH?
*SOS BRIGADE EMERGENCY MEETING
NO... THIS GOES DEEPER THAN THAT...
FOR INSTANCE, IF WE THINK OF MOTHER'S DAY AS AN "EVENT"...
CONSIDERING SUZUMIYA-SAN'S DEEP SUBCONSCIOUS...
...ISN'T IT THAT SHE WANTS TO BE CELEBRATED ON MOTHER'S DAY!?
OHH!!
IF THAT'S WHAT SHE WANTS, SHE'S BEING PRETTY DIRECT.

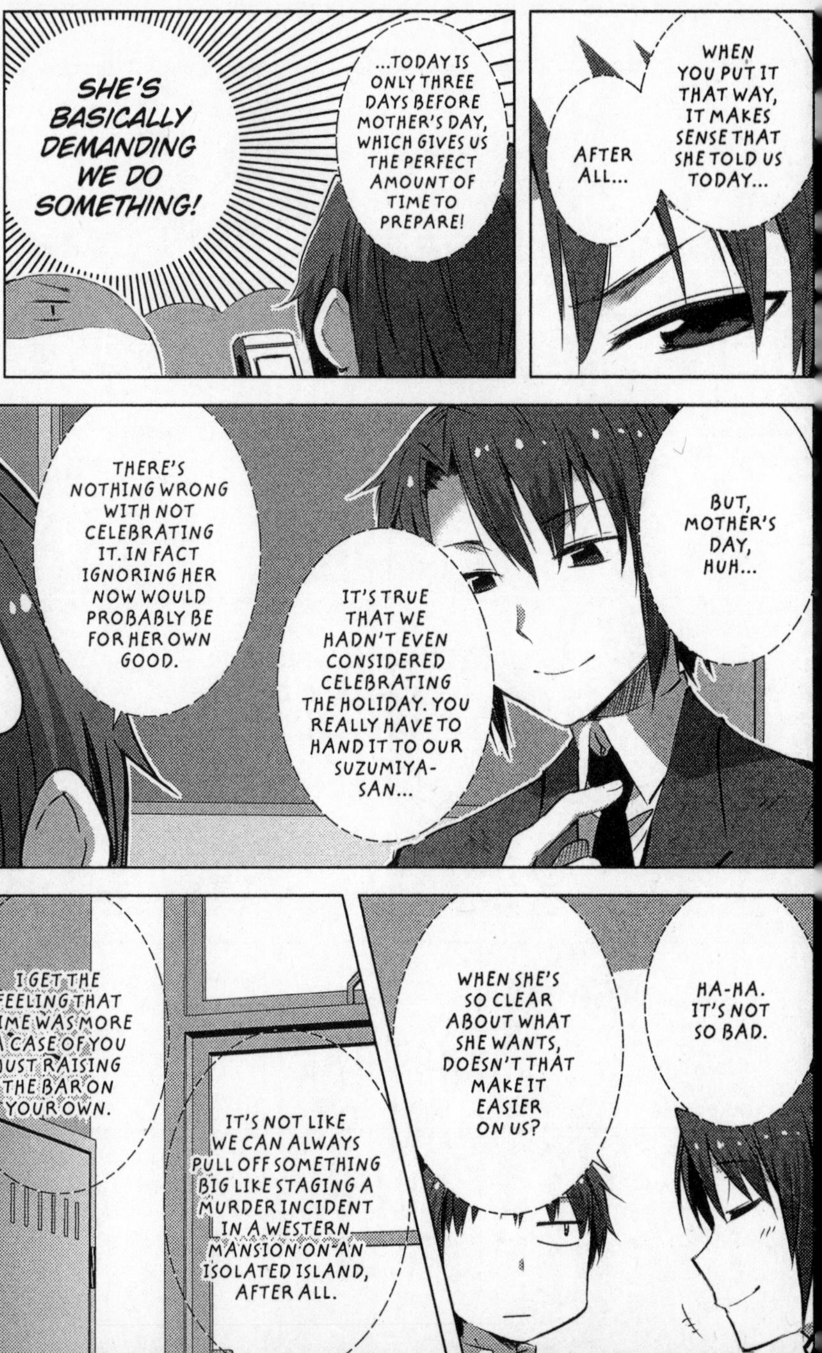
WHEN YOU PUT IT THAT WAY, IT MAKES SENSE THAT SHE TOLD US TODAY...
AFTER ALL...
...TODAY IS ONLY THREE DAYS BEFORE MOTHER'S DAY, WHICH GIVES US THE PERFECT AMOUNT OF TIME TO PREPARE!
SHE'S BASICALLY DEMANDING WE DO SOMETHING!
BUT, MOTHER'S DAY, HUH...
IT'S TRUE THAT WE HADN'T EVEN CONSIDERED CELEBRATING THE HOLIDAY. YOU REALLY HAVE TO HAND IT TO OUR SUZUMIYA-SAN...
THERE'S NOTHING WRONG WITH NOT CELEBRATING IT. IN FACT IGNORING HER NOW WOULD PROBABLY BE FOR HER OWN GOOD.
HA-HA. IT'S NOT SO BAD.
WHEN SHE'S SO CLEAR ABOUT WHAT SHE WANTS, DOESN'T THAT MAKE IT EASIER ON US?
I GET THE FEELING THAT TIME WAS MORE A CASE OF YOU JUST RAISING THE BAR ON YOUR OWN.
IT'S NOT LIKE WE CAN ALWAYS PULL OFF SOMETHING BIG LIKE STAGING A MURDER INCIDENT IN A WESTERN MANSION ON AN ISOLATED ISLAND, AFTER ALL.

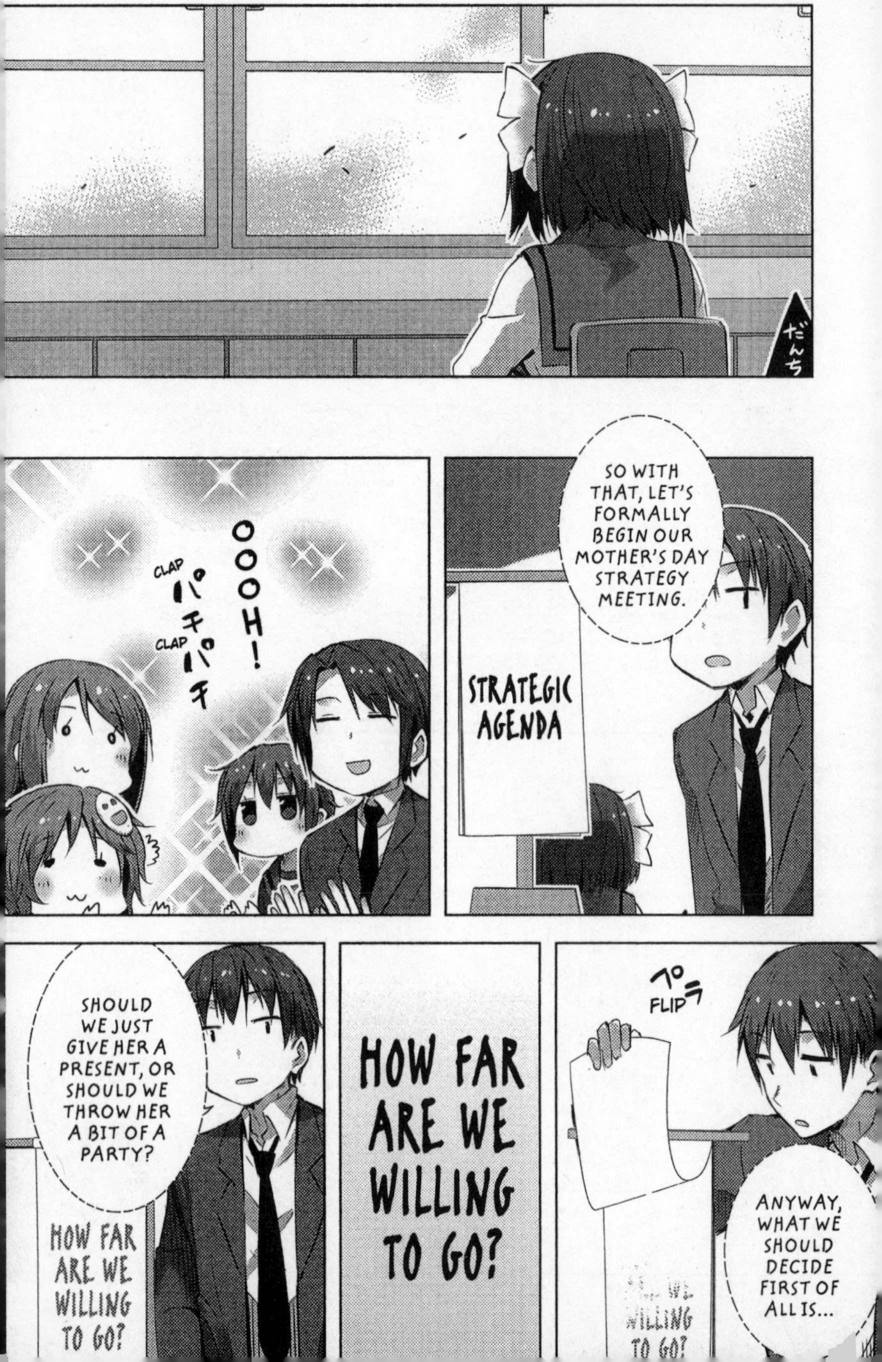
だんち
SO WITH THAT, LET'S FORMALLY BEGIN OUR MOTHER'S DAY STRATEGY MEETING.
STRATEGIC AGENDA
CLAP パチ CLAP パチ
OOOH!
ペラ FLIP
ANYWAY, WHAT WE SHOULD DECIDE FIRST OF ALL IS...
HOW FAR ARE WE WILLING TO GO?
SHOULD WE JUST GIVE HER A PRESENT, OR SHOULD WE THROW HER A BIT OF A PARTY?
HOW FAR ARE WE WILLING TO GO?

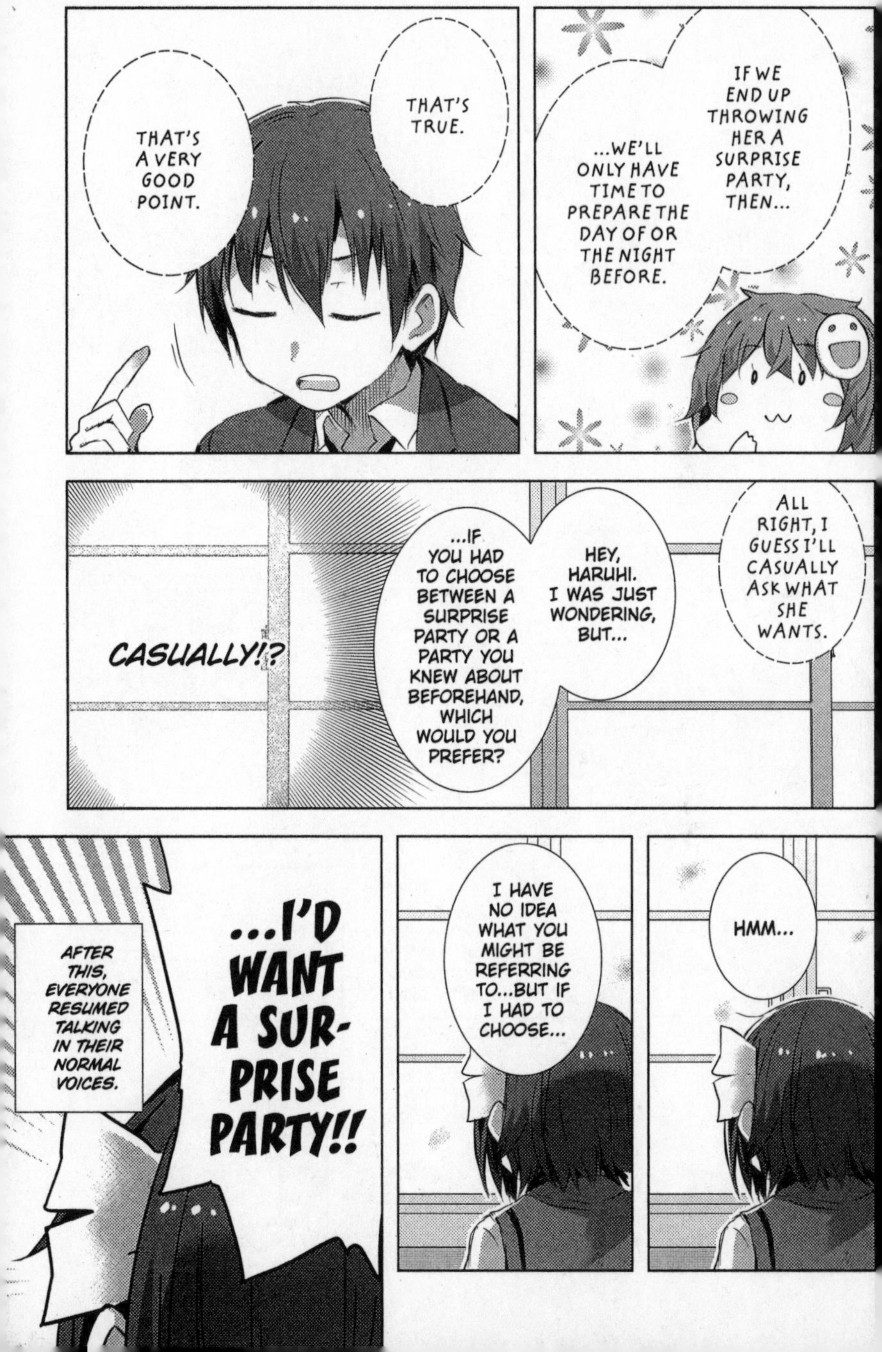
IF WE END UP THROWING HER A SURPRISE PARTY, THEN...
...WE'LL ONLY HAVE TIME TO PREPARE THE DAY OF OR THE NIGHT BEFORE.
THAT'S TRUE.
THAT'S A VERY GOOD POINT.
ALL RIGHT, I GUESS I'LL CASUALLY ASK WHAT SHE WANTS.
HEY, HARUHI. I WAS JUST WONDERING, BUT...
...IF YOU HAD TO CHOOSE BETWEEN A SURPRISE PARTY OR A PARTY YOU KNEW ABOUT BEFOREHAND, WHICH WOULD YOU PREFER?
CASUALLY!?
HMM...
I HAVE NO IDEA WHAT YOU MIGHT BE REFERRING TO...BUT IF I HAD TO CHOOSE...
...I'D WANT A SUR-PRISE PARTY!!
AFTER THIS, EVERYONE RESUMED TALKING IN THEIR NORMAL VOICES.

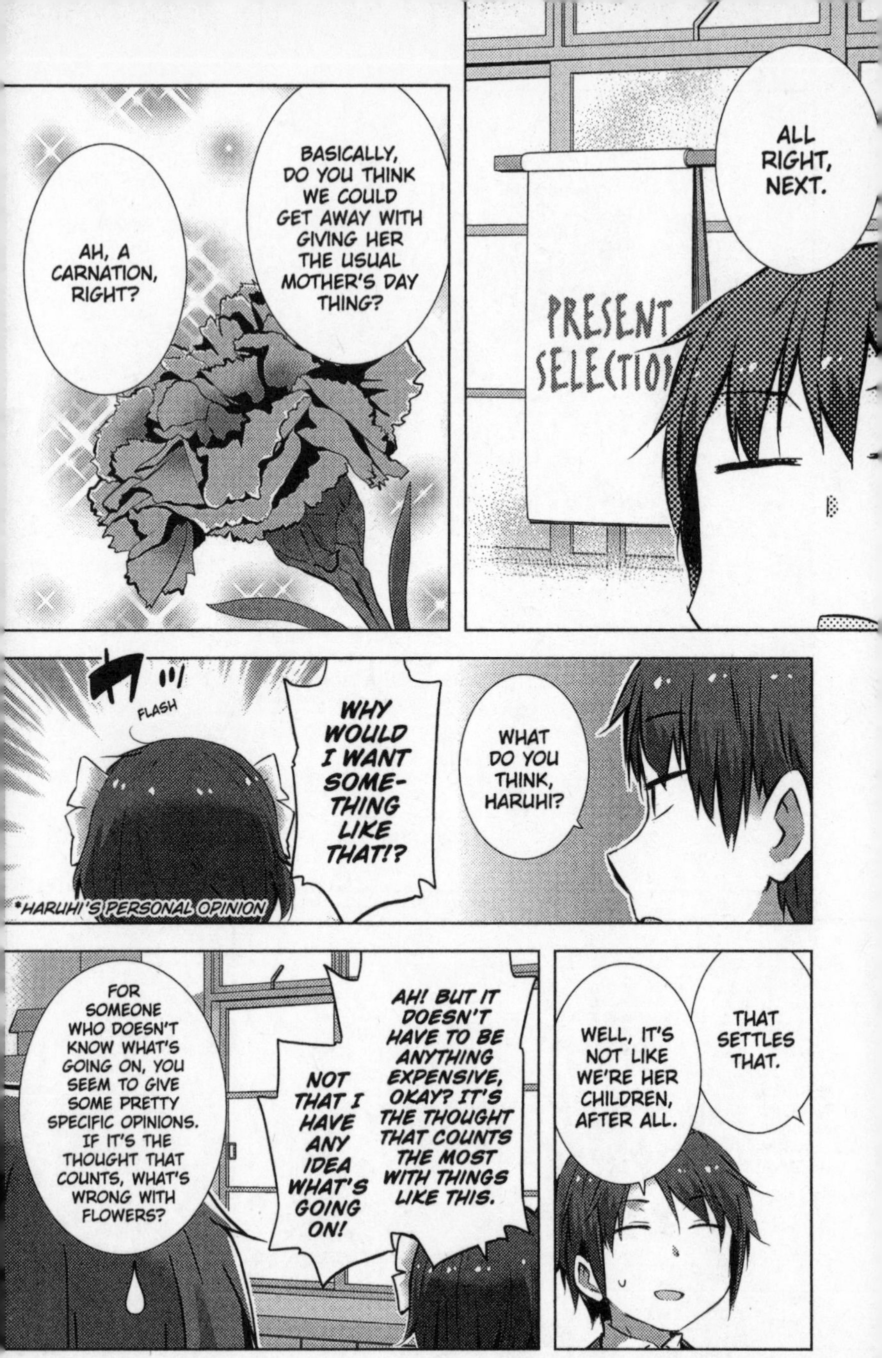
ALL RIGHT, NEXT.
PRESENT SELECTION
BASICALLY, DO YOU THINK WE COULD GET AWAY WITH GIVING HER THE USUAL MOTHER'S DAY THING?
AH, A CARNATION, RIGHT?
WHAT DO YOU THINK, HARUHI?
WHY WOULD I WANT SOMETHING LIKE THAT!?
FLASH
*HARUHI'S PERSONAL OPINION
THAT SETTLES THAT.
WELL, IT'S NOT LIKE WE'RE HER CHILDREN, AFTER ALL.
AH! BUT IT DOESN'T HAVE TO BE ANYTHING EXPENSIVE, OKAY? IT'S THE THOUGHT THAT COUNTS THE MOST WITH THINGS LIKE THIS.
NOT THAT I HAVE ANY IDEA WHAT'S GOING ON!
FOR SOMEONE WHO DOESN'T KNOW WHAT'S GOING ON, YOU SEEM TO GIVE SOME PRETTY SPECIFIC OPINIONS. IF IT'S THE THOUGHT THAT COUNTS, WHAT'S WRONG WITH FLOWERS?

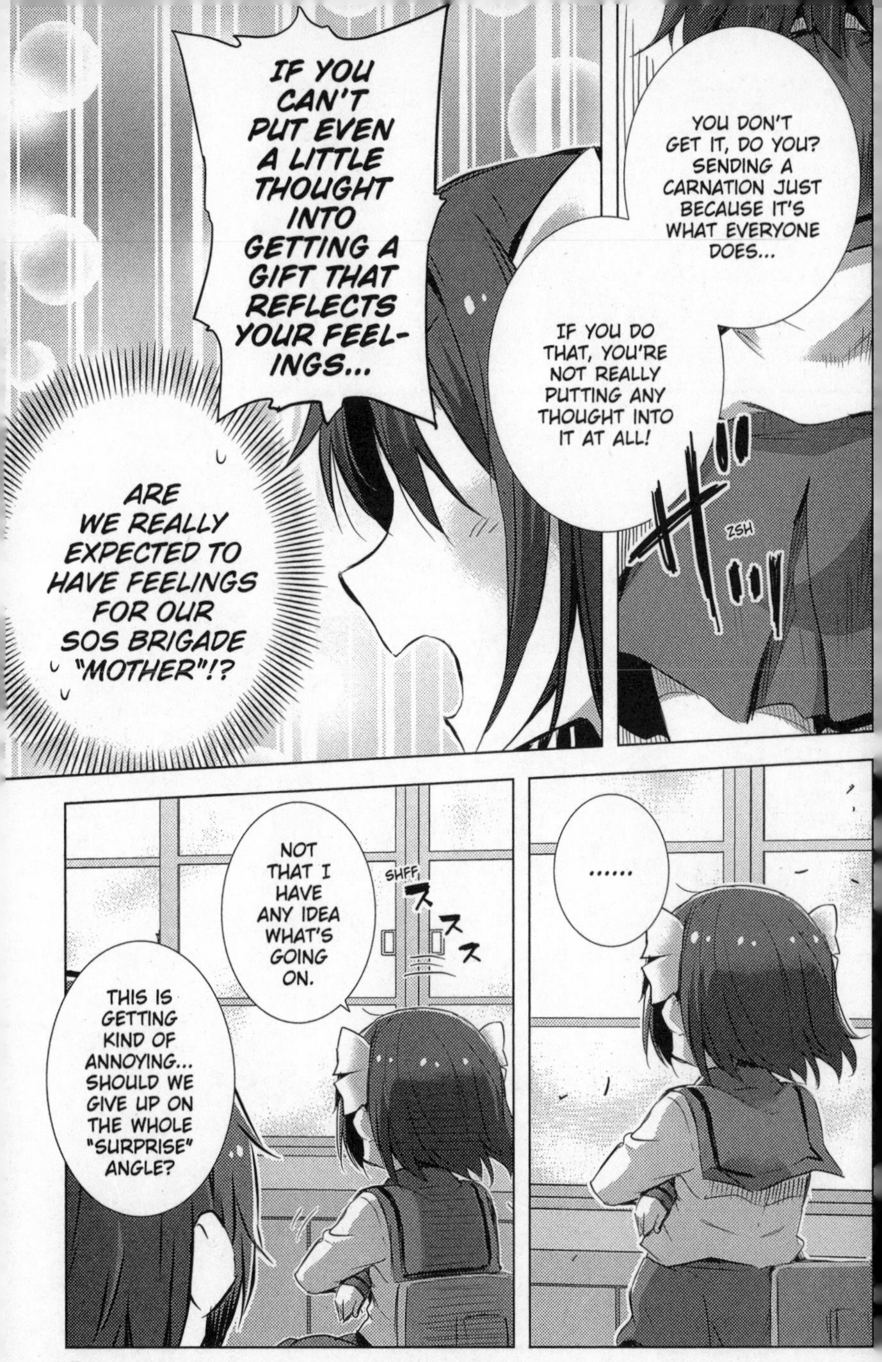
YOU DON'T GET IT, DO YOU? SENDING A CARNATION JUST BECAUSE IT'S WHAT EVERYONE DOES...
IF YOU DO THAT, YOU'RE NOT REALLY PUTTING ANY THOUGHT INTO IT AT ALL!
ZSH
IF YOU CAN'T PUT EVEN A LITTLE THOUGHT INTO GETTING A GIFT THAT REFLECTS YOUR FEEL-INGS...
ARE WE REALLY EXPECTED TO HAVE FEELINGS FOR OUR SOS BRIGADE "MOTHER"!?
......
NOT THAT I HAVE ANY IDEA WHAT'S GOING ON.
SHFF
THIS IS GETTING KIND OF ANNOYING... SHOULD WE GIVE UP ON THE WHOLE "SURPRISE" ANGLE?

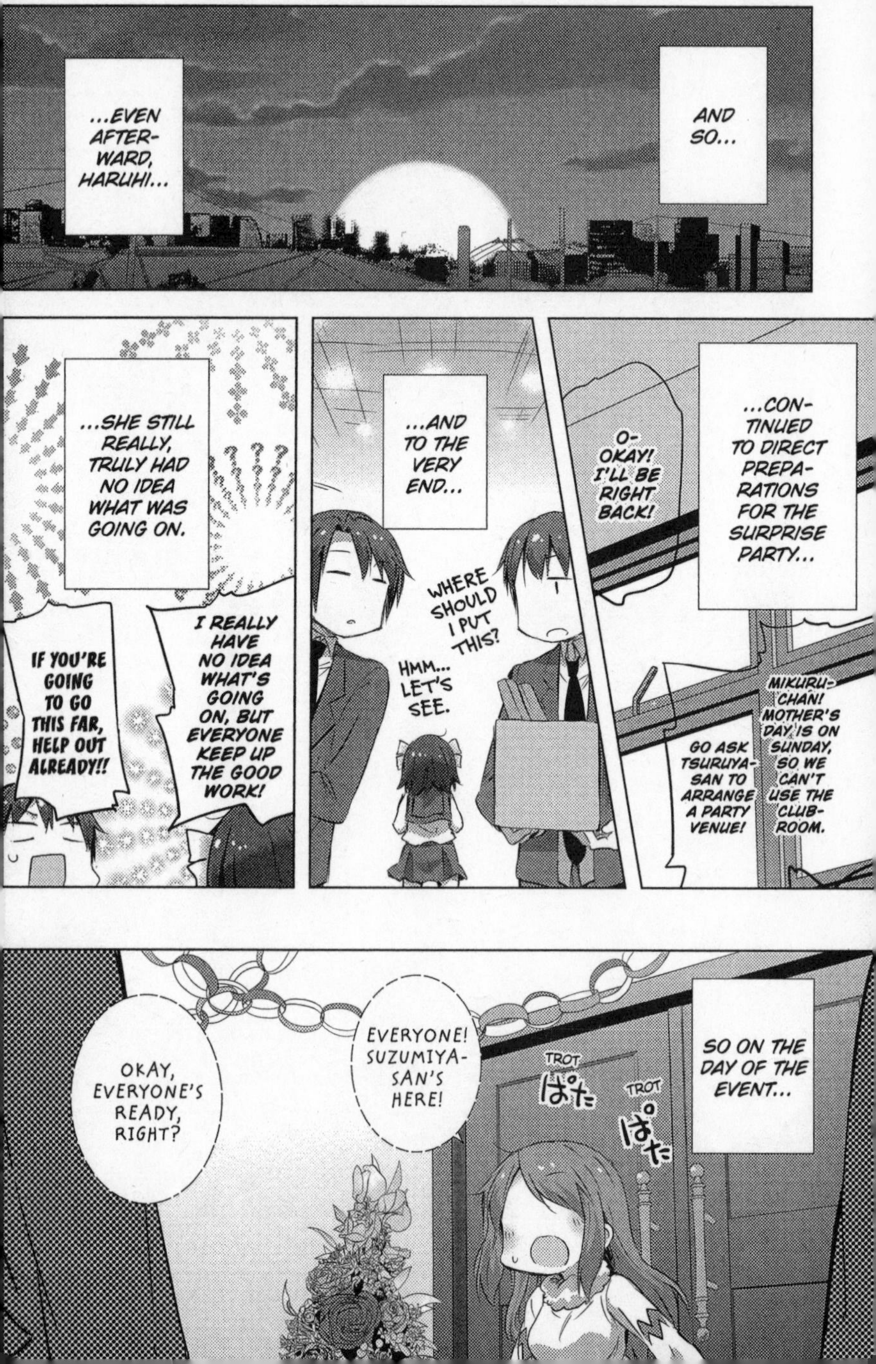
AND SO...
...EVEN AFTERWARD, HARUHI...
...CONTINUED TO DIRECT PREPARATIONS FOR THE SURPRISE PARTY...
O-OKAY! I'LL BE RIGHT BACK!
MIKURU-CHAN! MOTHER'S DAY IS ON SUNDAY, SO WE CAN'T USE THE CLUBROOM.
GO ASK TSURUYA-SAN TO ARRANGE A PARTY VENUE!
...AND TO THE VERY END...
WHERE SHOULD I PUT THIS?
HMM... LET'S SEE.
...SHE STILL REALLY, TRULY HAD NO IDEA WHAT WAS GOING ON.
I REALLY HAVE NO IDEA WHAT'S GOING ON, BUT EVERYONE KEEP UP THE GOOD WORK!
IF YOU'RE GOING TO GO THIS FAR, HELP OUT ALREADY!!
SO ON THE DAY OF THE EVENT...
TROT ぱた
TROT ぱた
EVERYONE! SUZUMIYA-SAN'S HERE!
OKAY, EVERYONE'S READY, RIGHT?

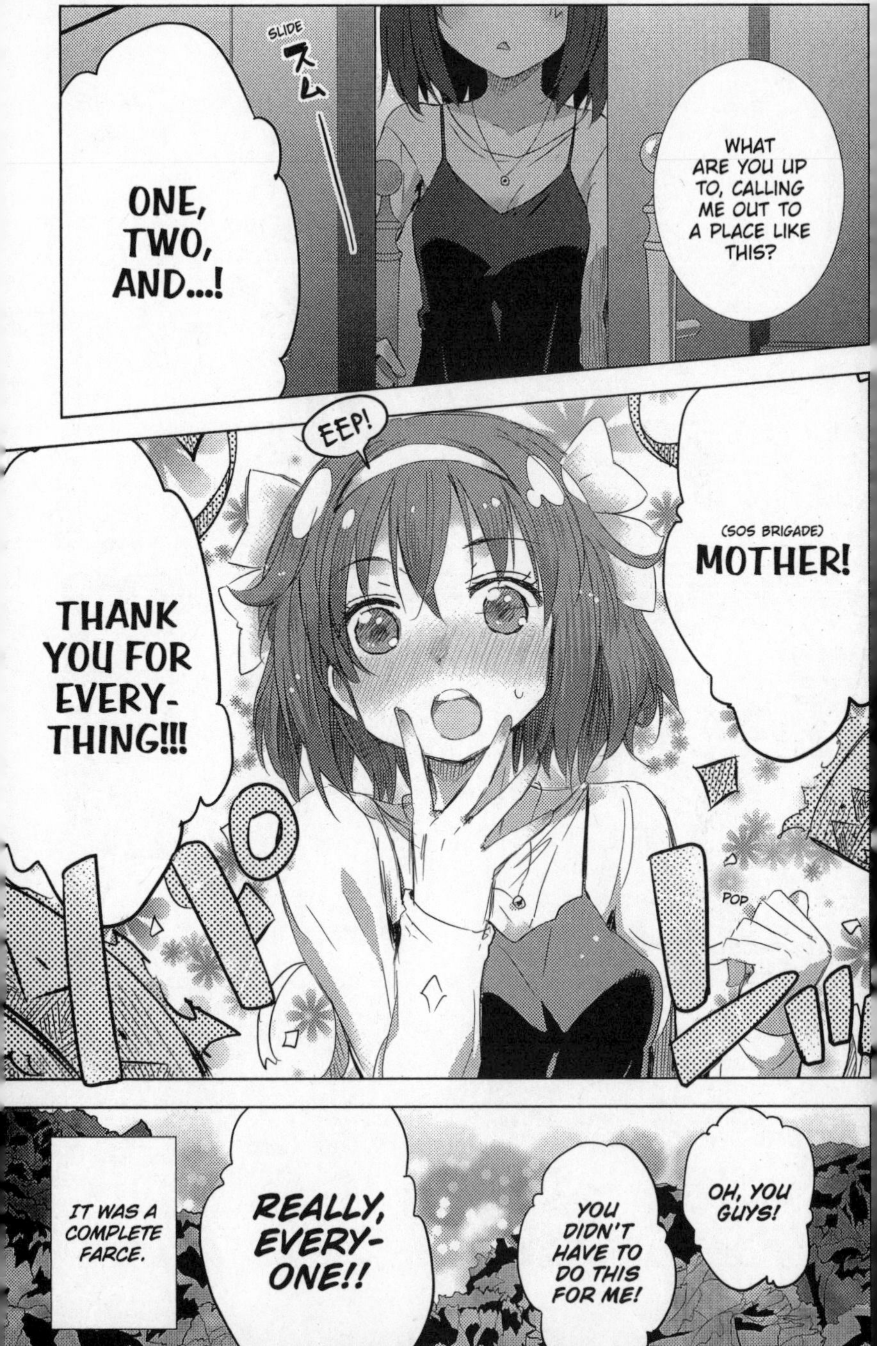
WHAT ARE YOU UP TO, CALLING ME OUT TO A PLACE LIKE THIS?
SLIDE スム
ONE, TWO, AND...!
(SOS BRIGADE) MOTHER!
EEP!
THANK YOU FOR EVERY-THING!!!
POP
OH, YOU GUYS!
YOU DIDN'T HAVE TO DO THIS FOR ME!
REALLY, EVERY-ONE!!
IT WAS A COMPLETE FARCE.

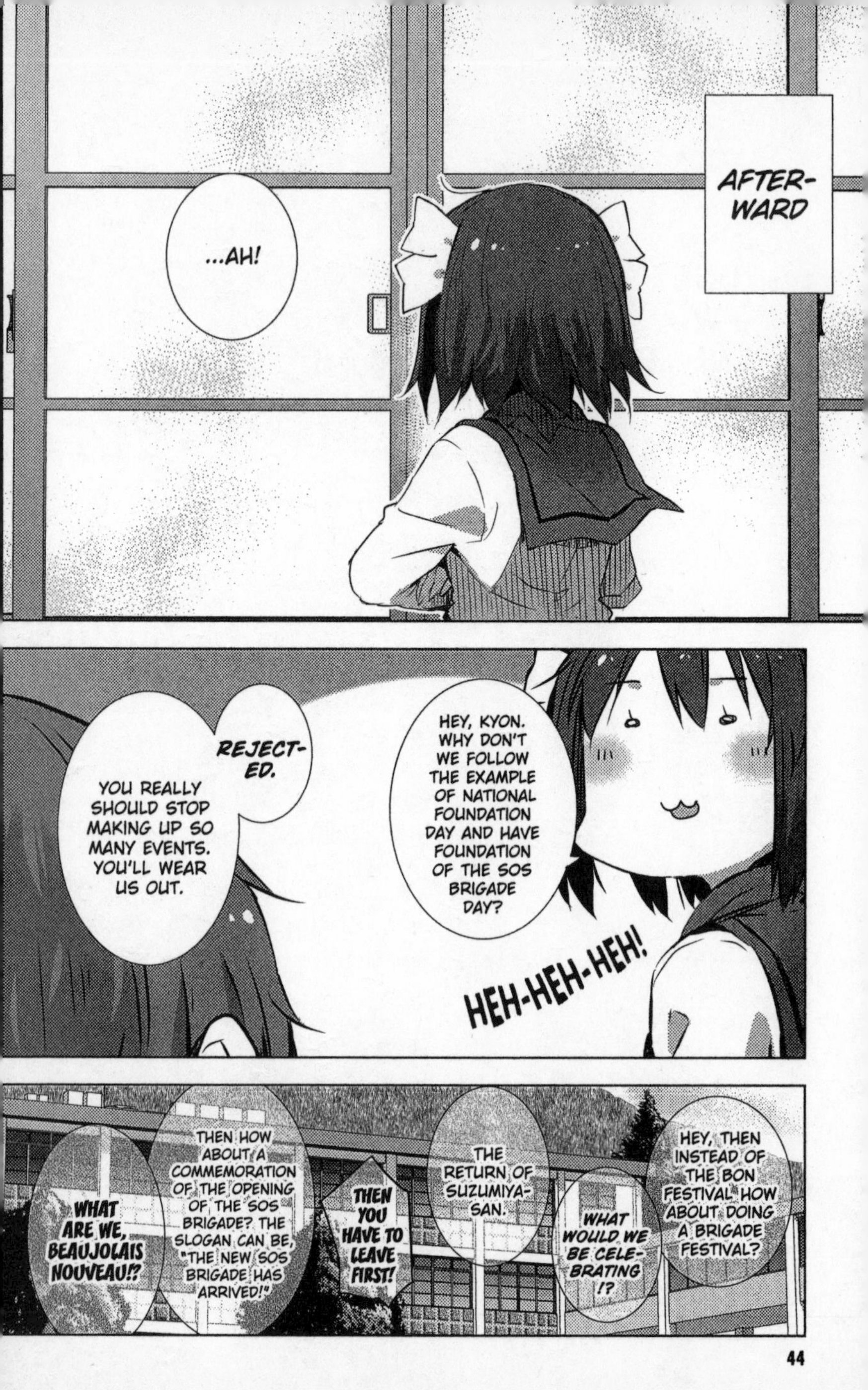
AFTER-WARD
...AH!
HEY, KYON. WHY DON'T WE FOLLOW THE EXAMPLE OF NATIONAL FOUNDATION DAY AND HAVE FOUNDATION OF THE SOS BRIGADE DAY?
REJECT-ED.
YOU REALLY SHOULD STOP MAKING UP SO MANY EVENTS. YOU'LL WEAR US OUT.
HEH-HEH-HEH!
HEY, THEN INSTEAD OF THE BON FESTIVAL HOW ABOUT DOING A BRIGADE FESTIVAL?
WHAT WOULD WE BE CELE-BRATING!?
THE RETURN OF SUZUMIYA-SAN.
THEN YOU HAVE TO LEAVE FIRST!
THEN HOW ABOUT A COMMEMORATION OF THE OPENING OF THE SOS BRIGADE? THE SLOGAN CAN BE, "THE NEW SOS BRIGADE HAS ARRIVED!"
WHAT ARE WE, BEAUJOLAIS NOUVEAU!?

I HAVE THE FEELING SHE'S FORGETTING A REALLY IMPORTANT EVENT.

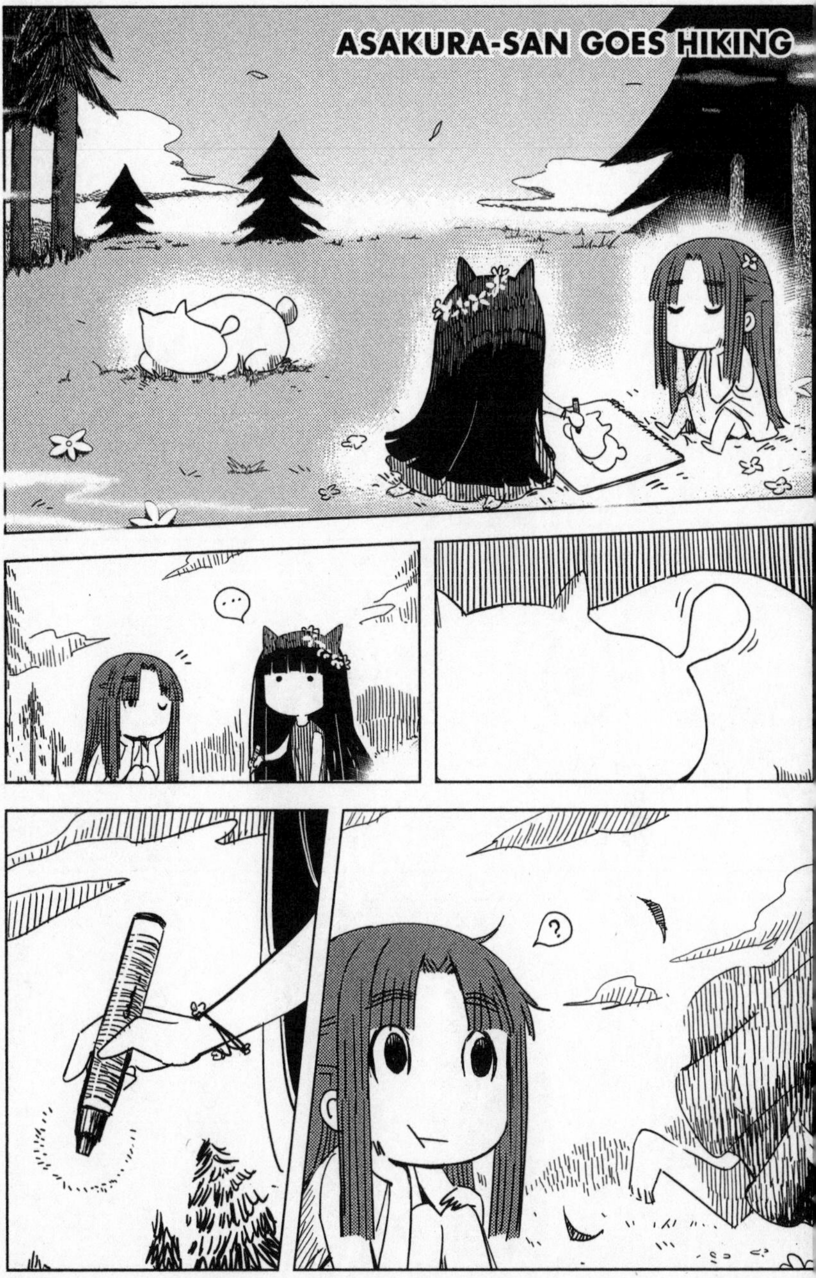
ASAKURA-SAN GOES HIKING
...
?

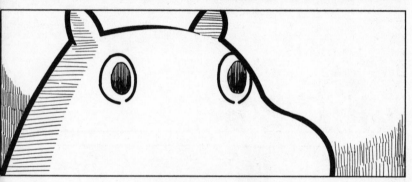

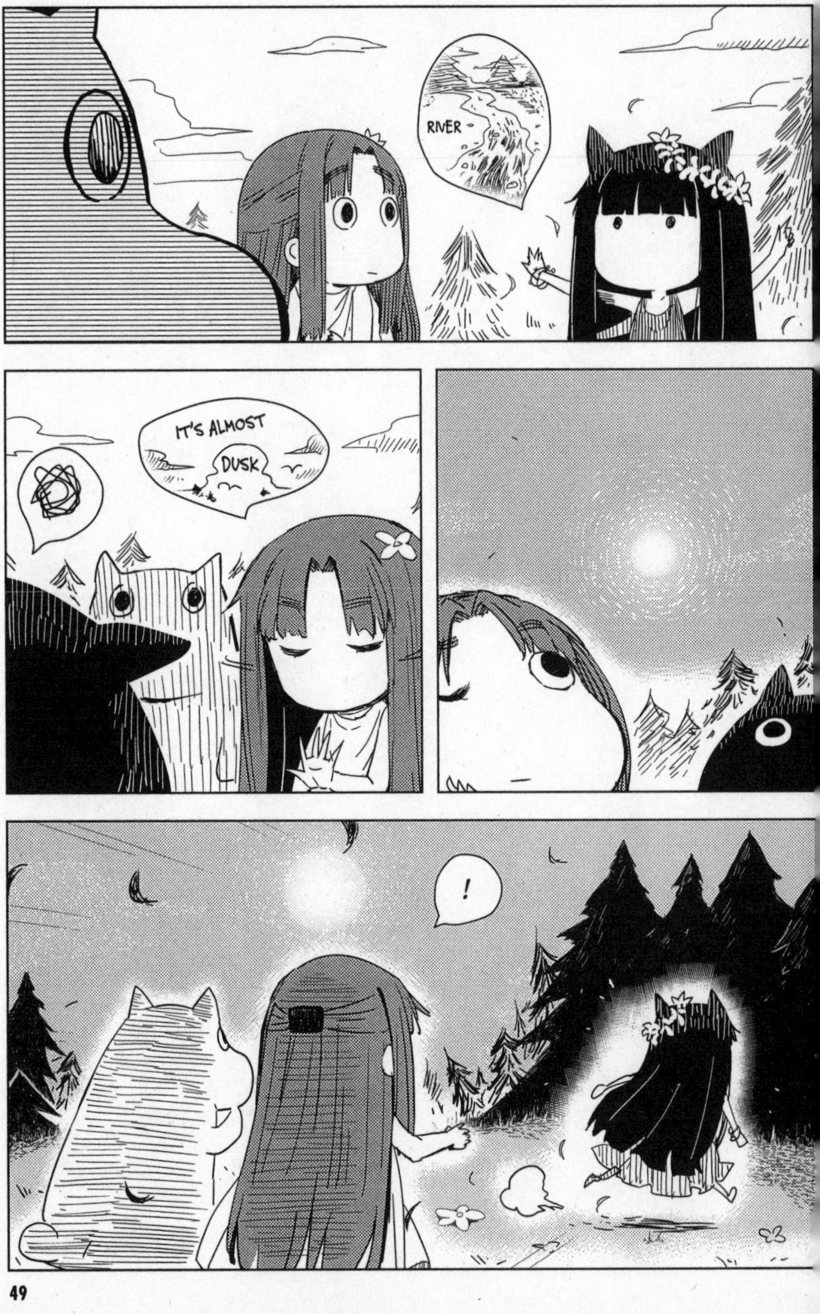
RIVER
IT'S ALMOST DUSK
!

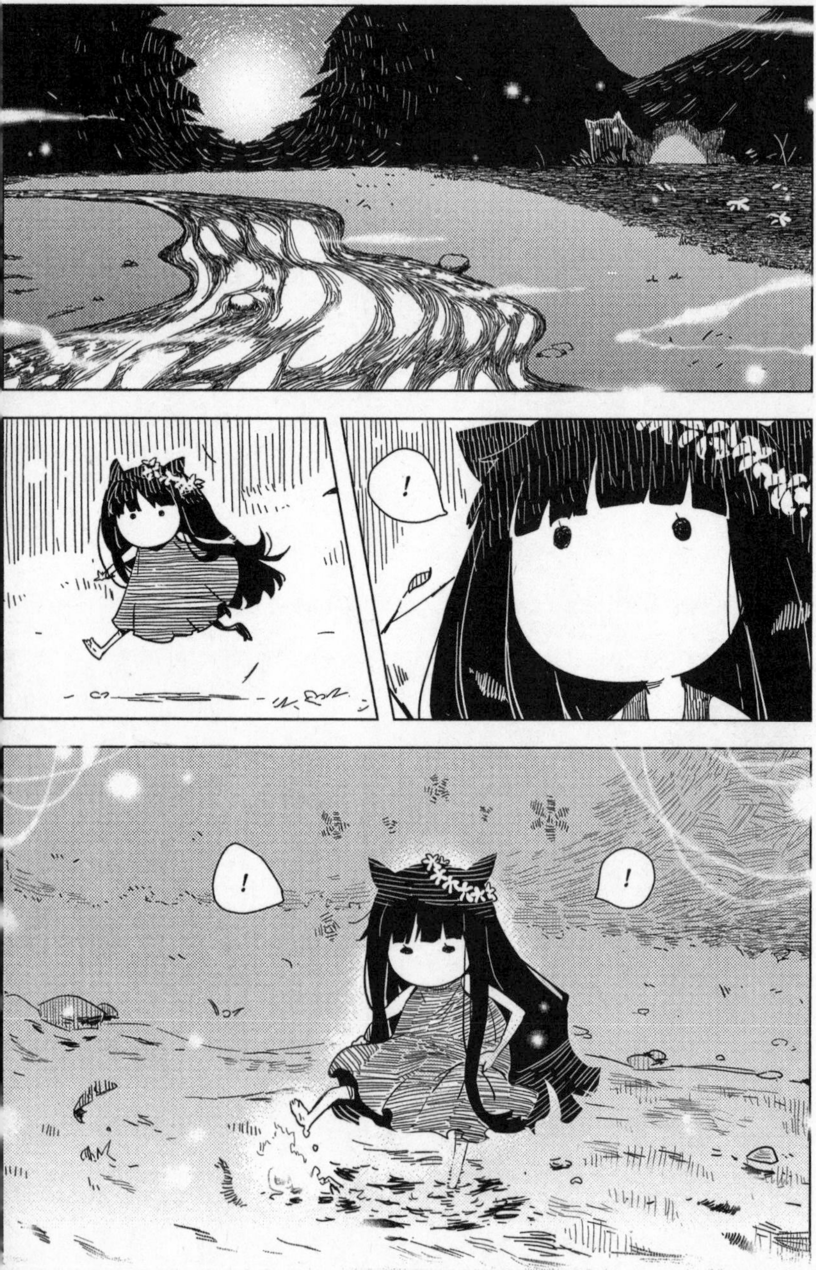
!
!
!

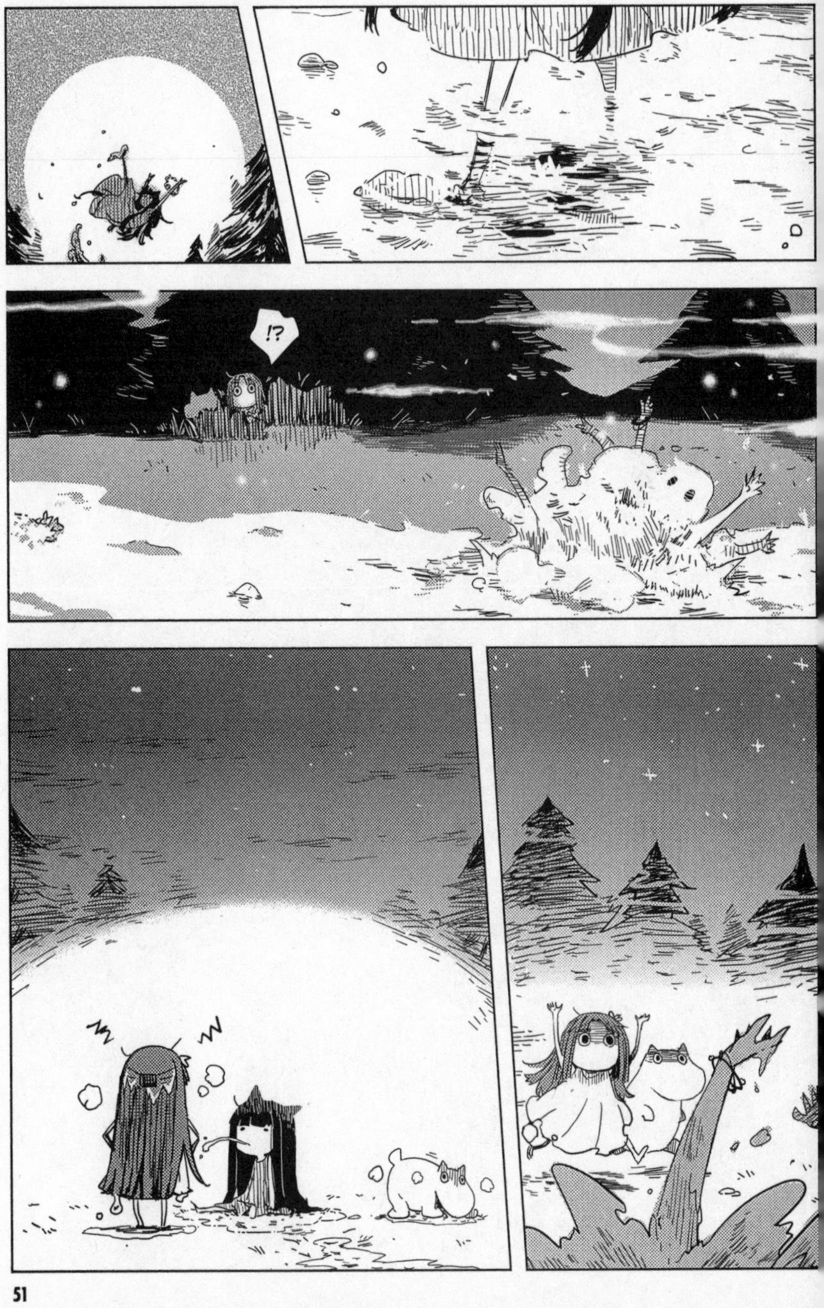
!?

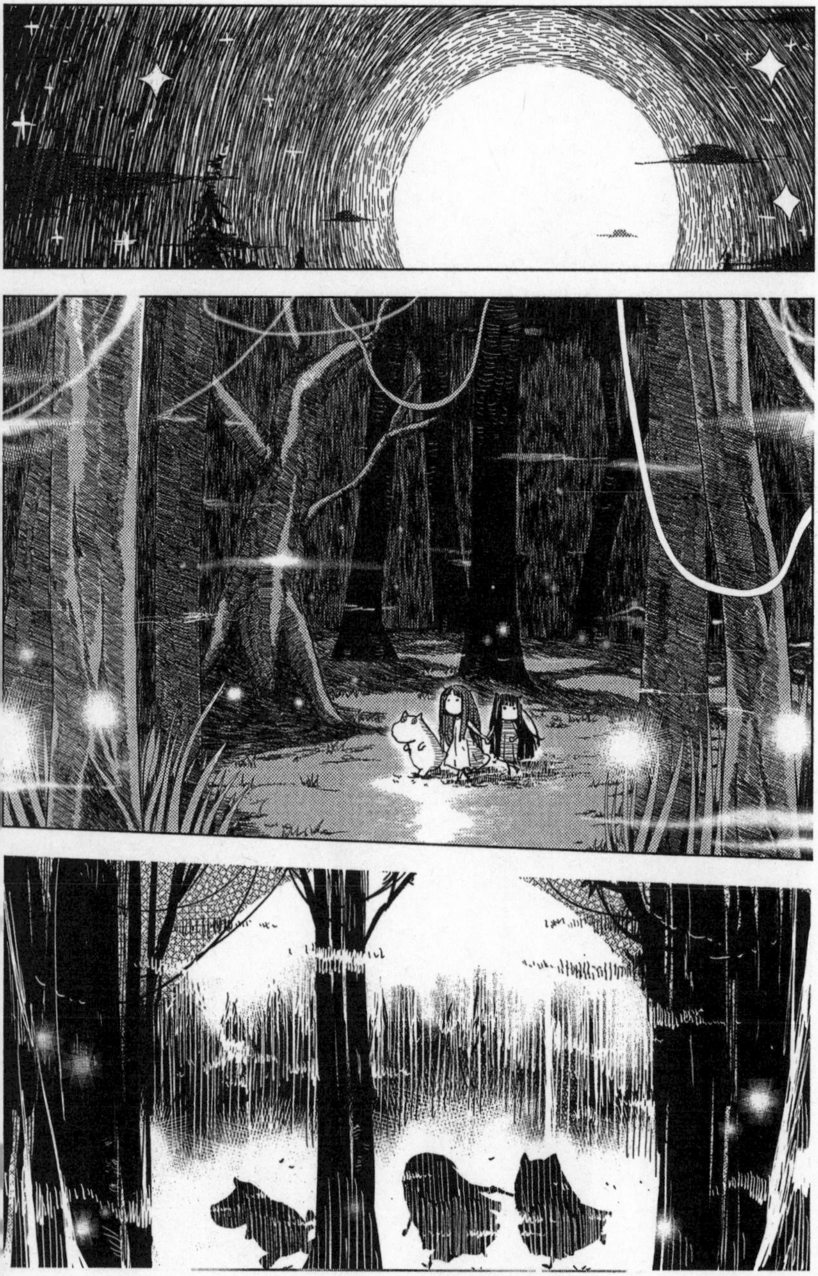

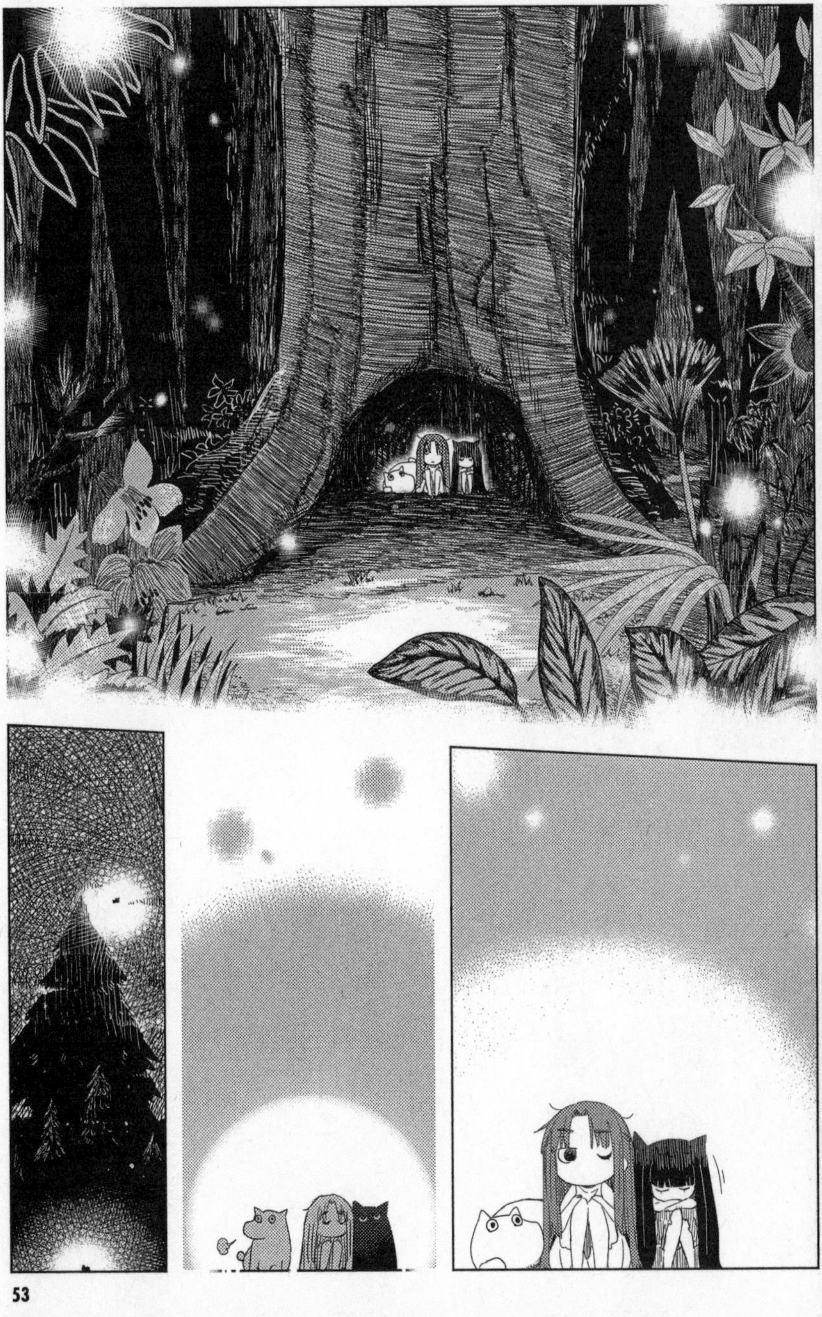

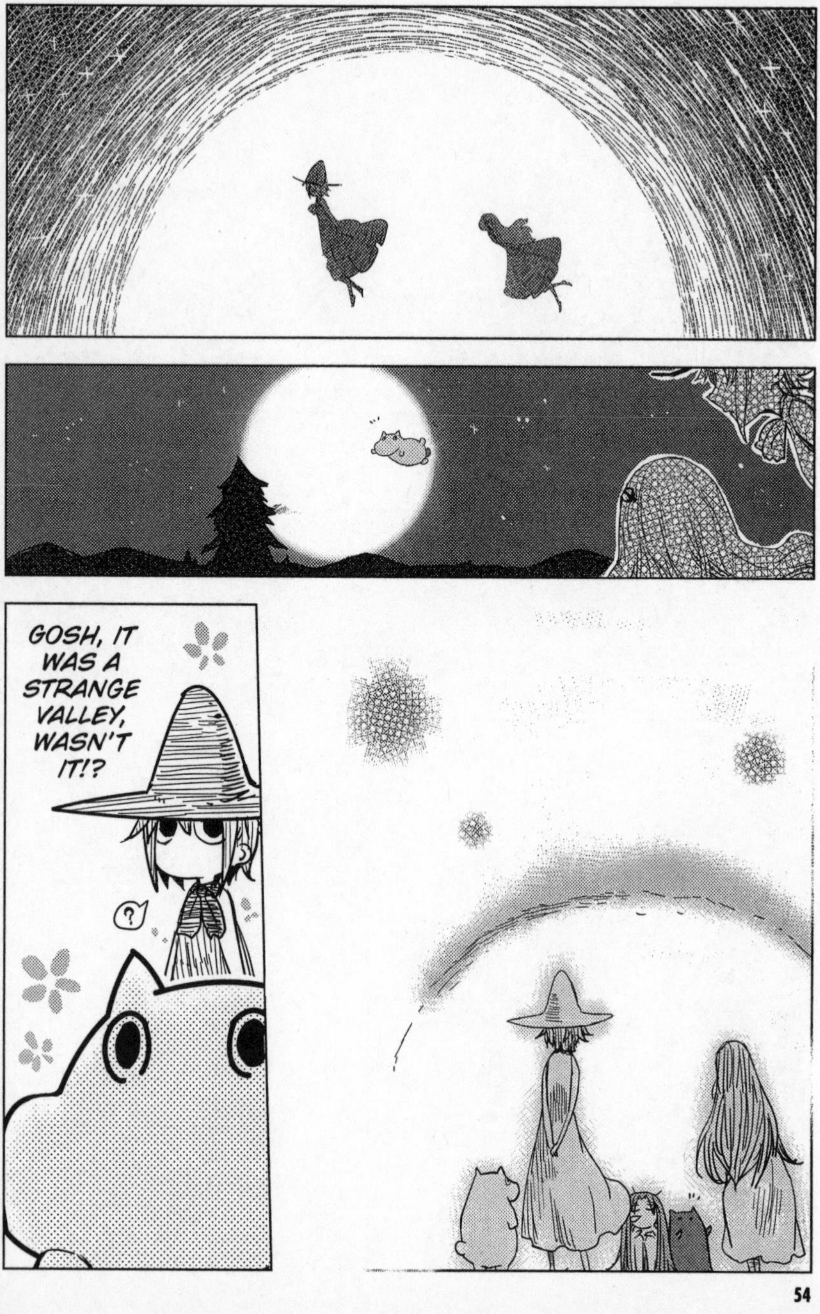
GOSH, IT WAS A STRANGE VALLEY, WASN'T IT!?
?

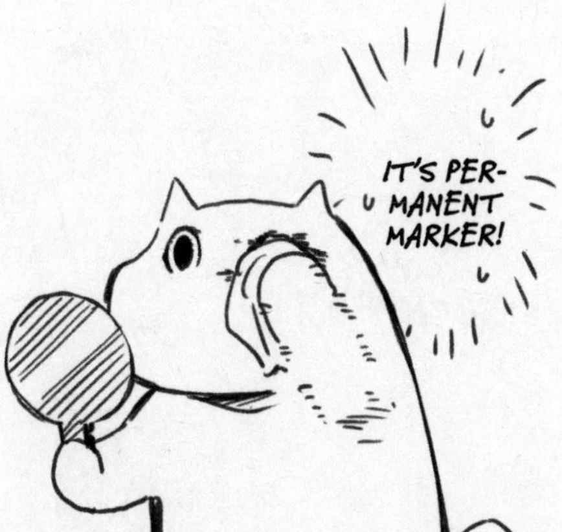
IT'S PERMANENT MARKER!

SUMMER VACATION!

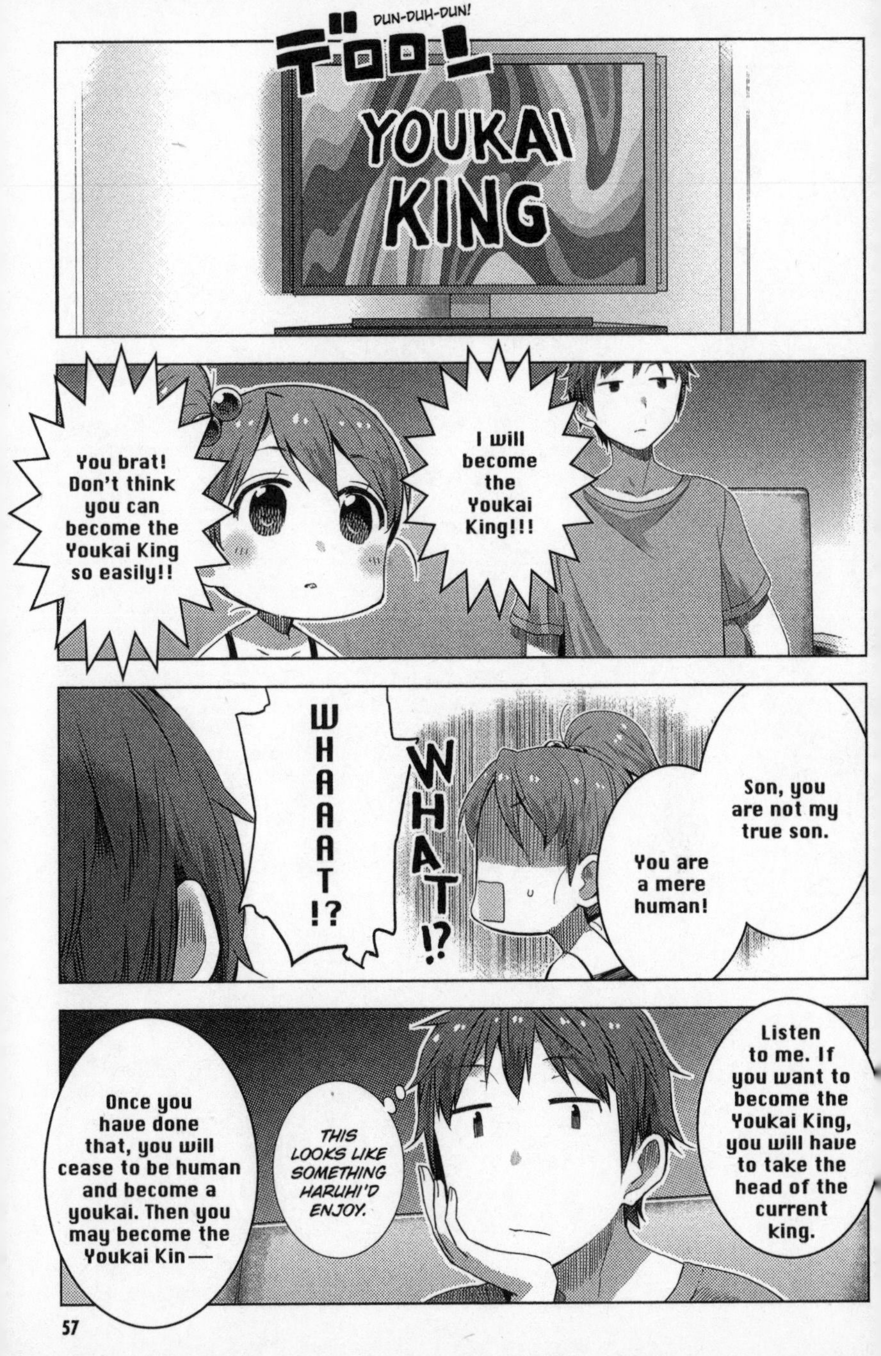
DUN-DUH-DUN!
YOUKAI KING
I will become the Youkai King!!!
You brat! Don't think you can become the Youkai King so easily!!
Son, you are not my true son.
You are a mere human!
WHAT!?
WHAAAAT!?
Listen to me. If you want to become the Youkai King, you will have to take the head of the current king.
THIS LOOKS LIKE SOMETHING HARUHI'D ENJOY.
Once you have done that, you will cease to be human and become a youkai. Then you may become the Youkai Kin—

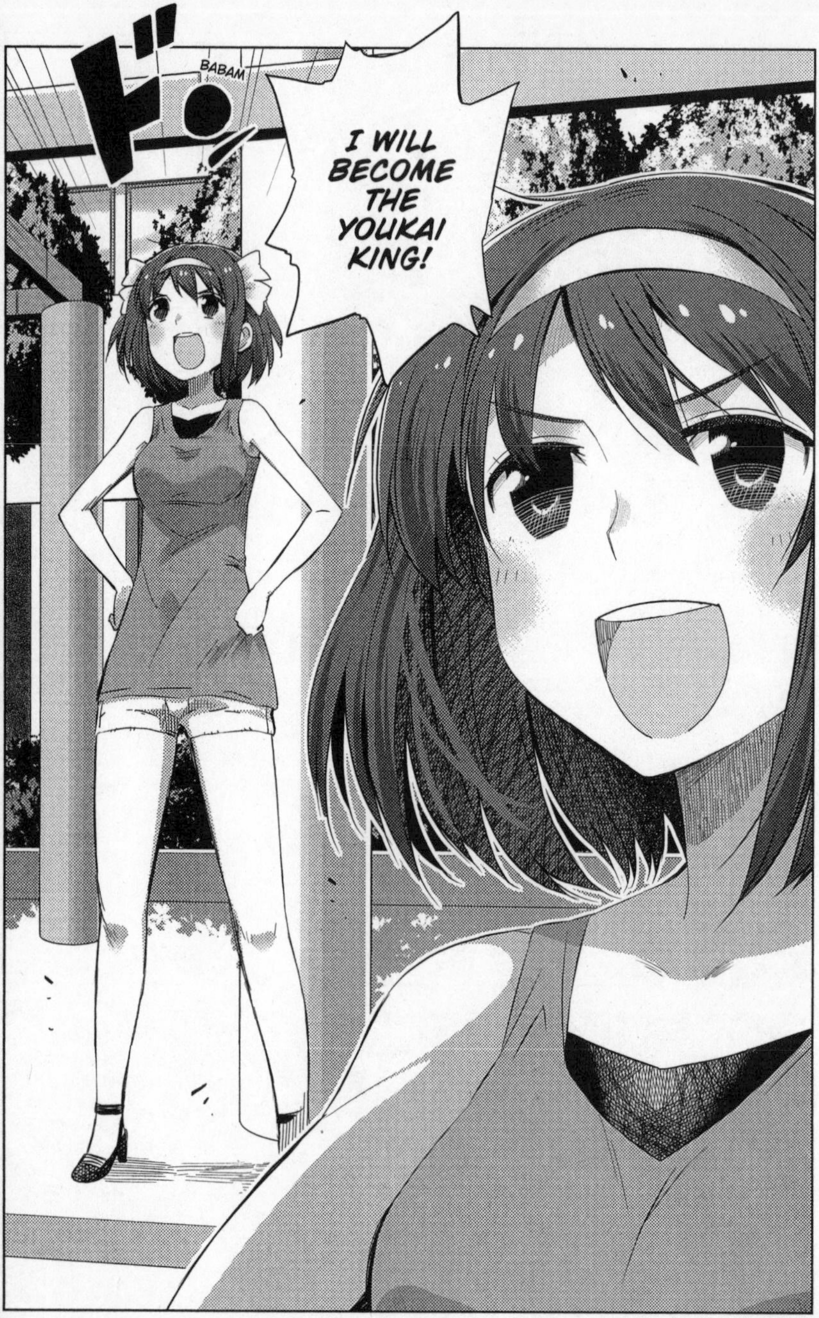
ドドン
BABAM
I WILL BECOME THE YOUKAI KING!

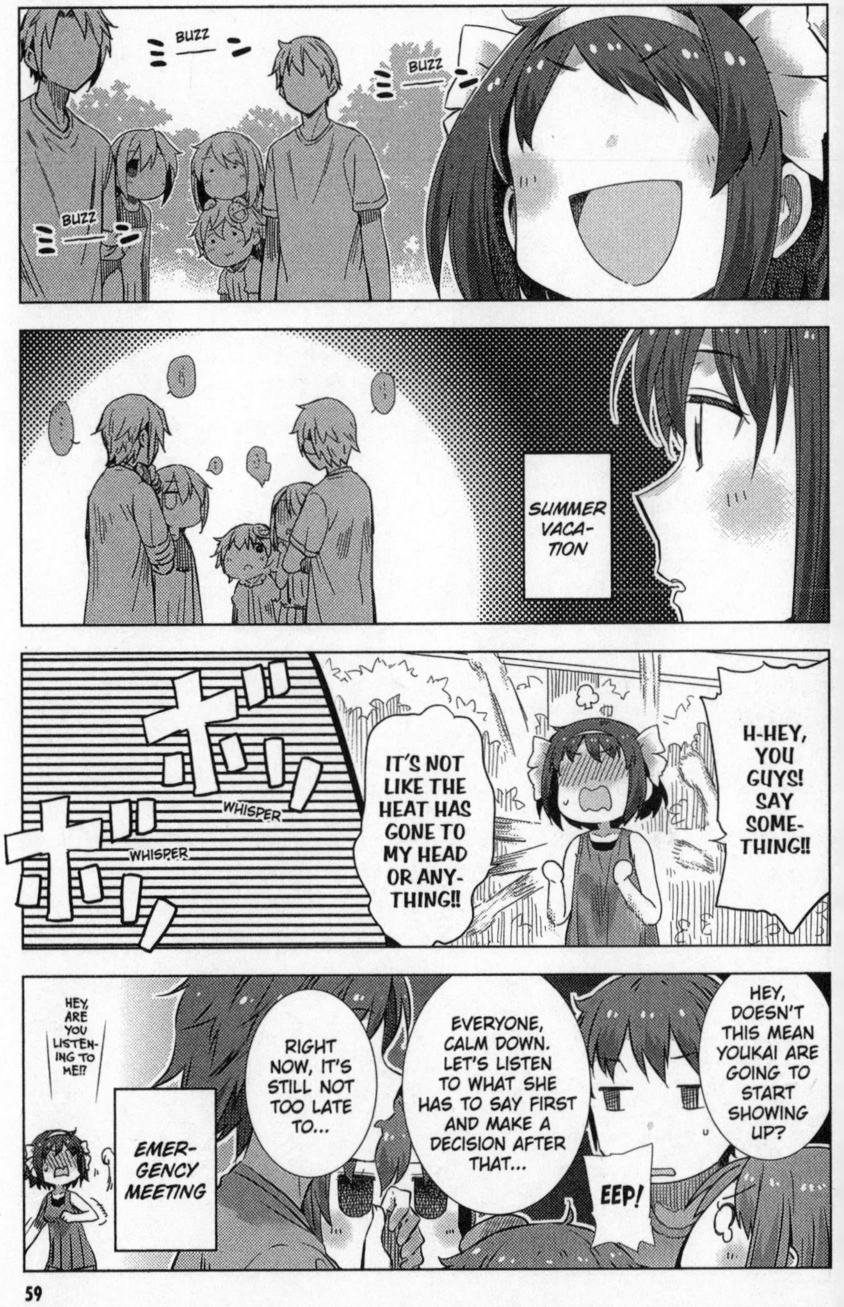
BUZZ
BUZZ
BUZZ
SUMMER VACA- TION
H-HEY, YOU GUYS! SAY SOME- THING!!
IT'S NOT LIKE THE HEAT HAS GONE TO MY HEAD OR ANY- THING!!
WHISPER
WHISPER
HEY, DOESN'T THIS MEAN YOUKAI ARE GOING TO START SHOWING UP?
EEP!
EVERYONE, CALM DOWN. LET'S LISTEN TO WHAT SHE HAS TO SAY FIRST AND MAKE A DECISION AFTER THAT...
RIGHT NOW, IT'S STILL NOT TOO LATE TO...
EMER- GENCY MEETING
HEY, ARE YOU LISTEN- ING TO ME!?

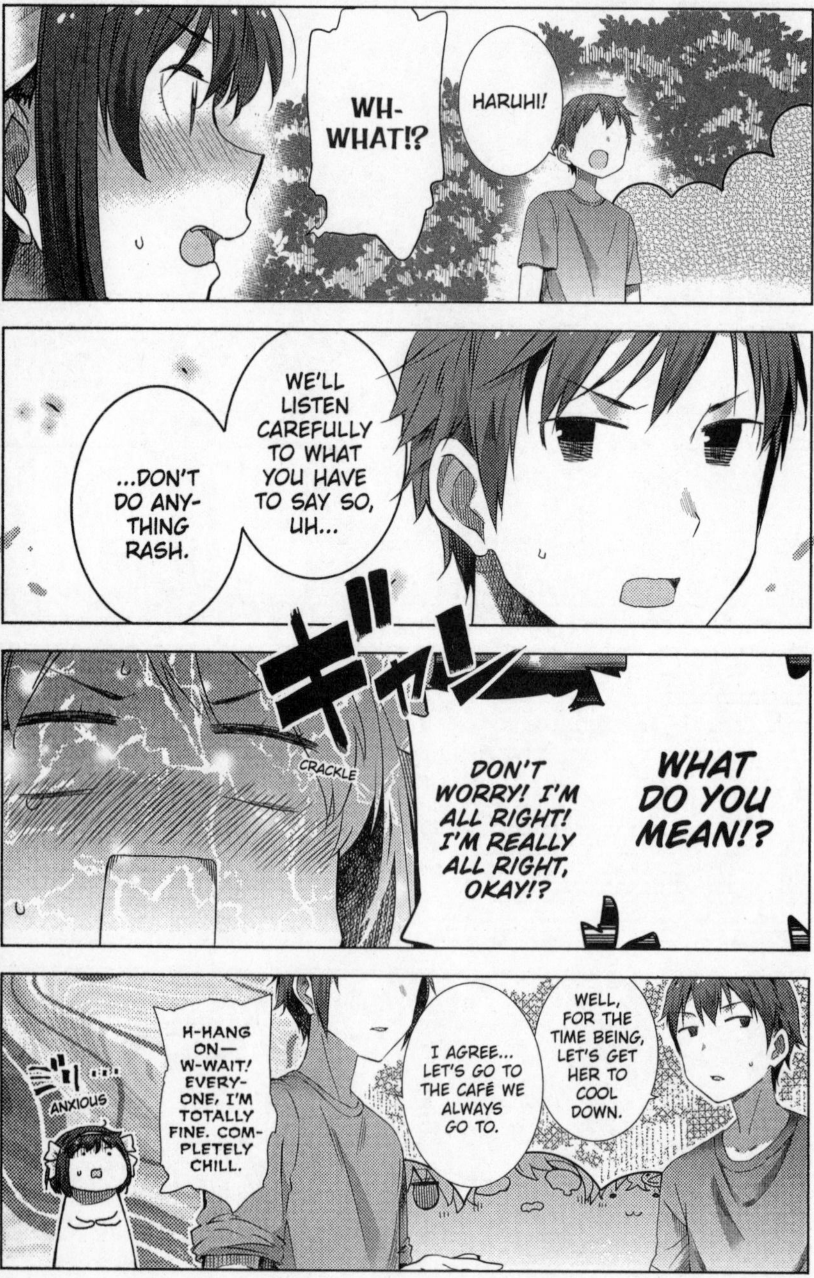
HARUHI!
WH-WHAT!?
WE'LL LISTEN CAREFULLY TO WHAT YOU HAVE TO SAY SO, UH...
...DON'T DO ANYTHING RASH.
WHAT DO YOU MEAN!?
DON'T WORRY! I'M ALL RIGHT! I'M REALLY ALL RIGHT, OKAY!?
CRACKLE
WELL, FOR THE TIME BEING, LET'S GET HER TO COOL DOWN.
I AGREE... LET'S GO TO THE CAFÉ WE ALWAYS GO TO.
H-HANG ON— W-WAIT! EVERYONE, I'M TOTALLY FINE. COMPLETELY CHILL.
ANXIOUS

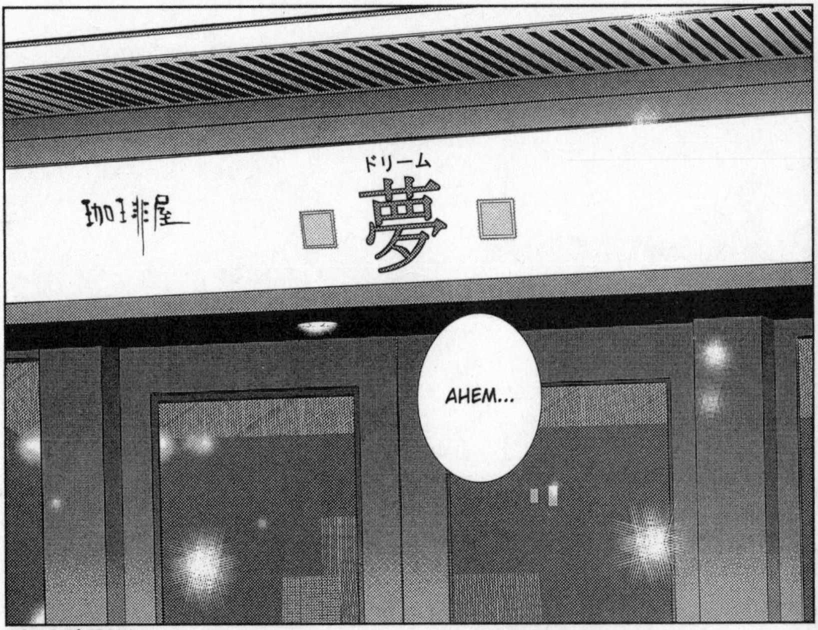
珈琲屋
ドリーム
夢
AHEM...

SIGN: CAFÉ DREAM

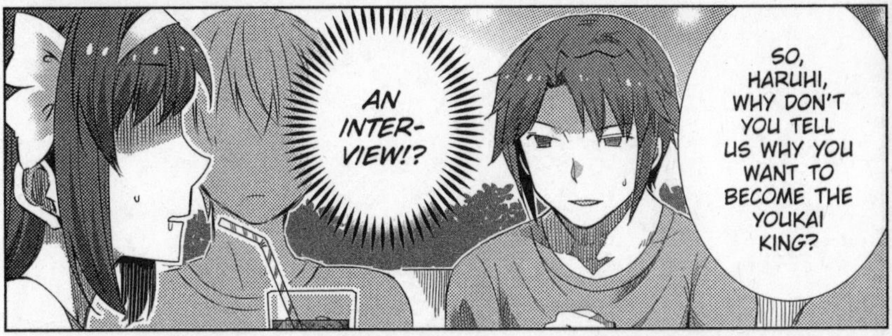
SO, HARUHI, WHY DON'T YOU TELL US WHY YOU WANT TO BECOME THE YOUKAI KING?
AN INTER-VIEW!?

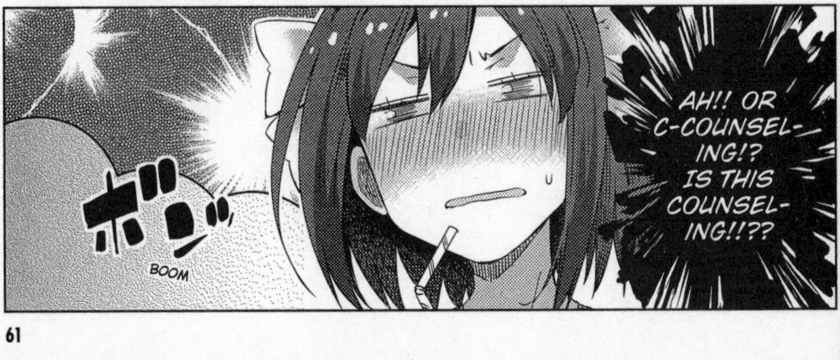
AH!! OR C-COUNSEL-ING!? IS THIS COUNSEL-ING!!??
BOOM

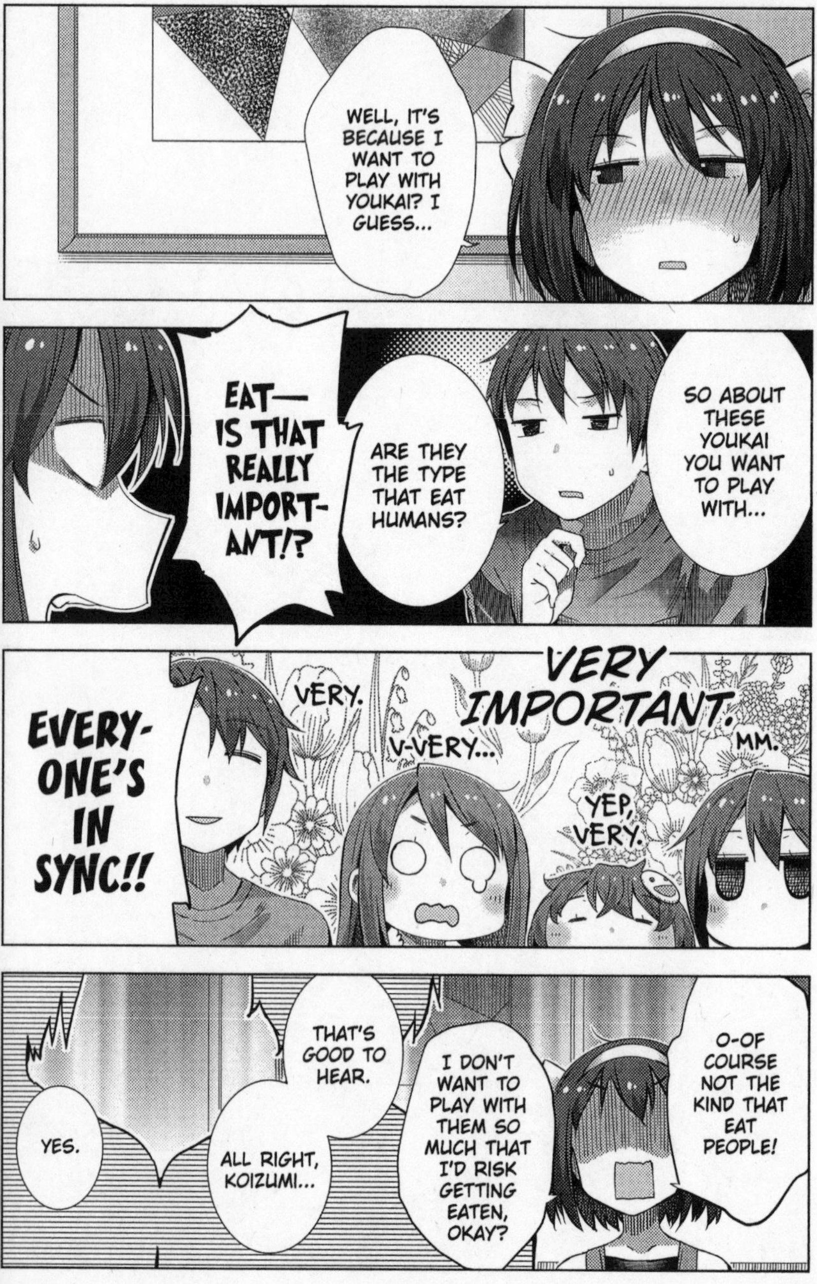
WELL, IT'S BECAUSE I WANT TO PLAY WITH YOUKAI? I GUESS...
SO ABOUT THESE YOUKAI YOU WANT TO PLAY WITH...
ARE THEY THE TYPE THAT EAT HUMANS?
EAT— IS THAT REALLY IMPORTANT!?
VERY IMPORTANT.
MM.
YEP, VERY.
V-VERY...
VERY.
EVERYONE'S IN SYNC!!
O-OF COURSE NOT THE KIND THAT EAT PEOPLE!
I DON'T WANT TO PLAY WITH THEM SO MUCH THAT I'D RISK GETTING EATEN, OKAY?
THAT'S GOOD TO HEAR.
ALL RIGHT, KOIZUMI...
YES.

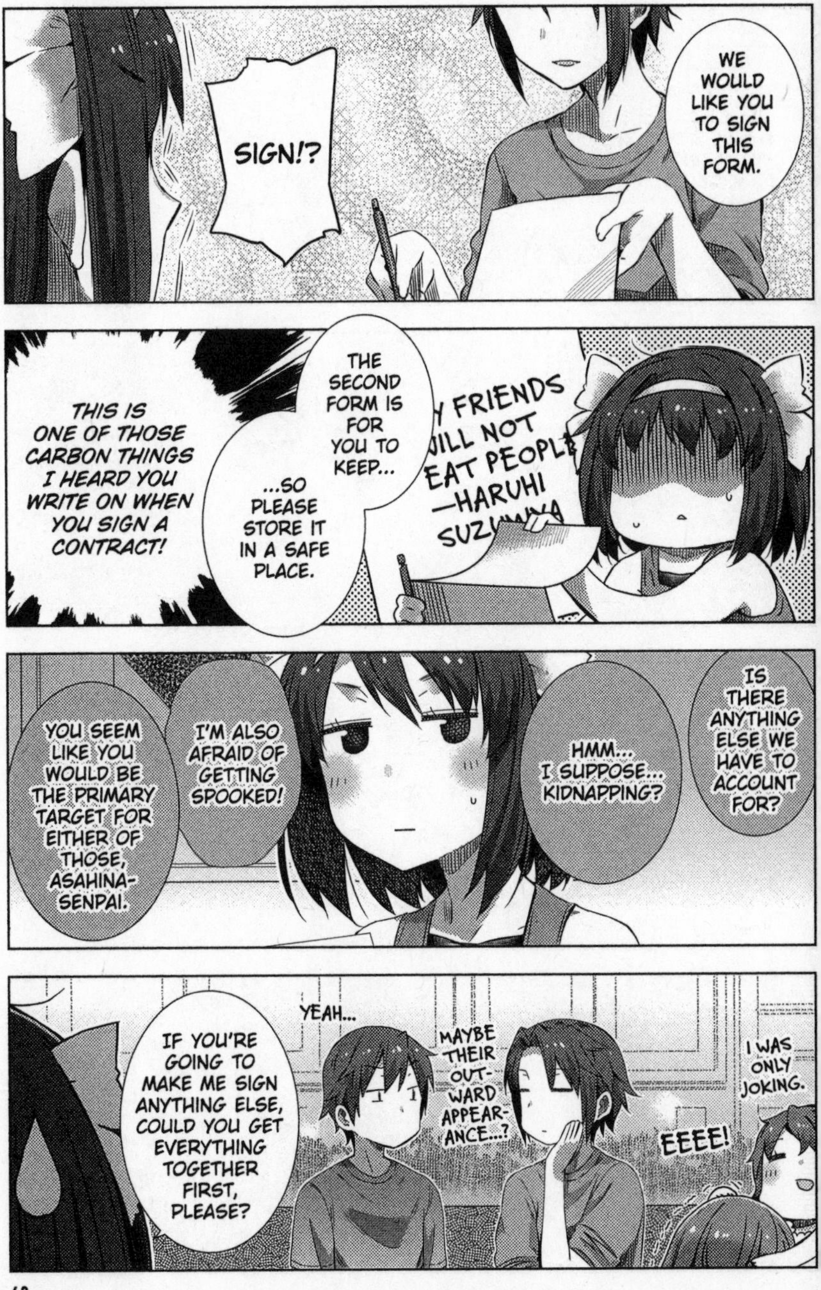
WE WOULD LIKE YOU TO SIGN THIS FORM.
SIGN!?
Y FRIENDS
ILL NOT
EAT PEOPL
—HARUHI
SUZU
THE SECOND FORM IS FOR YOU TO KEEP...
...SO PLEASE STORE IT IN A SAFE PLACE.
THIS IS ONE OF THOSE CARBON THINGS I HEARD YOU WRITE ON WHEN YOU SIGN A CONTRACT!
IS THERE ANYTHING ELSE WE HAVE TO ACCOUNT FOR?
HMM... I SUPPOSE... KIDNAPPING?
I'M ALSO AFRAID OF GETTING SPOOKED!
YOU SEEM LIKE YOU WOULD BE THE PRIMARY TARGET FOR EITHER OF THOSE, ASAHINA-SENPAI.
I WAS ONLY JOKING.
EEEE!
MAYBE THEIR OUT-WARD APPEARANCE...?
YEAH...
IF YOU'RE GOING TO MAKE ME SIGN ANYTHING ELSE, COULD YOU GET EVERYTHING TOGETHER FIRST, PLEASE?

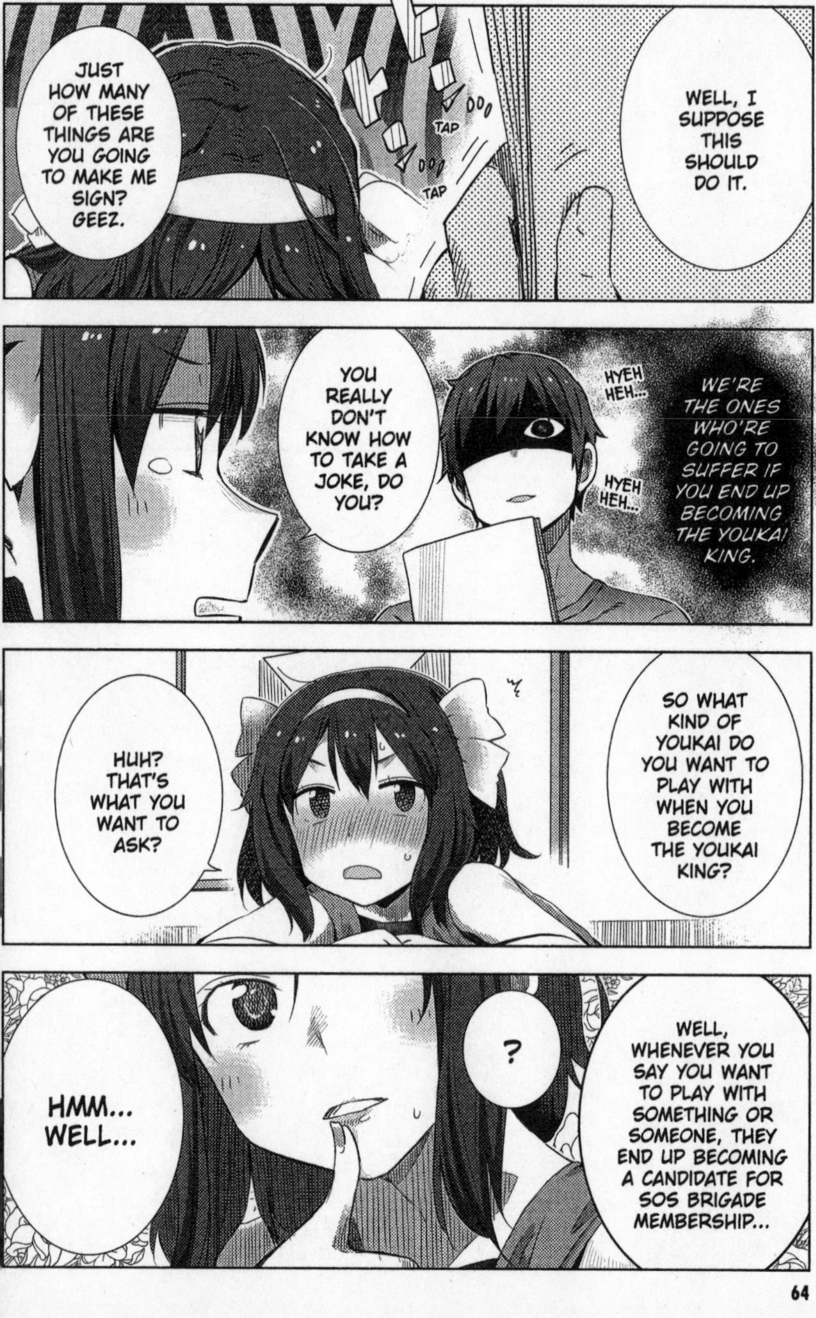
WELL, I SUPPOSE THIS SHOULD DO IT.
TAP
TAP
JUST HOW MANY OF THESE THINGS ARE YOU GOING TO MAKE ME SIGN? GEEZ.
WE'RE THE ONES WHO'RE GOING TO SUFFER IF YOU END UP BECOMING THE YOUKAI KING.
HYEH HEH...
HYEH HEH...
YOU REALLY DON'T KNOW HOW TO TAKE A JOKE, DO YOU?
SO WHAT KIND OF YOUKAI DO YOU WANT TO PLAY WITH WHEN YOU BECOME THE YOUKAI KING?
HUH? THAT'S WHAT YOU WANT TO ASK?
WELL, WHENEVER YOU SAY YOU WANT TO PLAY WITH SOMETHING OR SOMEONE, THEY END UP BECOMING A CANDIDATE FOR SOS BRIGADE MEMBERSHIP...
?
HMM... WELL...

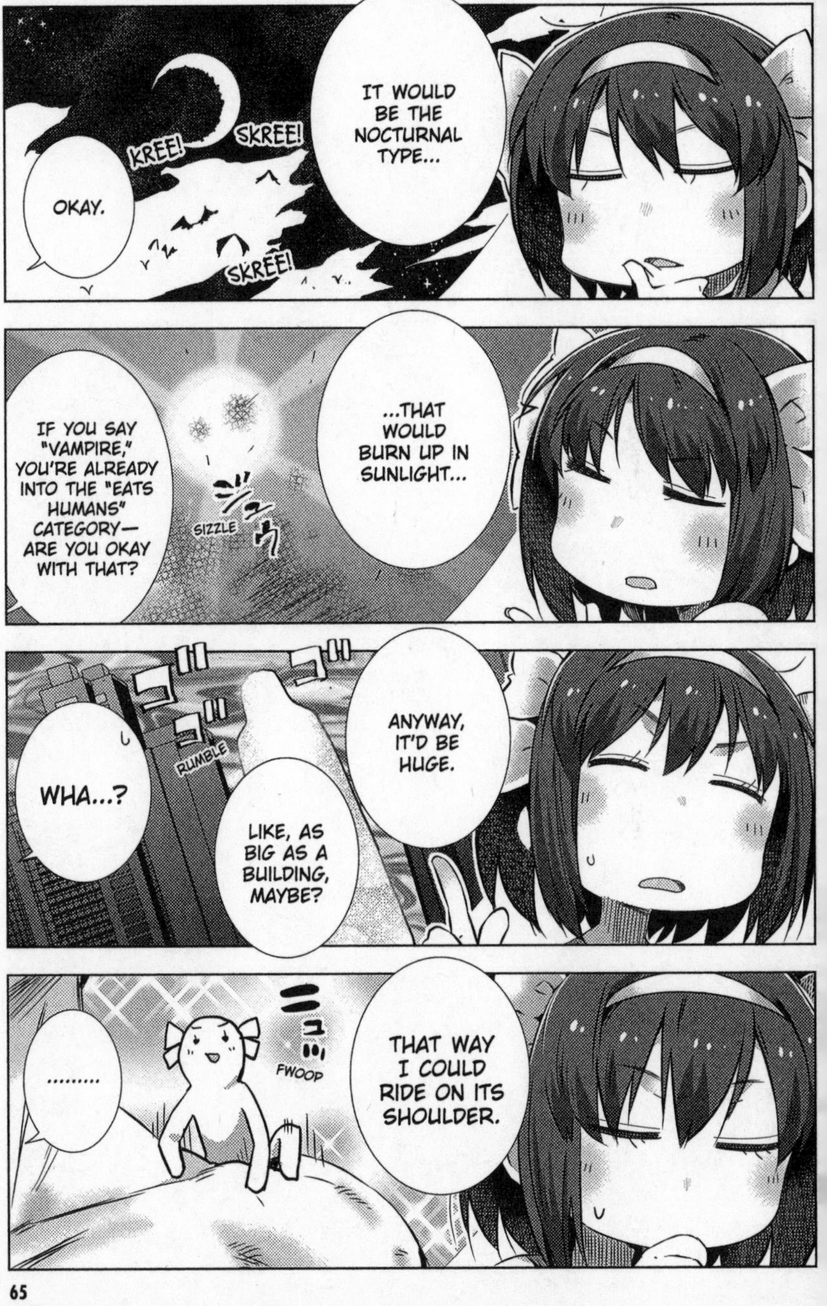
IT WOULD BE THE NOCTURNAL TYPE...
SKREE!
KREE!
OKAY.
SKREE!
...THAT WOULD BURN UP IN SUNLIGHT...
SIZZLE
IF YOU SAY "VAMPIRE," YOU'RE ALREADY INTO THE "EATS HUMANS" CATEGORY—ARE YOU OKAY WITH THAT?
ANYWAY, IT'D BE HUGE.
LIKE, AS BIG AS A BUILDING, MAYBE?
RUMBLE
WHA...?
THAT WAY I COULD RIDE ON ITS SHOULDER.
FWOOP
....

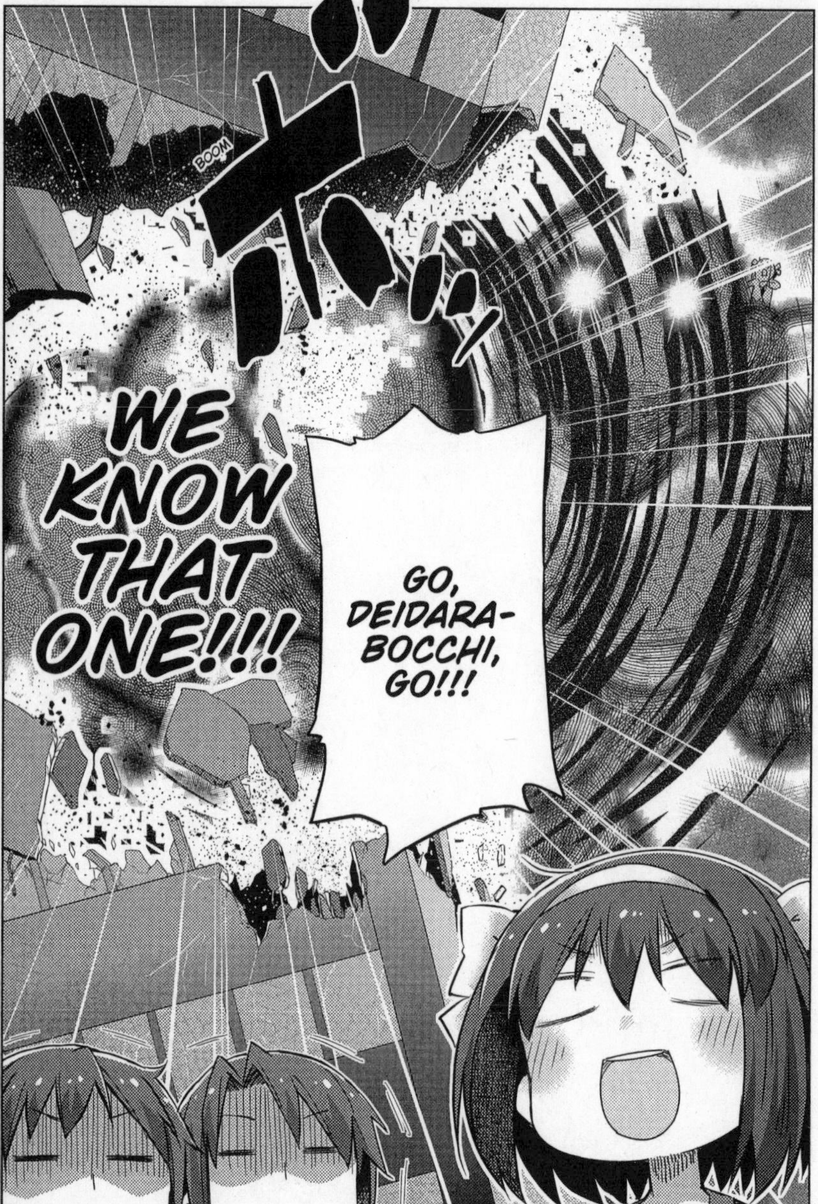
BOOM
GO, DEIDARA-BOCCHI, GO!!!
WE KNOW THAT ONE!!!!

NOTE: "DEIDARABOCCHI" (ALSO "DAIDARABOCCHI") IS AN ENORMOUS YOUKAI (MONSTER) FROM JAPANESE FOLKLORE.

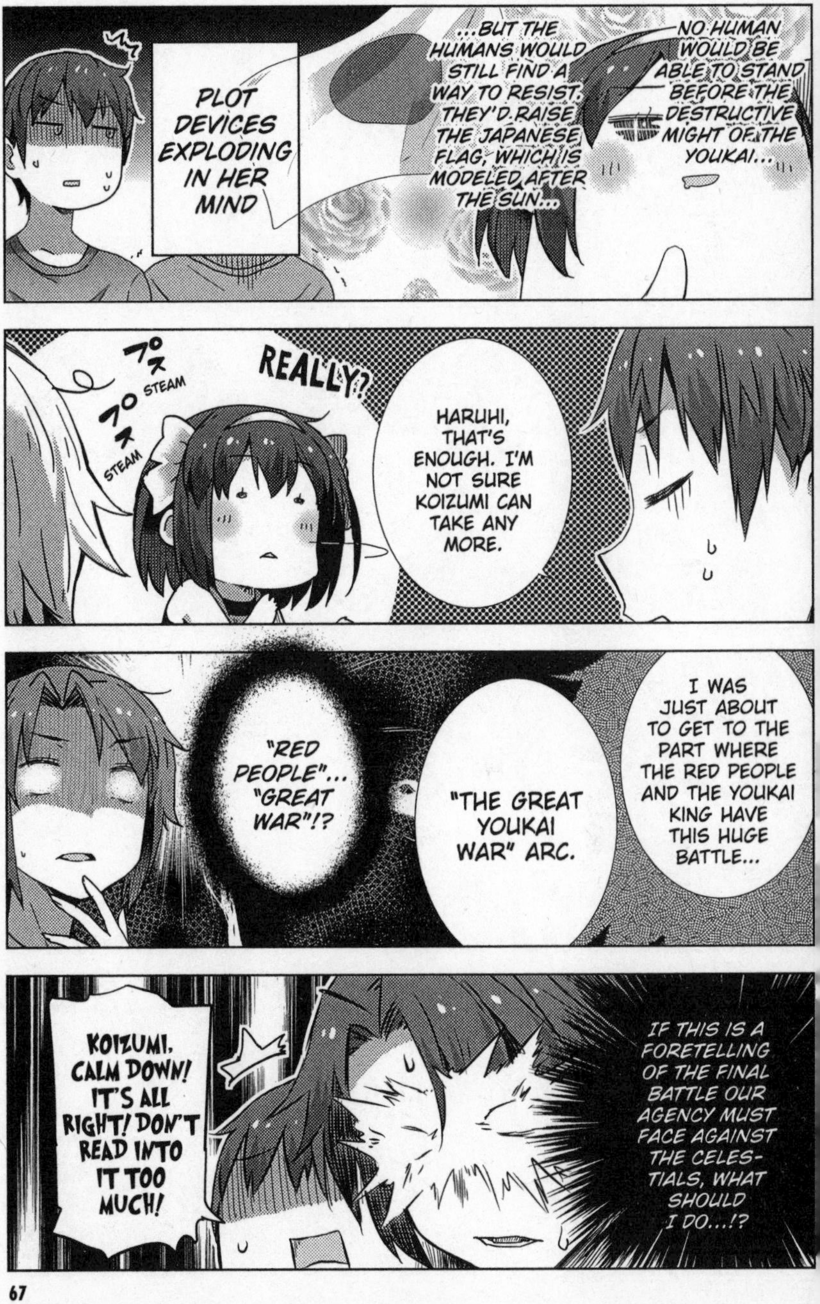
NO HUMAN WOULD BE ABLE TO STAND BEFORE THE DESTRUCTIVE MIGHT OF THE YOUKAI...
...BUT THE HUMANS WOULD STILL FIND A WAY TO RESIST. THEY'D RAISE THE JAPANESE FLAG, WHICH IS MODELED AFTER THE SUN...
PLOT DEVICES EXPLODING IN HER MIND
HARUHI, THAT'S ENOUGH. I'M NOT SURE KOIZUMI CAN TAKE ANY MORE.
REALLY?
プス STEAM
プス STEAM
I WAS JUST ABOUT TO GET TO THE PART WHERE THE RED PEOPLE AND THE YOUKAI KING HAVE THIS HUGE BATTLE...
"THE GREAT YOUKAI WAR" ARC.
"RED PEOPLE"... "GREAT WAR"!?
IF THIS IS A FORETELLING OF THE FINAL BATTLE OUR AGENCY MUST FACE AGAINST THE CELES-TIALS, WHAT SHOULD I DO...!?
KOIZUMI, CALM DOWN! IT'S ALL RIGHT! DON'T READ INTO IT TOO MUCH!

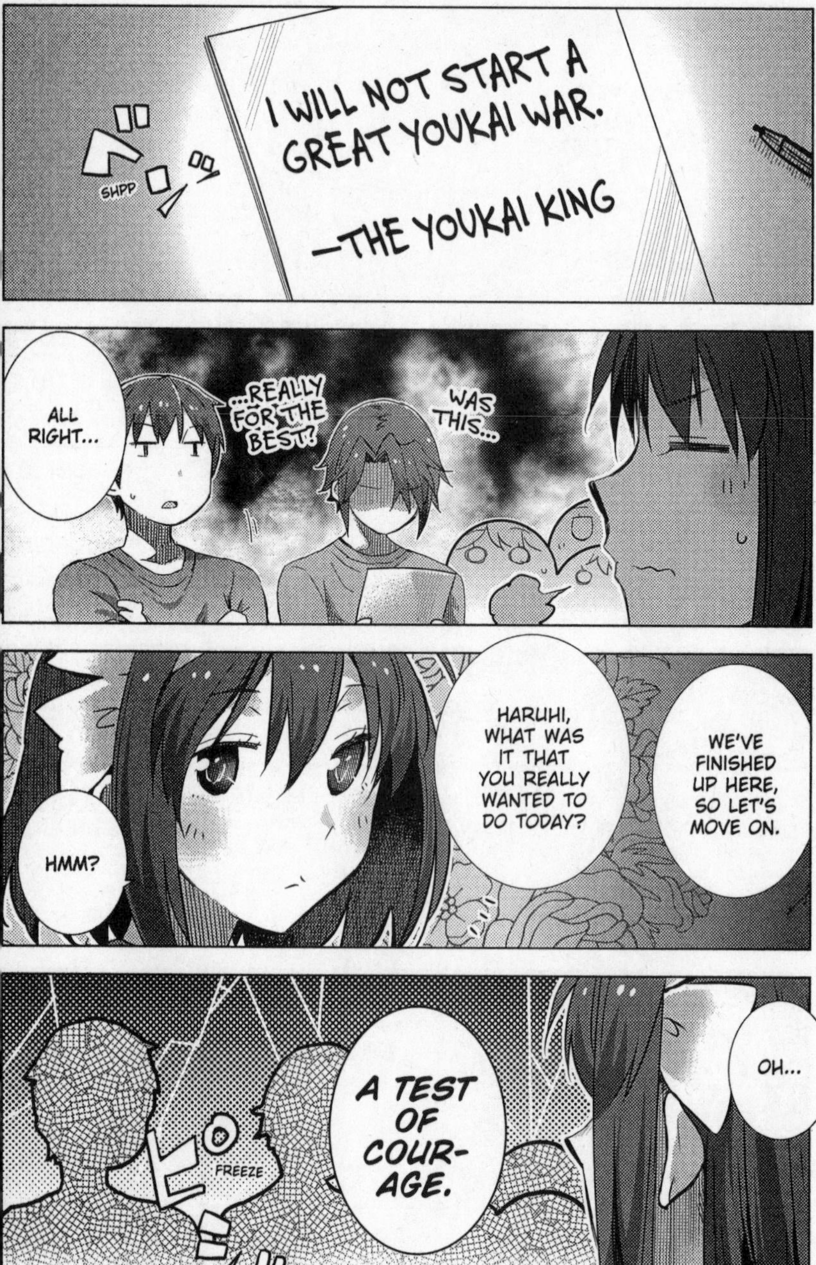
I WILL NOT START A GREAT YOUKAI WAR.
—THE YOUKAI KING
SHPP
WAS THIS...
...REALLY FOR THE BEST?
ALL RIGHT...
WE'VE FINISHED UP HERE, SO LET'S MOVE ON.
HARUHI, WHAT WAS IT THAT YOU REALLY WANTED TO DO TODAY?
HMM?
OH...
A TEST OF COUR-AGE.
FREEZE

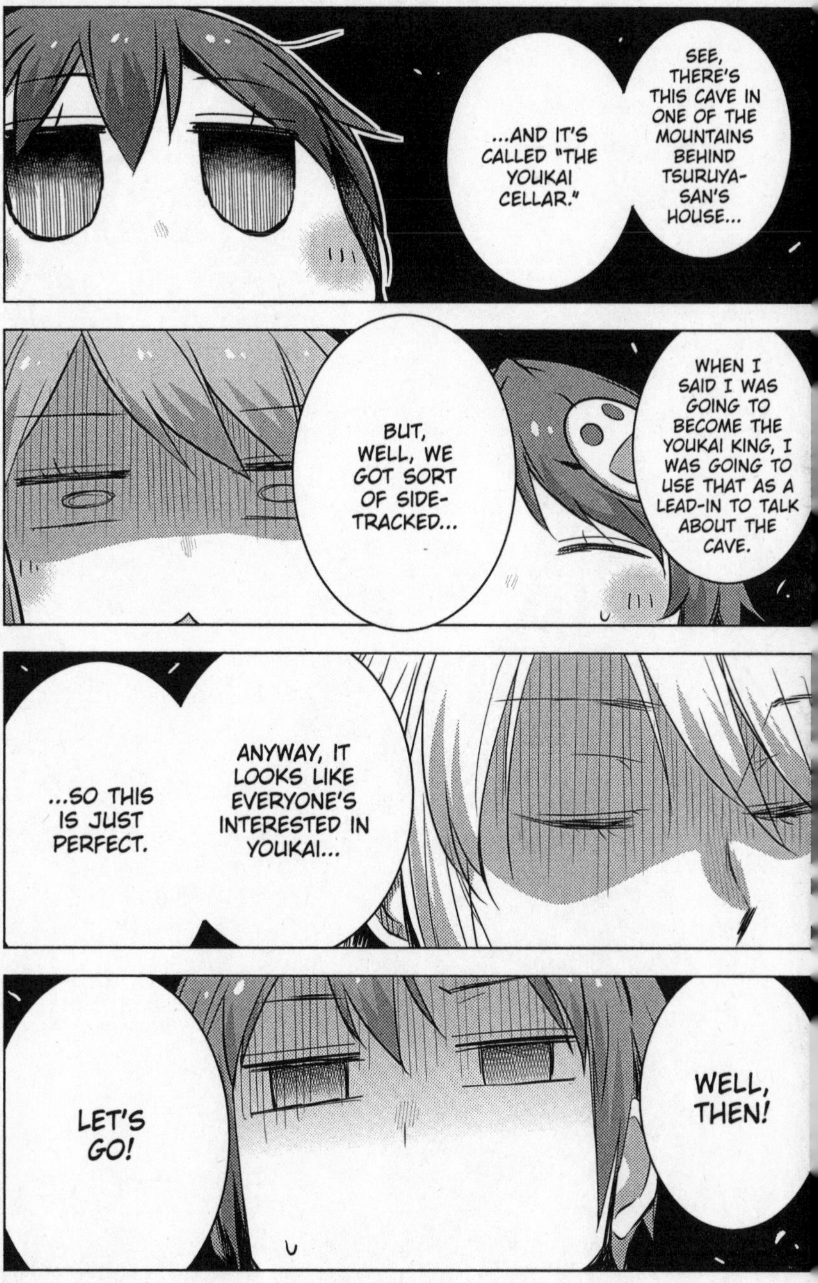
SEE, THERE'S THIS CAVE IN ONE OF THE MOUNTAINS BEHIND TSURUYA-SAN'S HOUSE...
...AND IT'S CALLED "THE YOUKAI CELLAR."
WHEN I SAID I WAS GOING TO BECOME THE YOUKAI KING, I WAS GOING TO USE THAT AS A LEAD-IN TO TALK ABOUT THE CAVE.
BUT, WELL, WE GOT SORT OF SIDE-TRACKED...
ANYWAY, IT LOOKS LIKE EVERYONE'S INTERESTED IN YOUKAI...
...SO THIS IS JUST PERFECT.
WELL, THEN!
LET'S GO!

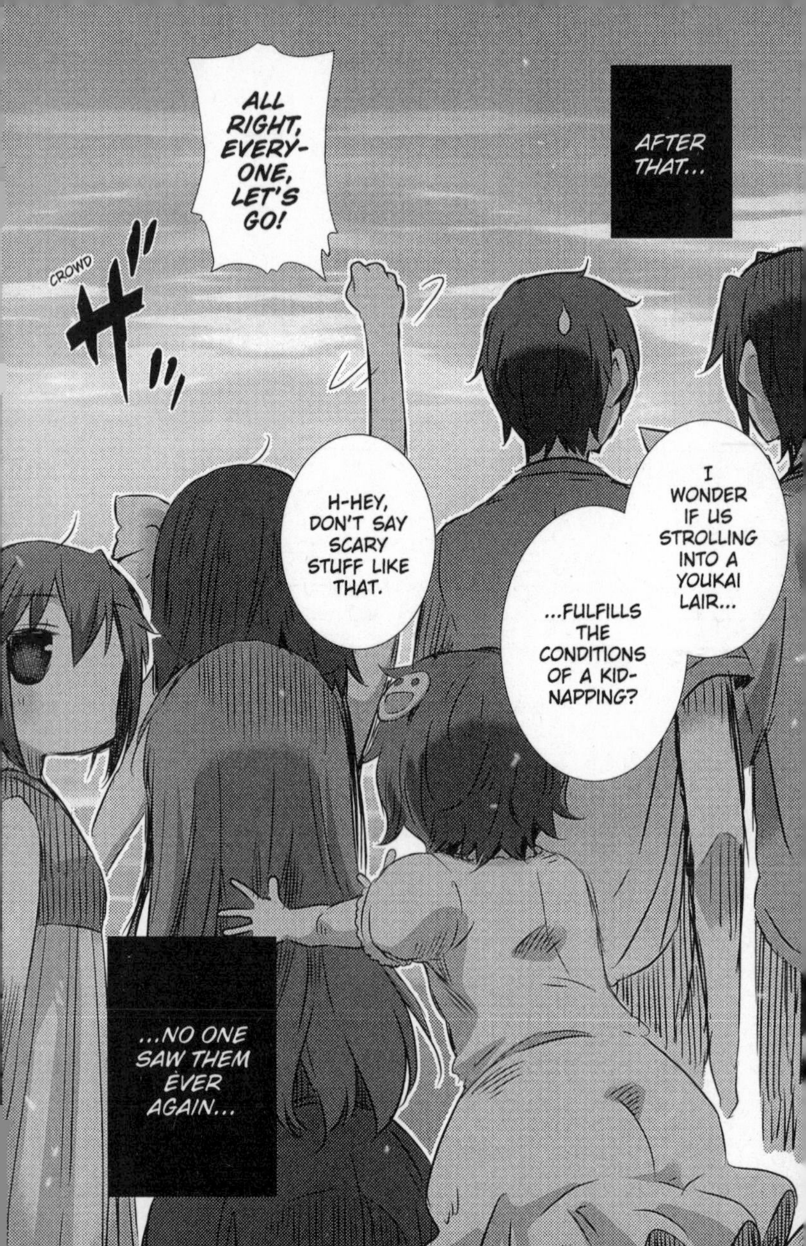
AFTER THAT...
ALL RIGHT, EVERYONE, LET'S GO!
CROWD
I WONDER IF US STROLLING INTO A YOUKAI LAIR...
...FULFILLS THE CONDITIONS OF A KIDNAPPING?
H-HEY, DON'T SAY SCARY STUFF LIKE THAT.
...NO ONE SAW THEM EVER AGAIN...

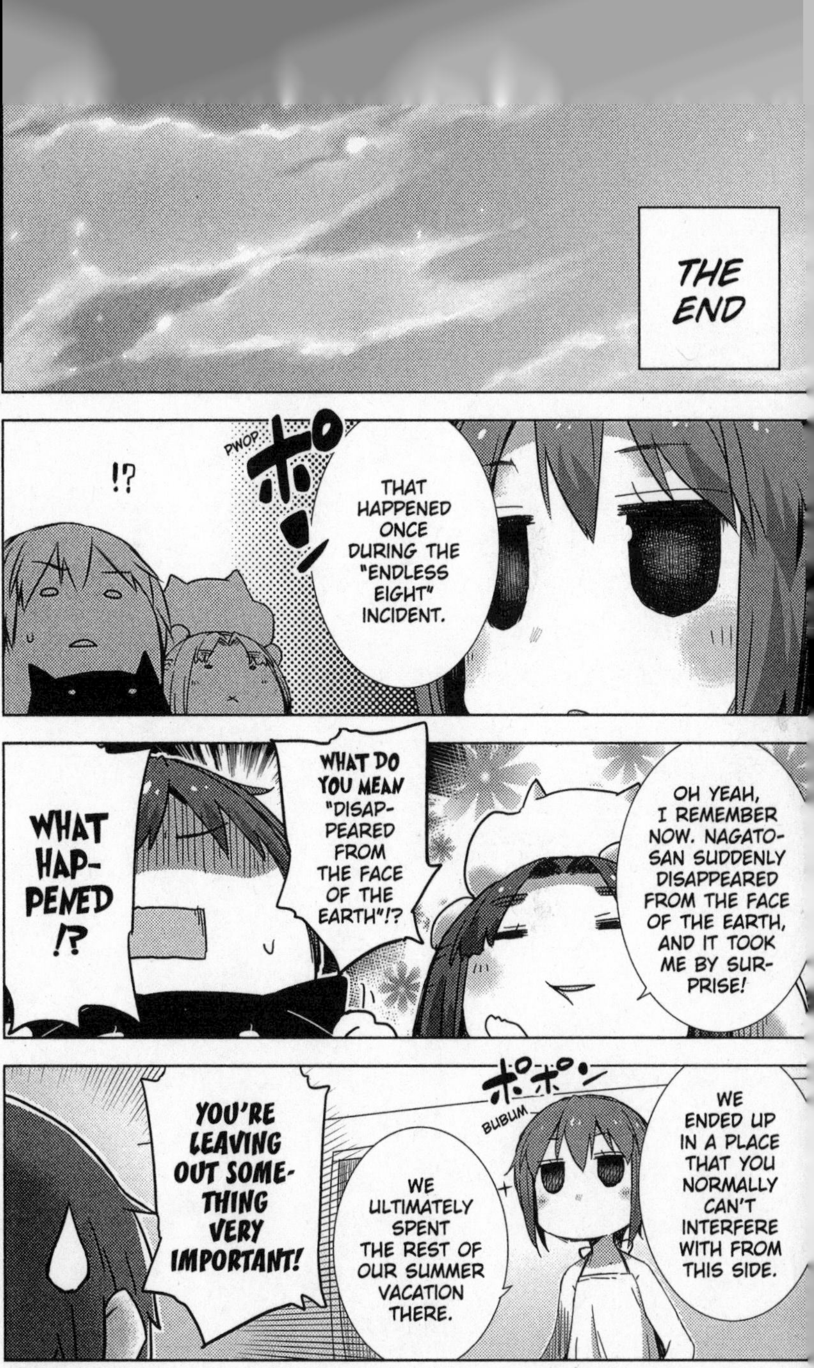
THE END
THAT HAPPENED ONCE DURING THE "ENDLESS EIGHT" INCIDENT.
PWOP
!?
OH YEAH, I REMEMBER NOW. NAGATO-SAN SUDDENLY DISAPPEARED FROM THE FACE OF THE EARTH, AND IT TOOK ME BY SURPRISE!
WHAT DO YOU MEAN "DISAPPEARED FROM THE FACE OF THE EARTH"!?
WHAT HAPPENED!?
BUBUM
WE ENDED UP IN A PLACE THAT YOU NORMALLY CAN'T INTERFERE WITH FROM THIS SIDE.
WE ULTIMATELY SPENT THE REST OF OUR SUMMER VACATION THERE.
YOU'RE LEAVING OUT SOMETHING VERY IMPORTANT!

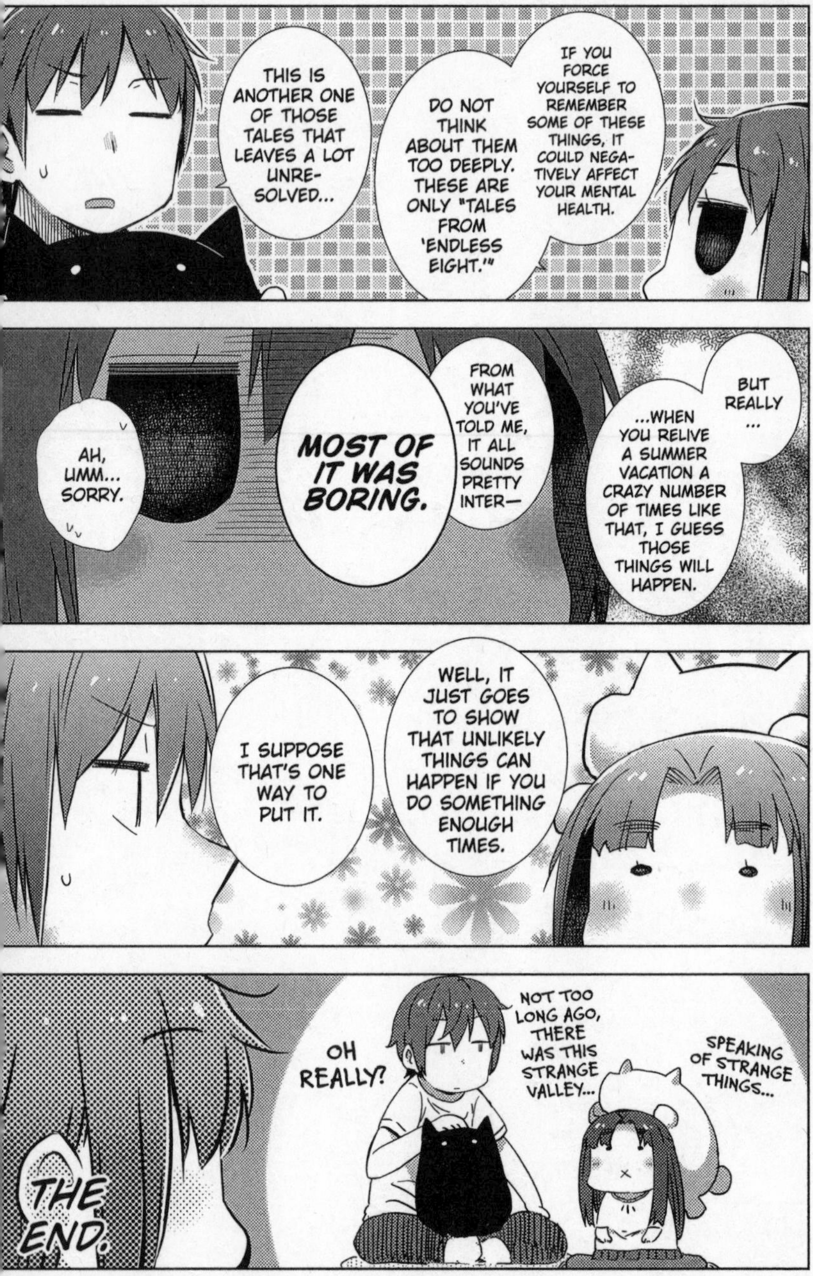
IF YOU FORCE YOURSELF TO REMEMBER SOME OF THESE THINGS, IT COULD NEGA-TIVELY AFFECT YOUR MENTAL HEALTH.
DO NOT THINK ABOUT THEM TOO DEEPLY. THESE ARE ONLY "TALES FROM 'ENDLESS EIGHT.'"
THIS IS ANOTHER ONE OF THOSE TALES THAT LEAVES A LOT UNRE-SOLVED...
BUT REALLY...
...WHEN YOU RELIVE A SUMMER VACATION A CRAZY NUMBER OF TIMES LIKE THAT, I GUESS THOSE THINGS WILL HAPPEN.
FROM WHAT YOU'VE TOLD ME, IT ALL SOUNDS PRETTY INTER—
MOST OF IT WAS BORING.
AH, UMM... SORRY.
WELL, IT JUST GOES TO SHOW THAT UNLIKELY THINGS CAN HAPPEN IF YOU DO SOMETHING ENOUGH TIMES.
I SUPPOSE THAT'S ONE WAY TO PUT IT.
SPEAKING OF STRANGE THINGS...
NOT TOO LONG AGO, THERE WAS THIS STRANGE VALLEY...
OH REALLY?
THE END.

TALES
FROM
"END-
LESS
EIGHT"

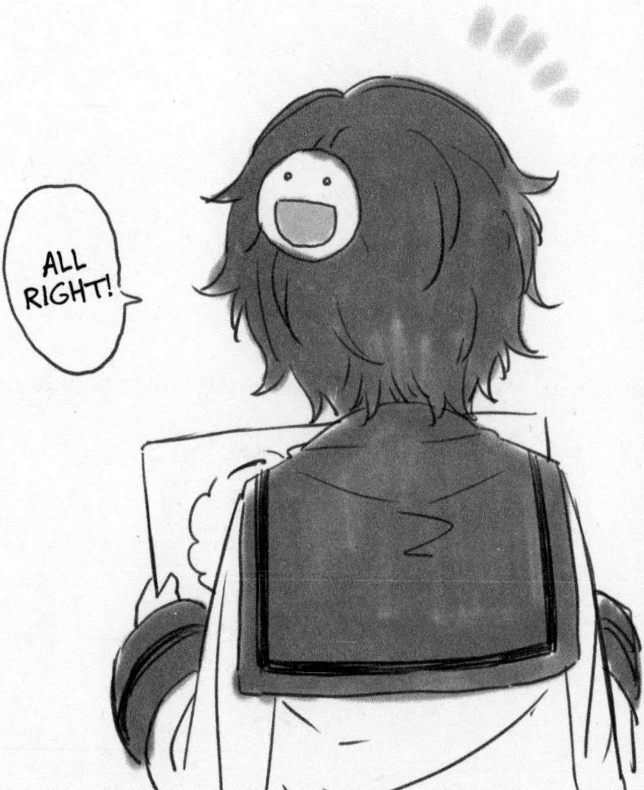
ALL RIGHT!

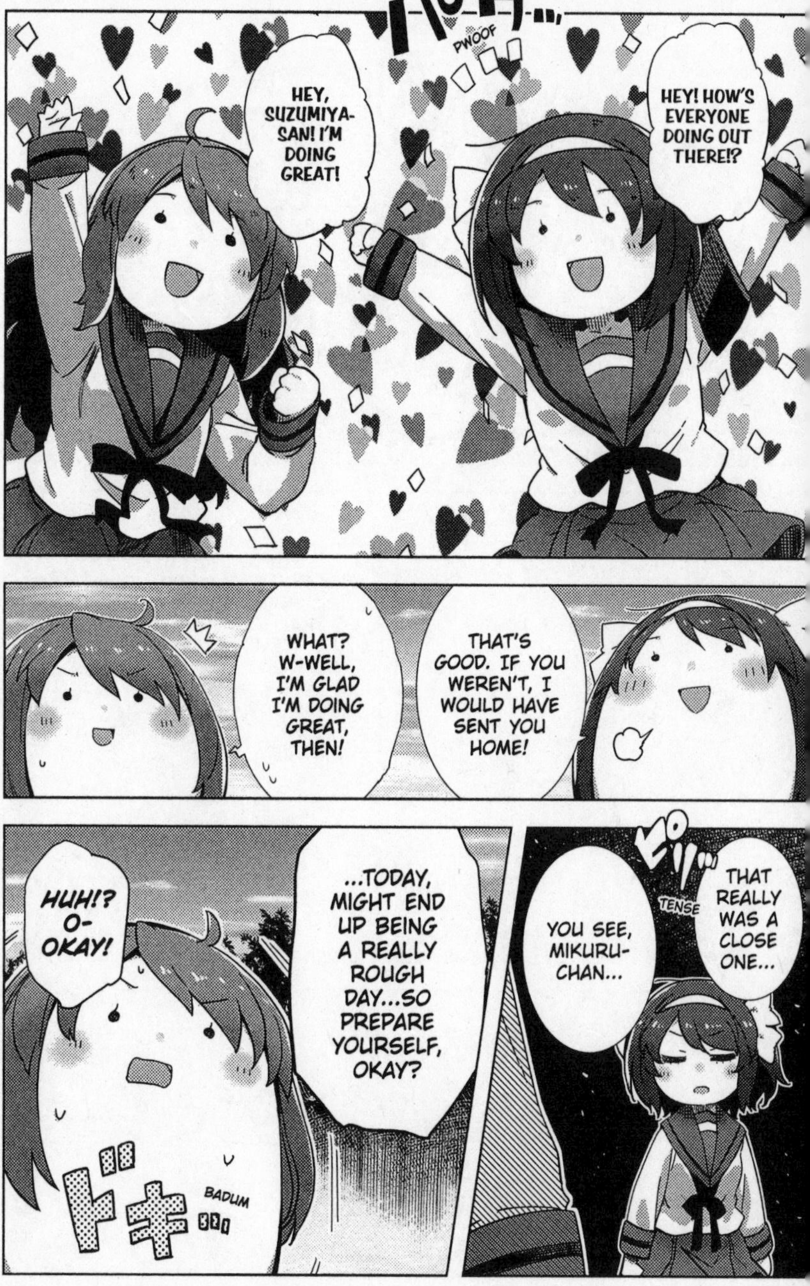
PWOOF
HEY! HOW'S EVERYONE DOING OUT THERE!?
HEY, SUZUMIYA-SAN! I'M DOING GREAT!
THAT'S GOOD. IF YOU WEREN'T, I WOULD HAVE SENT YOU HOME!
WHAT? W-WELL, I'M GLAD I'M DOING GREAT, THEN!
TENSE
THAT REALLY WAS A CLOSE ONE...
YOU SEE, MIKURU-CHAN...
...TODAY, MIGHT END UP BEING A REALLY ROUGH DAY...SO PREPARE YOURSELF, OKAY?
HUH!? O-OKAY!
BADUM

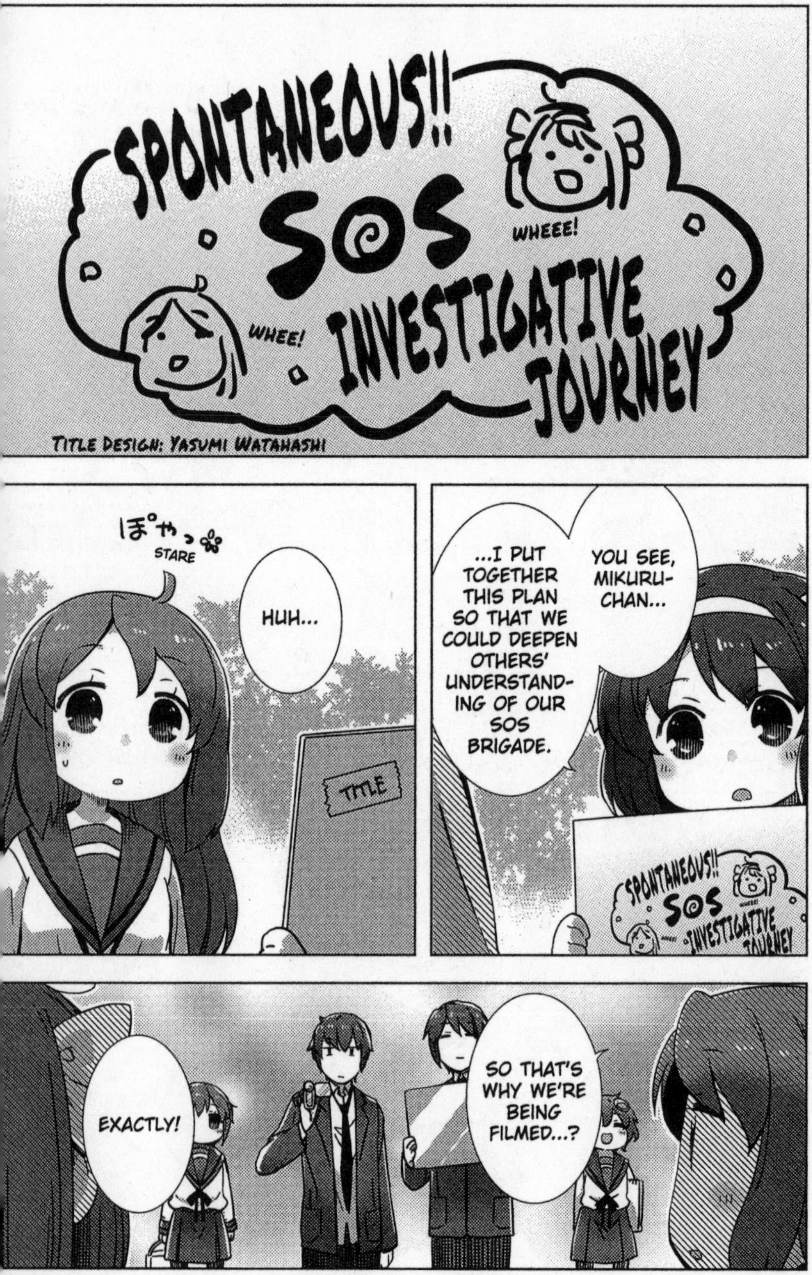
SPONTANEOUS!! SOS INVESTIGATIVE JOURNEY
WHEEE!
WHEE!
TITLE DESIGN: YASUMI WATAHASHI
YOU SEE, MIKURU-CHAN...
...I PUT TOGETHER THIS PLAN SO THAT WE COULD DEEPEN OTHERS' UNDERSTANDING OF OUR SOS BRIGADE.
SPONTANEOUS!! SOS INVESTIGATIVE JOURNEY
ぽやっ
STARE
HUH...
TITLE
SO THAT'S WHY WE'RE BEING FILMED...?
EXACTLY!

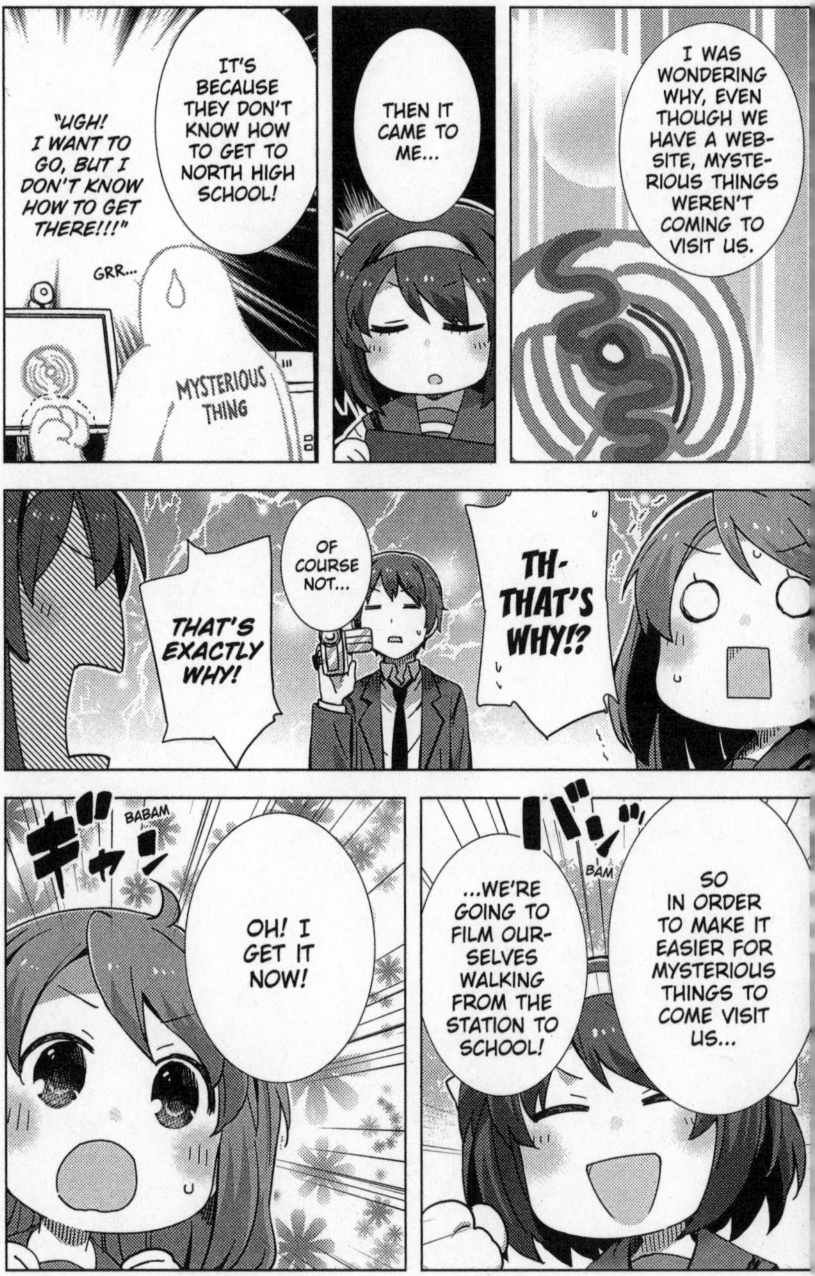
I WAS WONDERING WHY, EVEN THOUGH WE HAVE A WEB-SITE, MYSTE-RIOUS THINGS WEREN'T COMING TO VISIT US.
THEN IT CAME TO ME...
IT'S BECAUSE THEY DON'T KNOW HOW TO GET TO NORTH HIGH SCHOOL!
"UGH! I WANT TO GO, BUT I DON'T KNOW HOW TO GET THERE!!!"
GRR...
MYSTERIOUS THING
TH-THAT'S WHY!?
OF COURSE NOT...
THAT'S EXACTLY WHY!
バン
BAM
SO IN ORDER TO MAKE IT EASIER FOR MYSTERIOUS THINGS TO COME VISIT US...
...WE'RE GOING TO FILM OUR-SELVES WALKING FROM THE STATION TO SCHOOL!
ギャン
BABAM
OH! I GET IT NOW!

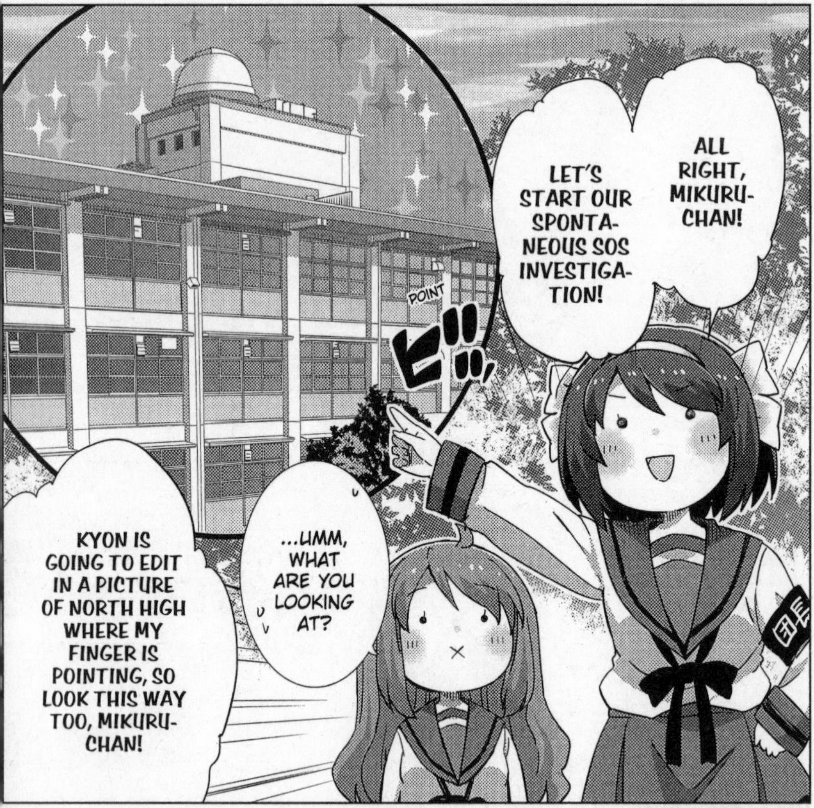
ALL RIGHT, MIKURU-CHAN!
LET'S START OUR SPONTANEOUS SOS INVESTIGATION!
POINT
...UMM, WHAT ARE YOU LOOKING AT?
KYON IS GOING TO EDIT IN A PICTURE OF NORTH HIGH WHERE MY FINGER IS POINTING, SO LOOK THIS WAY TOO, MIKURU-CHAN!

ARMBAND: BRIGADE CHIEF

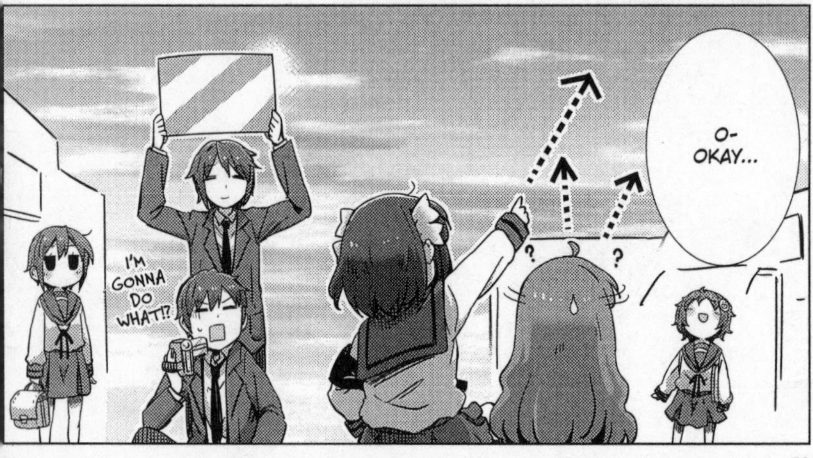
O-OKAY...
I'M GONNA DO WHAT!?

ROUTE TO SCHOOL

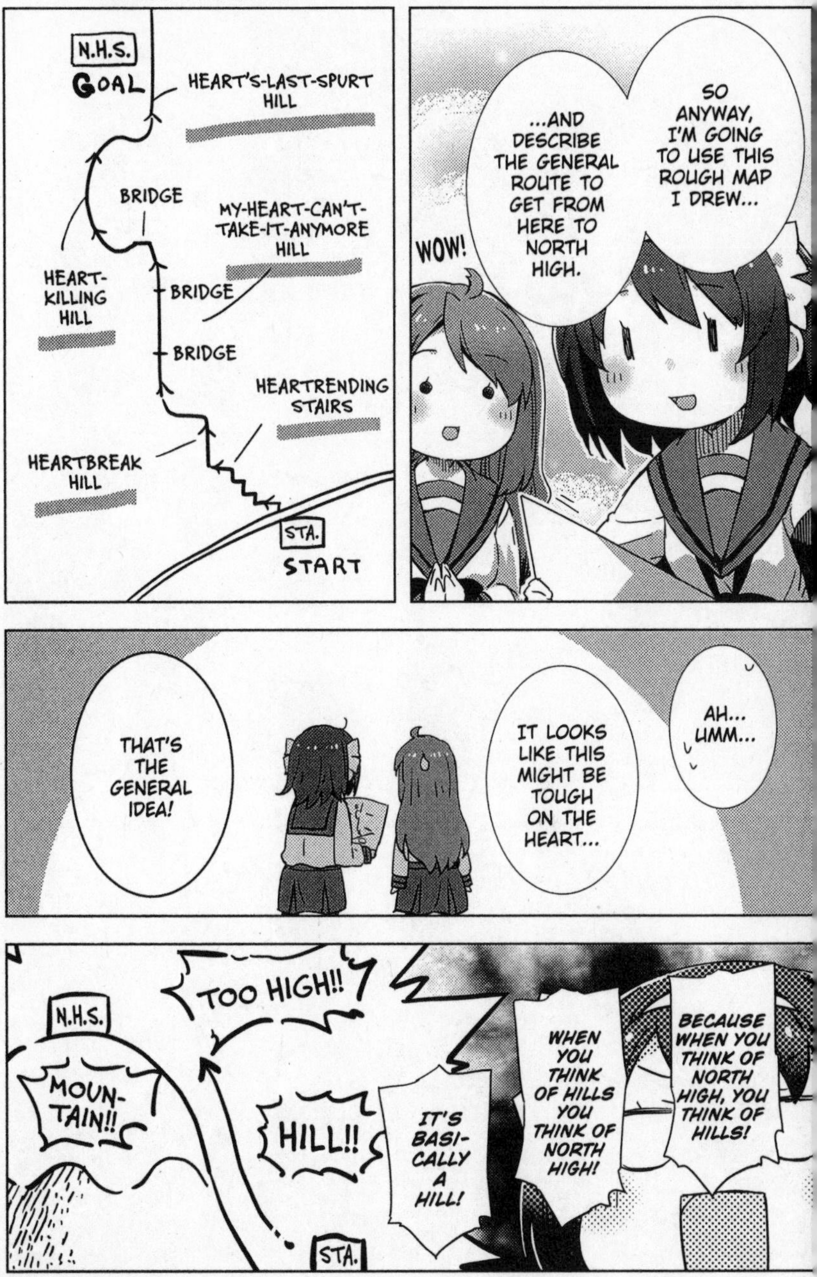
SO ANYWAY, I'M GOING TO USE THIS ROUGH MAP I DREW...
...AND DESCRIBE THE GENERAL ROUTE TO GET FROM HERE TO NORTH HIGH.
WOW!
N.H.S.
GOAL
HEART'S-LAST-SPURT HILL
BRIDGE
MY-HEART-CAN'T-TAKE-IT-ANYMORE HILL
HEART-KILLING HILL
BRIDGE
BRIDGE
HEARTRENDING STAIRS
HEARTBREAK HILL
STA.
START
AH... UMM...
IT LOOKS LIKE THIS MIGHT BE TOUGH ON THE HEART...
THAT'S THE GENERAL IDEA!
BECAUSE WHEN YOU THINK OF NORTH HIGH, YOU THINK OF HILLS!
WHEN YOU THINK OF HILLS YOU THINK OF NORTH HIGH!
IT'S BASICALLY A HILL!
HILL!!
TOO HIGH!!
N.H.S.
MOUN-TAIN!!
STA.

*NOT TO SCALE

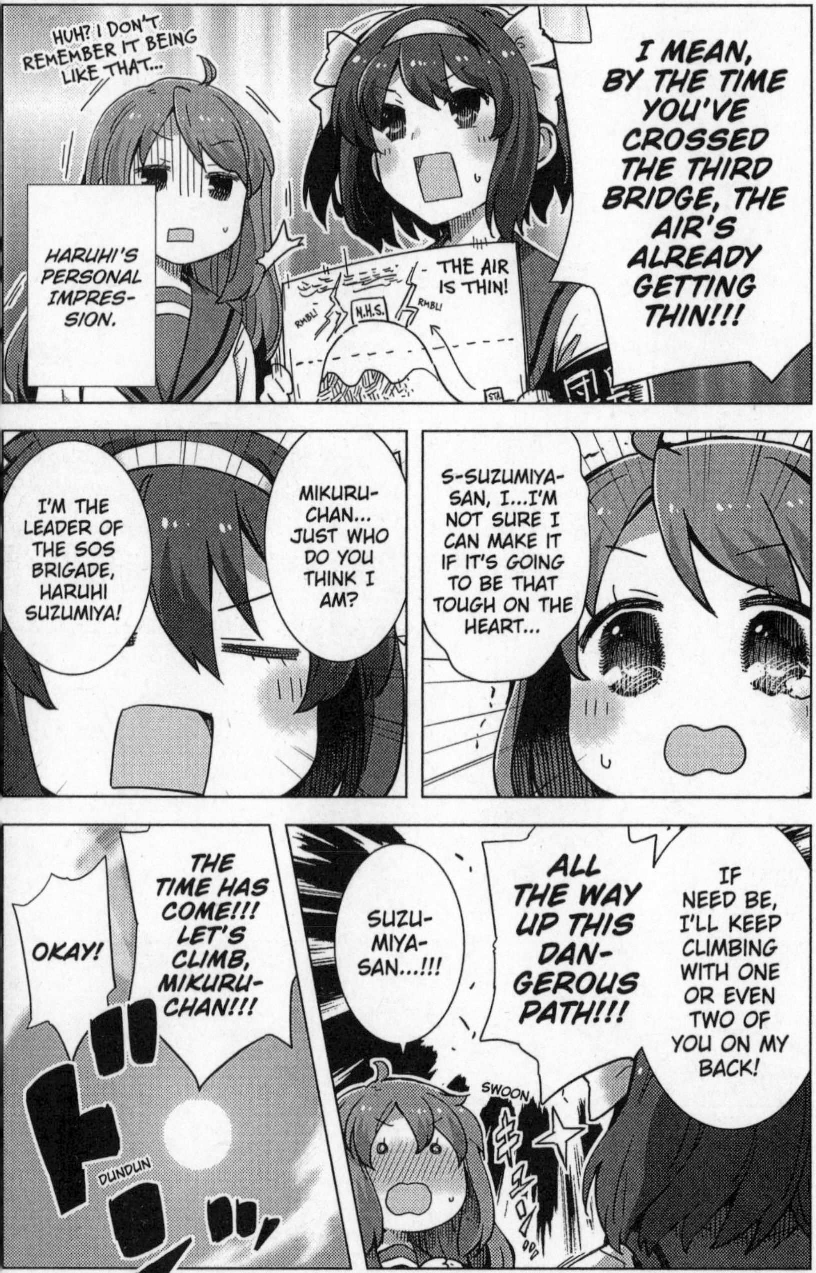
I MEAN, BY THE TIME YOU'VE CROSSED THE THIRD BRIDGE, THE AIR'S ALREADY GETTING THIN!!!
THE AIR IS THIN!
RMBL!
N.H.S.
RMBL!
HUH? I DON'T REMEMBER IT BEING LIKE THAT...
HARUHI'S PERSONAL IMPRES-SION.
S-SUZUMIYA-SAN, I...I'M NOT SURE I CAN MAKE IT IF IT'S GOING TO BE THAT TOUGH ON THE HEART...
MIKURU-CHAN... JUST WHO DO YOU THINK I AM?
I'M THE LEADER OF THE SOS BRIGADE, HARUHI SUZUMIYA!
IF NEED BE, I'LL KEEP CLIMBING WITH ONE OR EVEN TWO OF YOU ON MY BACK!
ALL THE WAY UP THIS DAN-GEROUS PATH!!!
SUZU-MIYA-SAN...!!!
SWOON
THE TIME HAS COME!!! LET'S CLIMB, MIKURU-CHAN!!!
OKAY!
DUNDUN

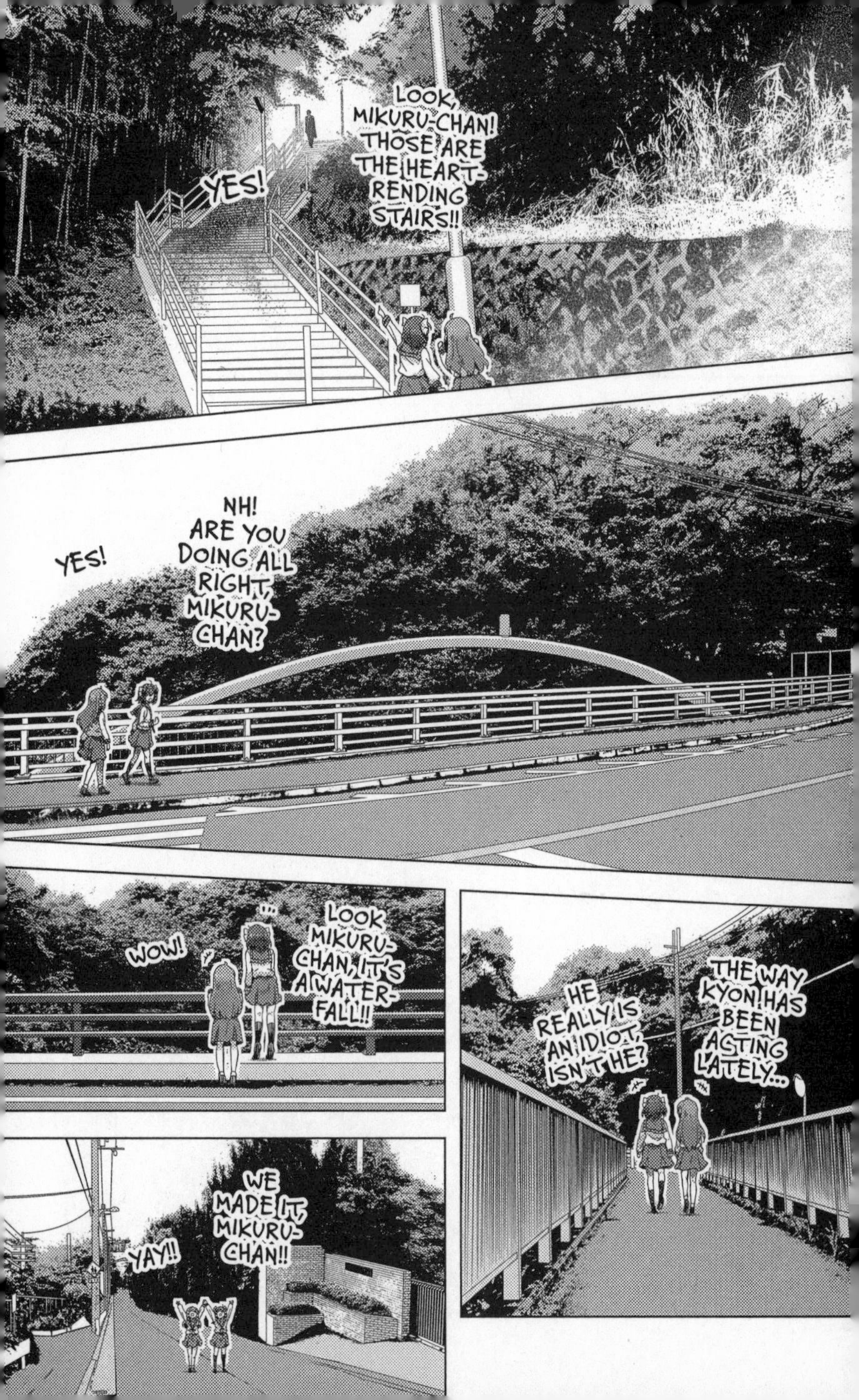
LOOK, MIKURU-CHAN! THOSE ARE THE HEART-RENDING STAIRS!!
YES!
NH! ARE YOU DOING ALL RIGHT, MIKURU-CHAN?
YES!
THE WAY KYON HAS BEEN ACTING LATELY...
HE REALLY IS AN IDIOT, ISN'T HE?
...
LOOK MIKURU-CHAN, IT'S A WATERFALL!!
WOW!
WE MADE IT, MIKURU-CHAN!!
YAY!!

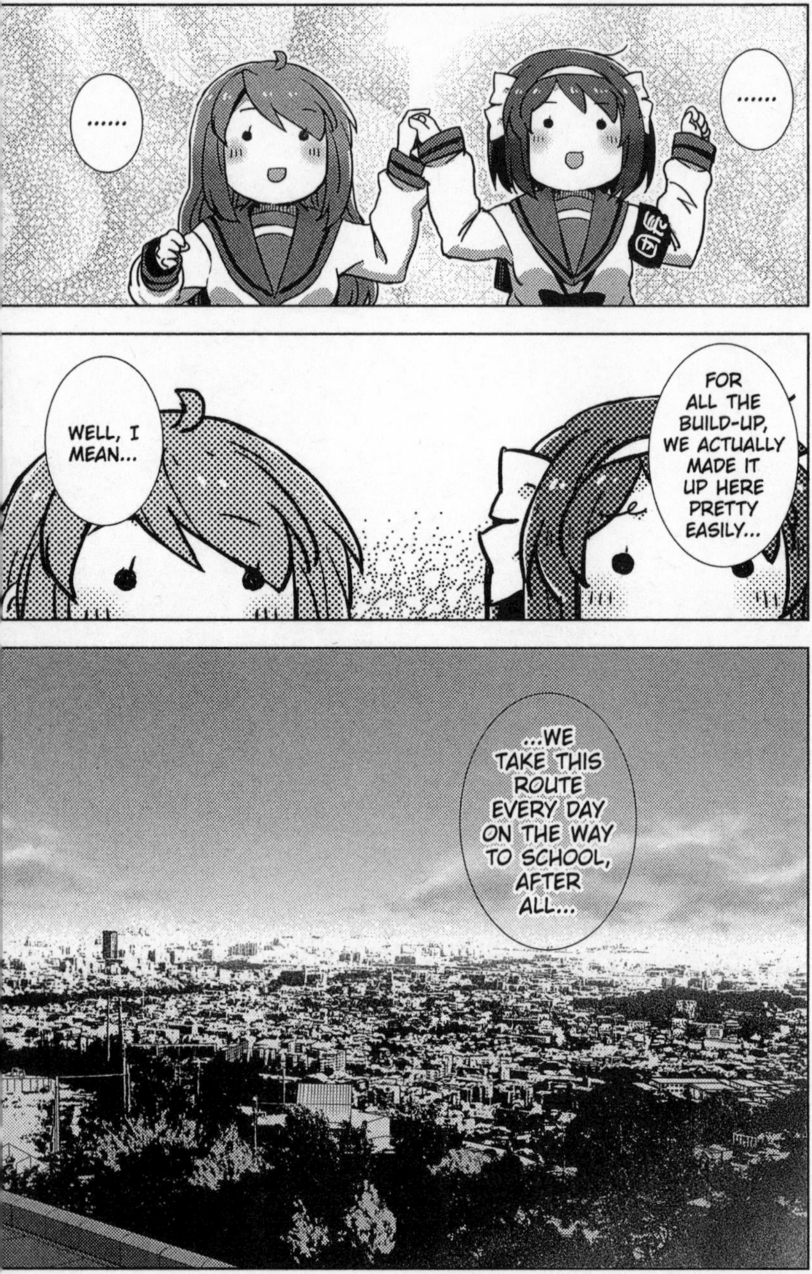
......
......
FOR ALL THE BUILD-UP, WE ACTUALLY MADE IT UP HERE PRETTY EASILY...
WELL, I MEAN...
...WE TAKE THIS ROUTE EVERY DAY ON THE WAY TO SCHOOL, AFTER ALL...

FOR THE TENTH VOLUME OF HARUHI-CHAN, I WAS FINALLY ABLE TO GO ON-SITE TO GATHER MATERIAL.

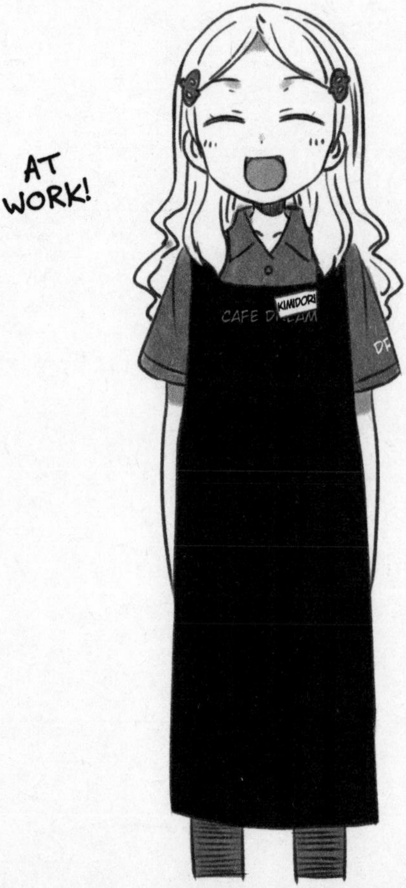
AT WORK!
KIMIDORI

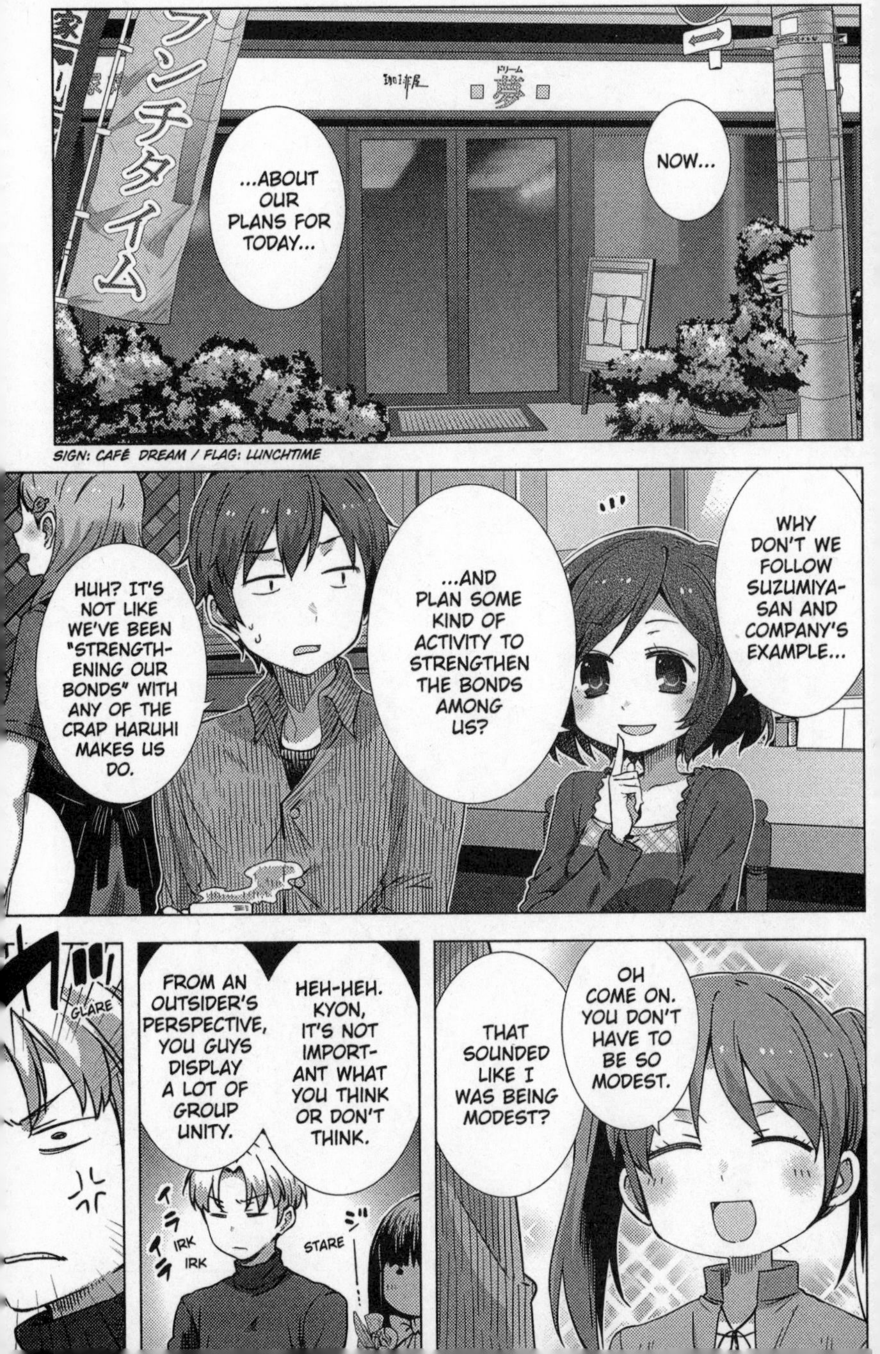
NOW...
...ABOUT OUR PLANS FOR TODAY...
SIGN: CAFÉ DREAM / FLAG: LUNCHTIME
...
WHY DON'T WE FOLLOW SUZUMIYA-SAN AND COMPANY'S EXAMPLE...
...AND PLAN SOME KIND OF ACTIVITY TO STRENGTHEN THE BONDS AMONG US?
HUH? IT'S NOT LIKE WE'VE BEEN "STRENGTH-ENING OUR BONDS" WITH ANY OF THE CRAP HARUHI MAKES US DO.
OH COME ON. YOU DON'T HAVE TO BE SO MODEST.
THAT SOUNDED LIKE I WAS BEING MODEST?
HEH-HEH. KYON, IT'S NOT IMPORT-ANT WHAT YOU THINK OR DON'T THINK.
FROM AN OUTSIDER'S PERSPECTIVE, YOU GUYS DISPLAY A LOT OF GROUP UNITY.
STARE
IRK
IRK
GLARE

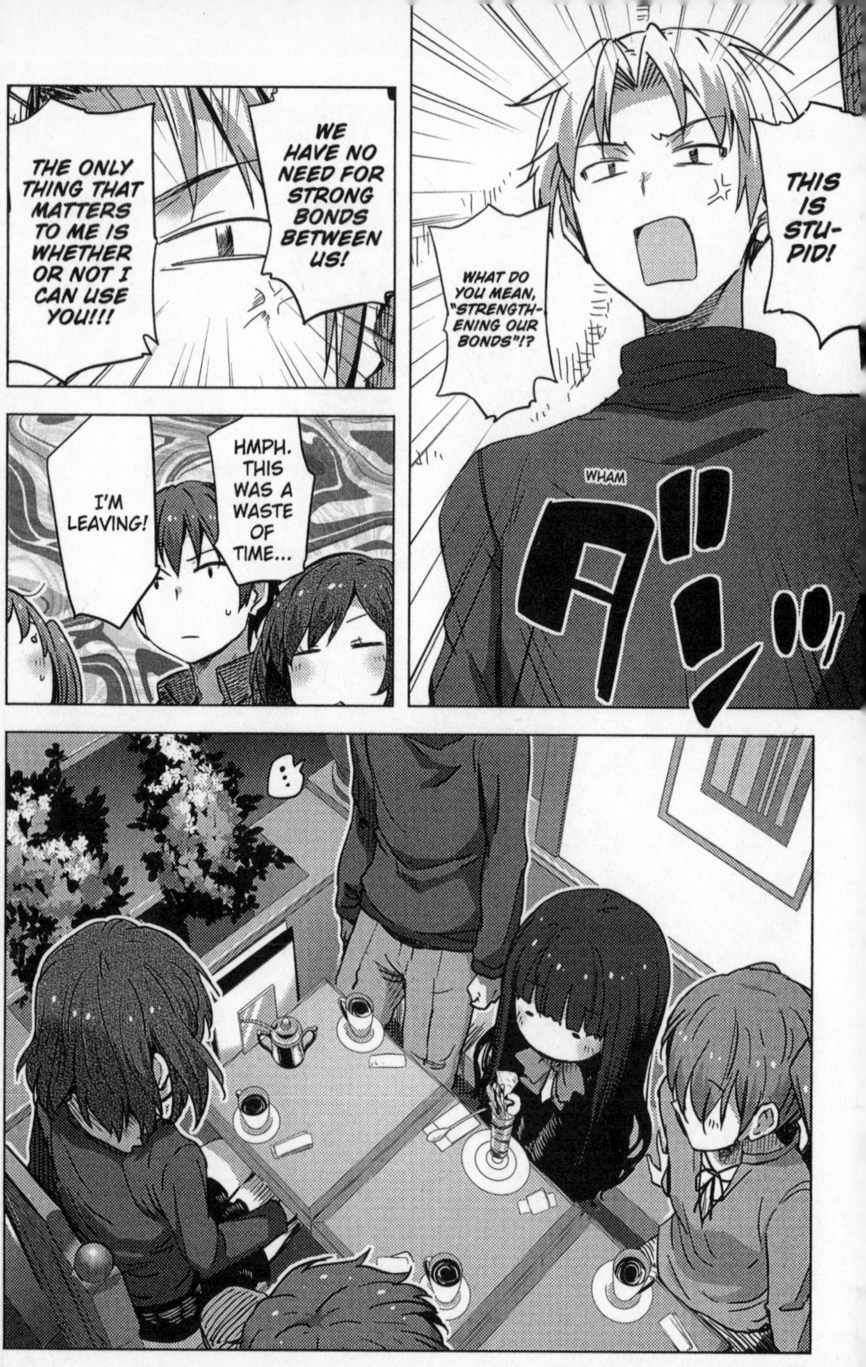
THIS IS STU-PID!
WHAT DO YOU MEAN, "STRENGTH-ENING OUR BONDS"!?
WHAM
WE HAVE NO NEED FOR STRONG BONDS BETWEEN US!
THE ONLY THING THAT MATTERS TO ME IS WHETHER OR NOT I CAN USE YOU!!!
HMPH. THIS WAS A WASTE OF TIME...
I'M LEAVING!
...

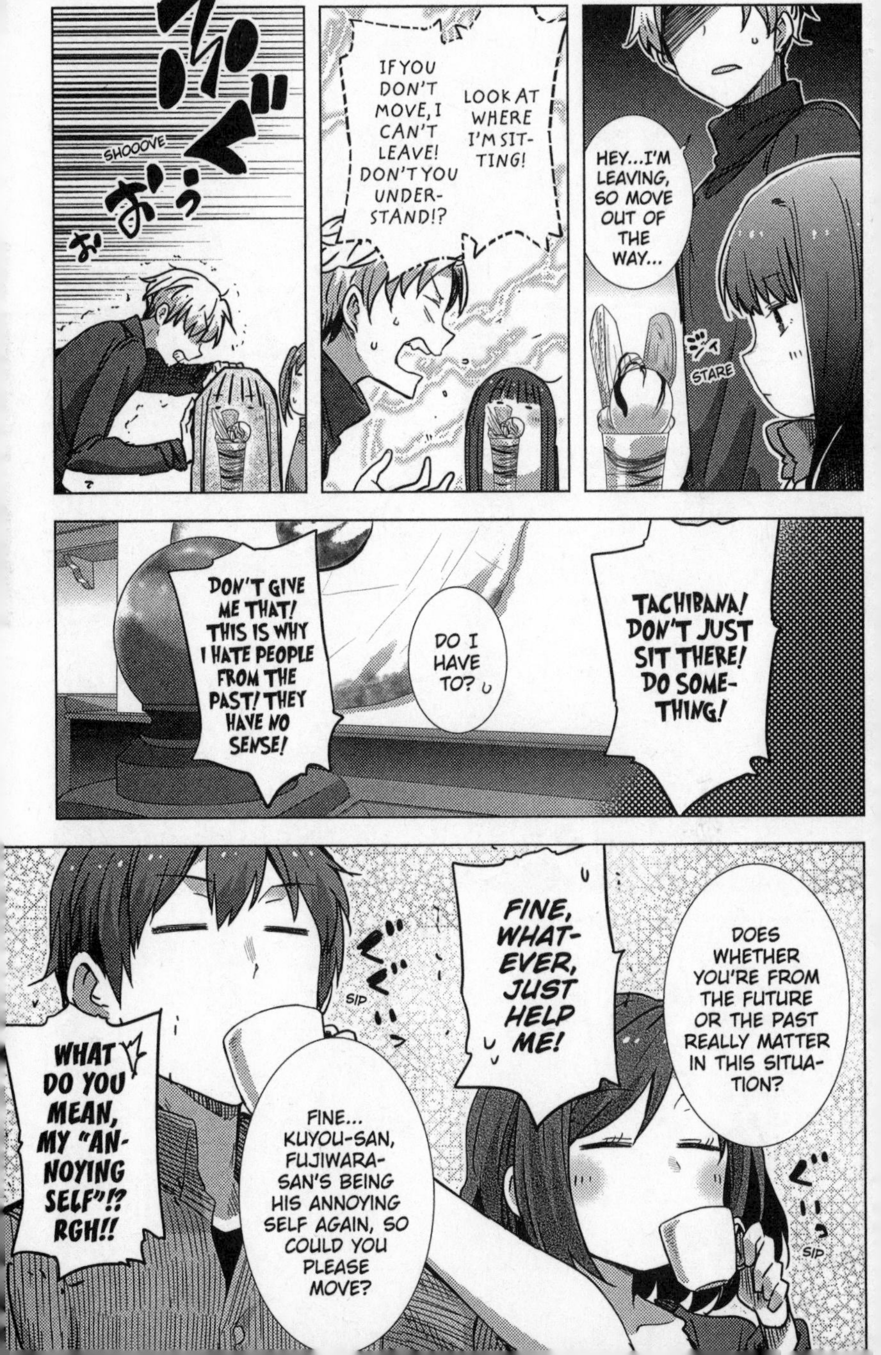
HEY...I'M LEAVING, SO MOVE OUT OF THE WAY...
STARE
LOOK AT WHERE I'M SIT-TING!
IF YOU DON'T MOVE, I CAN'T LEAVE! DON'T YOU UNDER-STAND!?
SHOOOVE
TACHIBANA! DON'T JUST SIT THERE! DO SOME-THING!
DO I HAVE TO?
DON'T GIVE ME THAT! THIS IS WHY I HATE PEOPLE FROM THE PAST! THEY HAVE NO SENSE!
DOES WHETHER YOU'RE FROM THE FUTURE OR THE PAST REALLY MATTER IN THIS SITUA-TION?
SIP
FINE, WHAT-EVER, JUST HELP ME!
FINE... KUYOU-SAN, FUJIWARA-SAN'S BEING HIS ANNOYING SELF AGAIN, SO COULD YOU PLEASE MOVE?
SIP
WHAT DO YOU MEAN, MY "AN-NOYING SELF"!? RGH!!

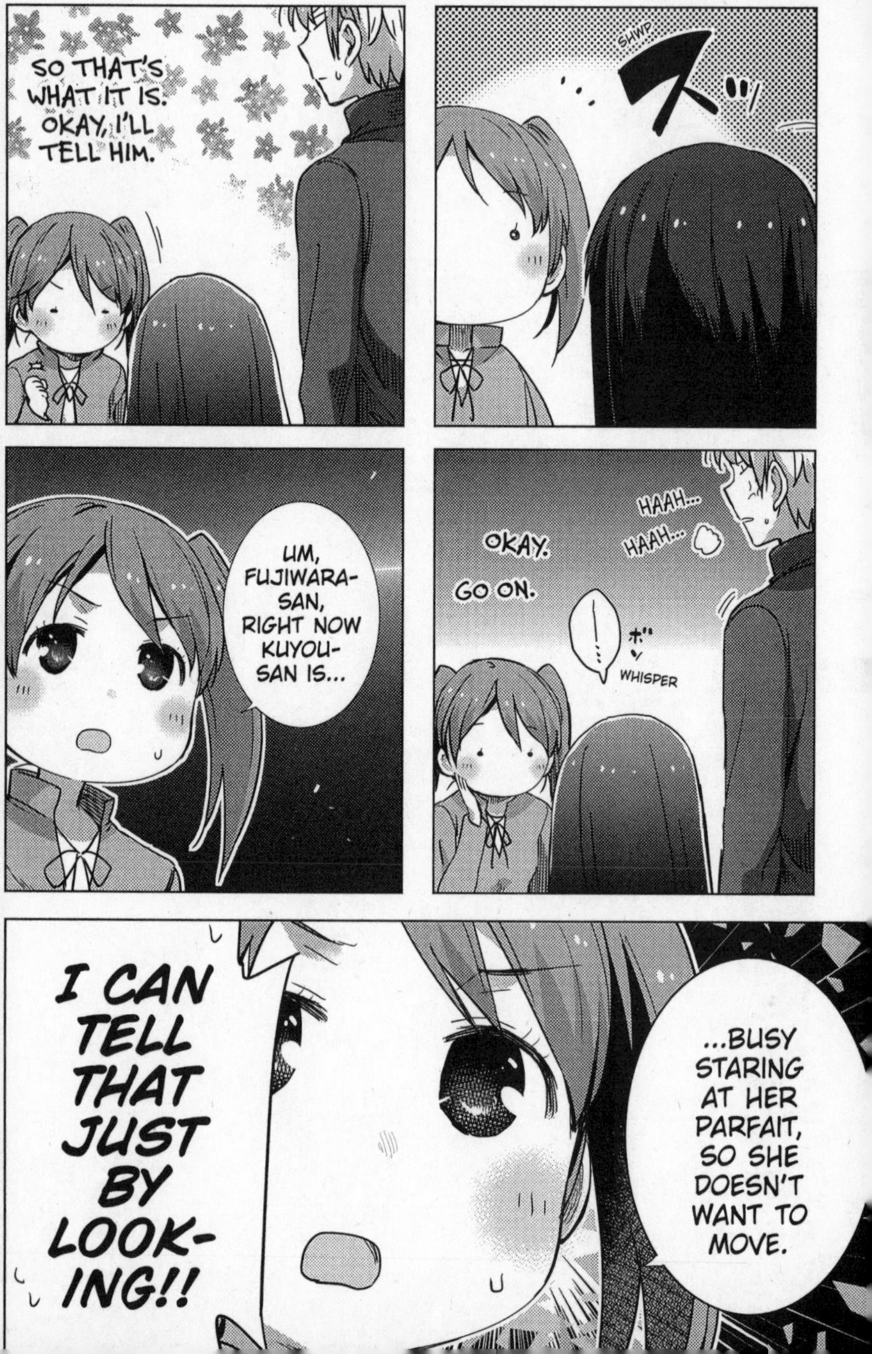
SHWP
...
SO THAT'S WHAT IT IS. OKAY, I'LL TELL HIM.
HAAH... HAAH...
OKAY.
GO ON.
!
WHISPER
UM, FUJIWARA-SAN, RIGHT NOW KUYOU-SAN IS...
...BUSY STARING AT HER PARFAIT, SO SHE DOESN'T WANT TO MOVE.
I CAN TELL THAT JUST BY LOOKING!!

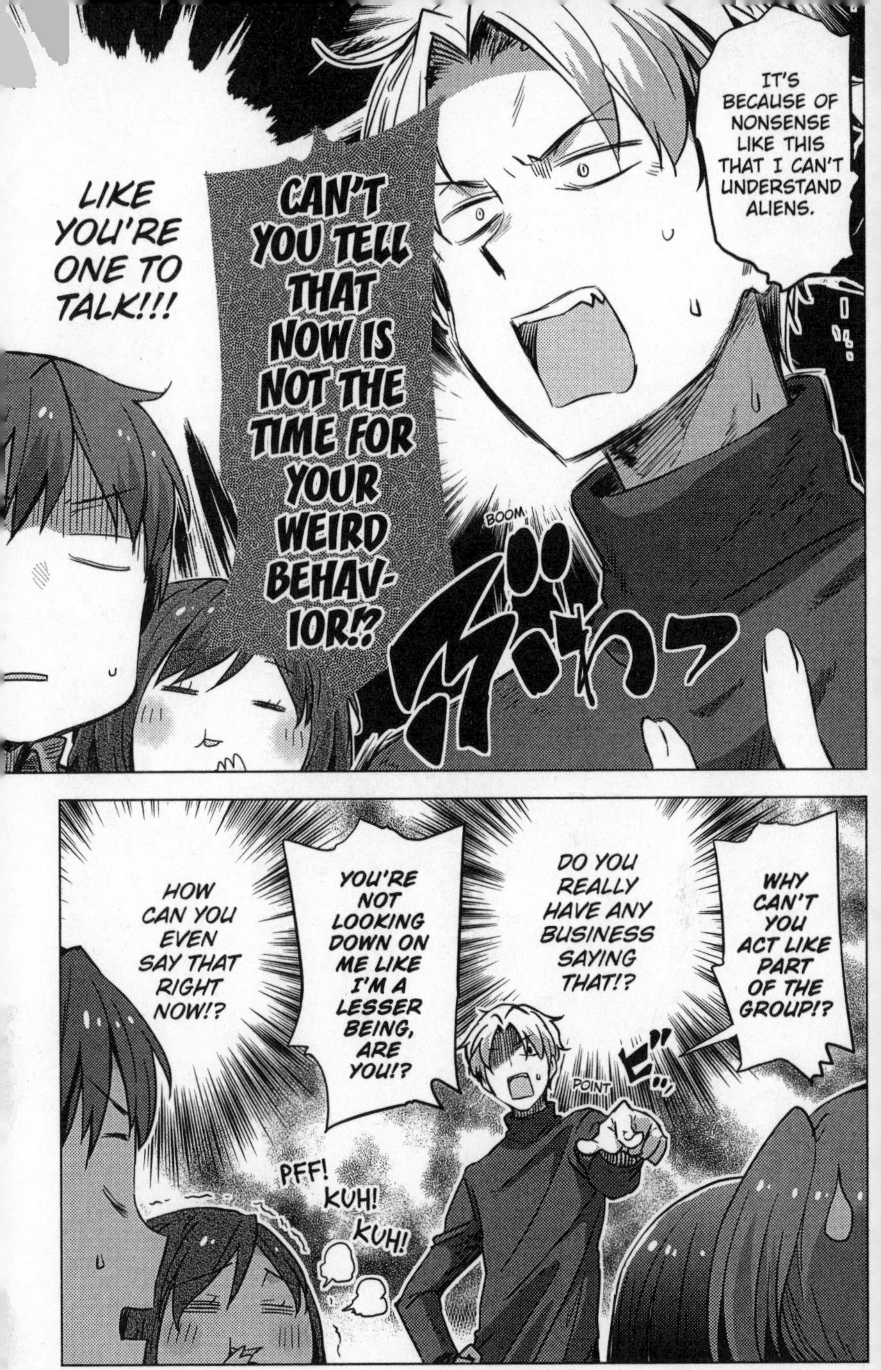
IT'S BECAUSE OF NONSENSE LIKE THIS THAT I CAN'T UNDERSTAND ALIENS.
CAN'T YOU TELL THAT NOW IS NOT THE TIME FOR YOUR WEIRD BEHAV-IOR!?
BOOM
LIKE YOU'RE ONE TO TALK!!!
WHY CAN'T YOU ACT LIKE PART OF THE GROUP!?
DO YOU REALLY HAVE ANY BUSINESS SAYING THAT!?
POINT
YOU'RE NOT LOOKING DOWN ON ME LIKE I'M A LESSER BEING, ARE YOU!?
HOW CAN YOU EVEN SAY THAT RIGHT NOW!?
PFF! KUH! KUH!

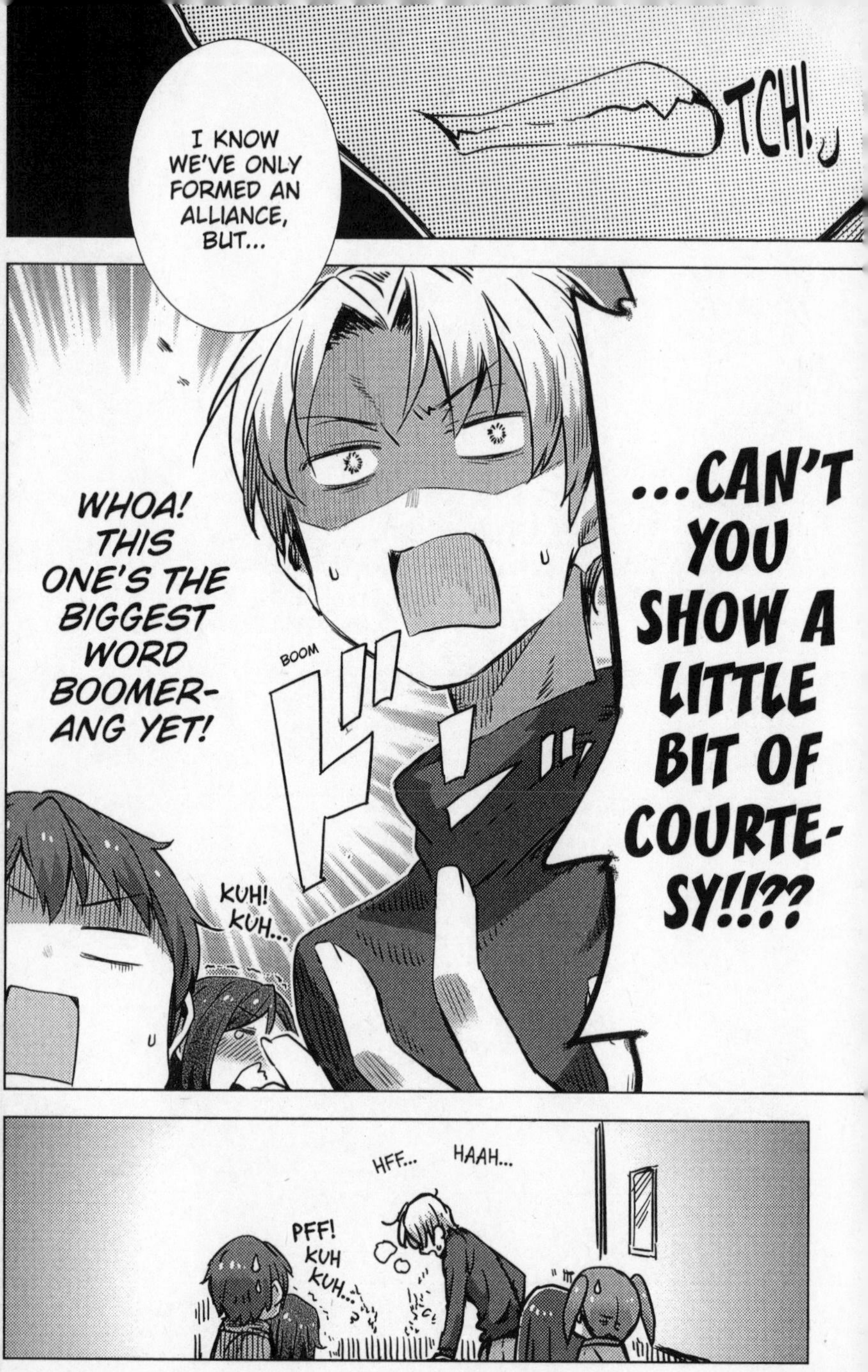
TCH!
I KNOW WE'VE ONLY FORMED AN ALLIANCE, BUT...
...CAN'T YOU SHOW A LITTLE BIT OF COURTE-SY!!??
BOOM
WHOA! THIS ONE'S THE BIGGEST WORD BOOMER-ANG YET!
KUH! KUH...
HAAH...
HFF...
PFF! KUH KUH...

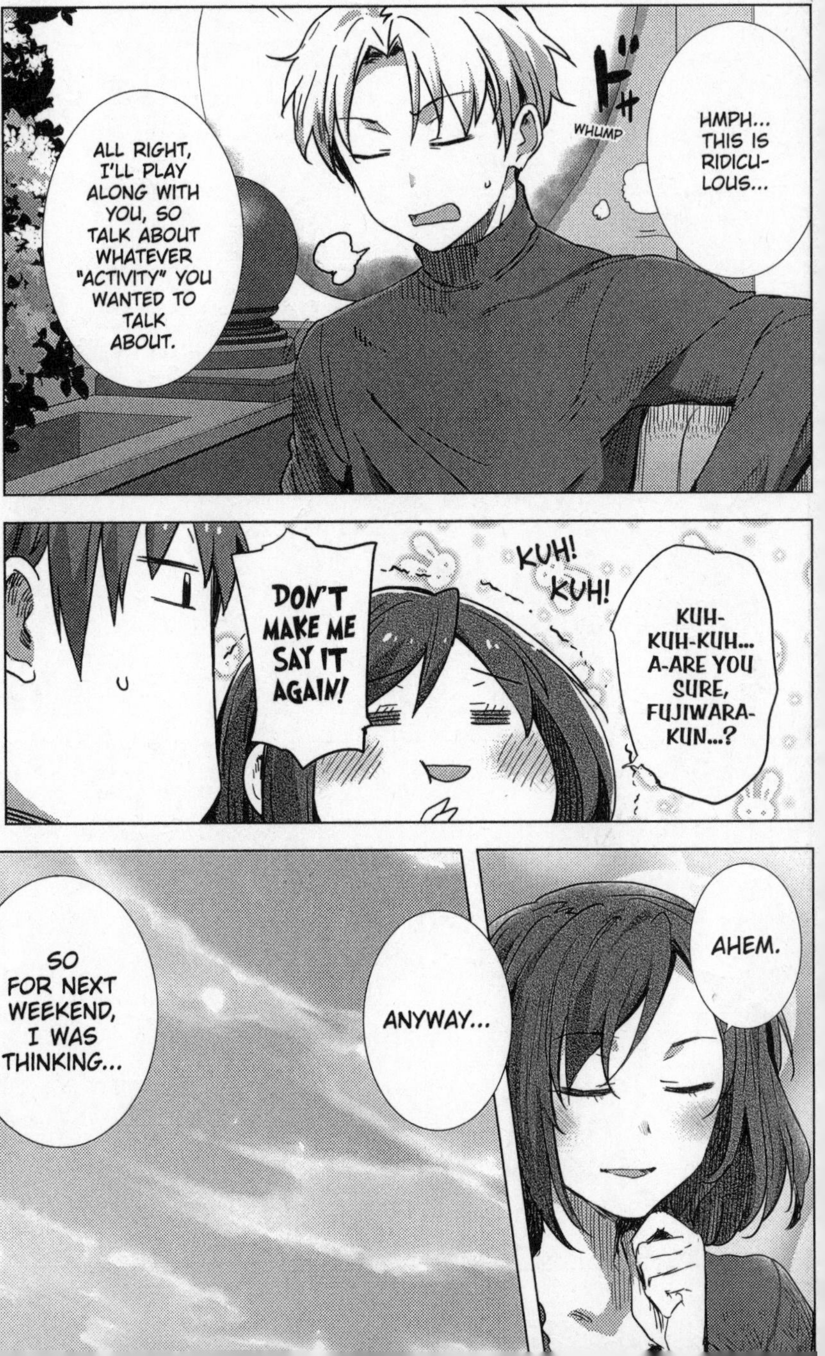
HMPH... THIS IS RIDICULOUS...
WHUMP
ALL RIGHT, I'LL PLAY ALONG WITH YOU, SO TALK ABOUT WHATEVER "ACTIVITY" YOU WANTED TO TALK ABOUT.
KUH! KUH!
KUH-KUH-KUH... A-ARE YOU SURE, FUJIWARA-KUN...?
DON'T MAKE ME SAY IT AGAIN!
AHEM.
ANYWAY...
SO FOR NEXT WEEKEND, I WAS THINKING...

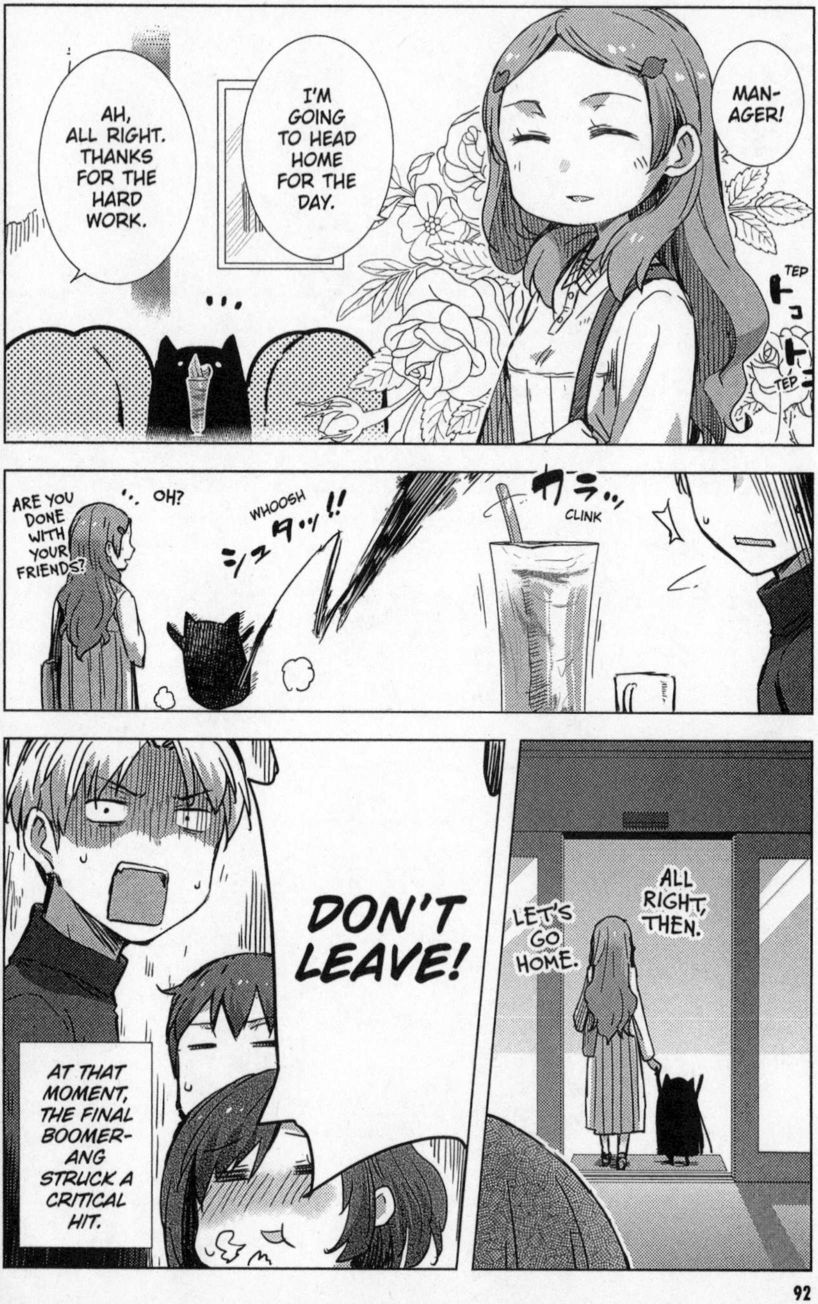
MAN-AGER!
TEP
TEP
I'M GOING TO HEAD HOME FOR THE DAY.
AH, ALL RIGHT. THANKS FOR THE HARD WORK.
...
CLINK
WHOOSH
... OH?
ARE YOU DONE WITH YOUR FRIENDS?
ALL RIGHT, THEN.
LET'S GO HOME.
DON'T LEAVE!
AT THAT MOMENT, THE FINAL BOOMER-ANG STRUCK A CRITICAL HIT.

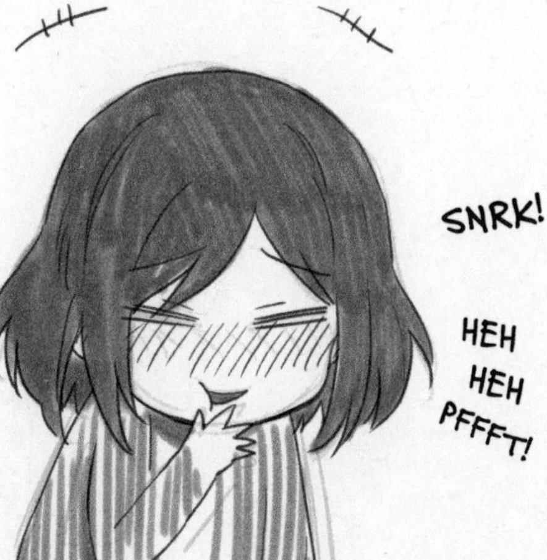
SNRK!
HEH
HEH
PFFFT!

WHEEE!

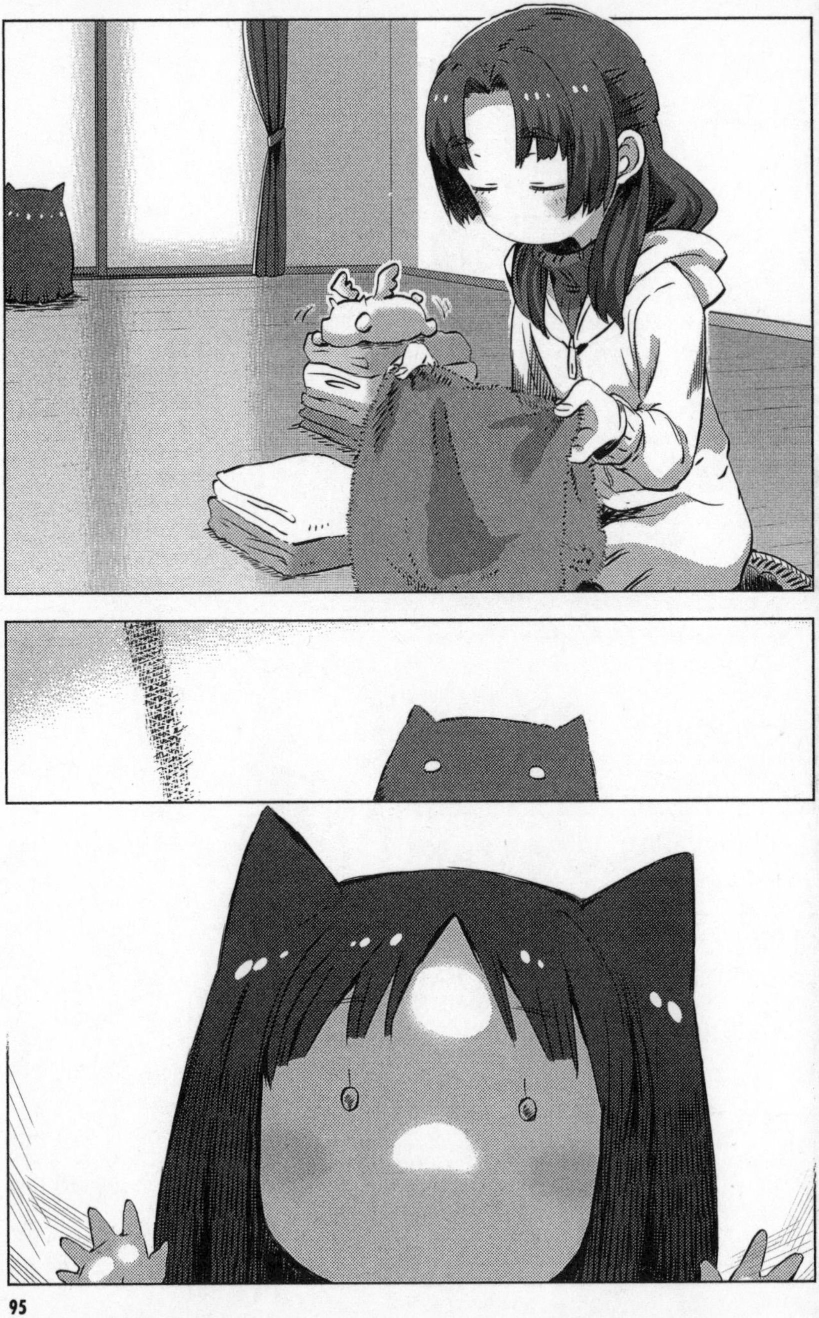

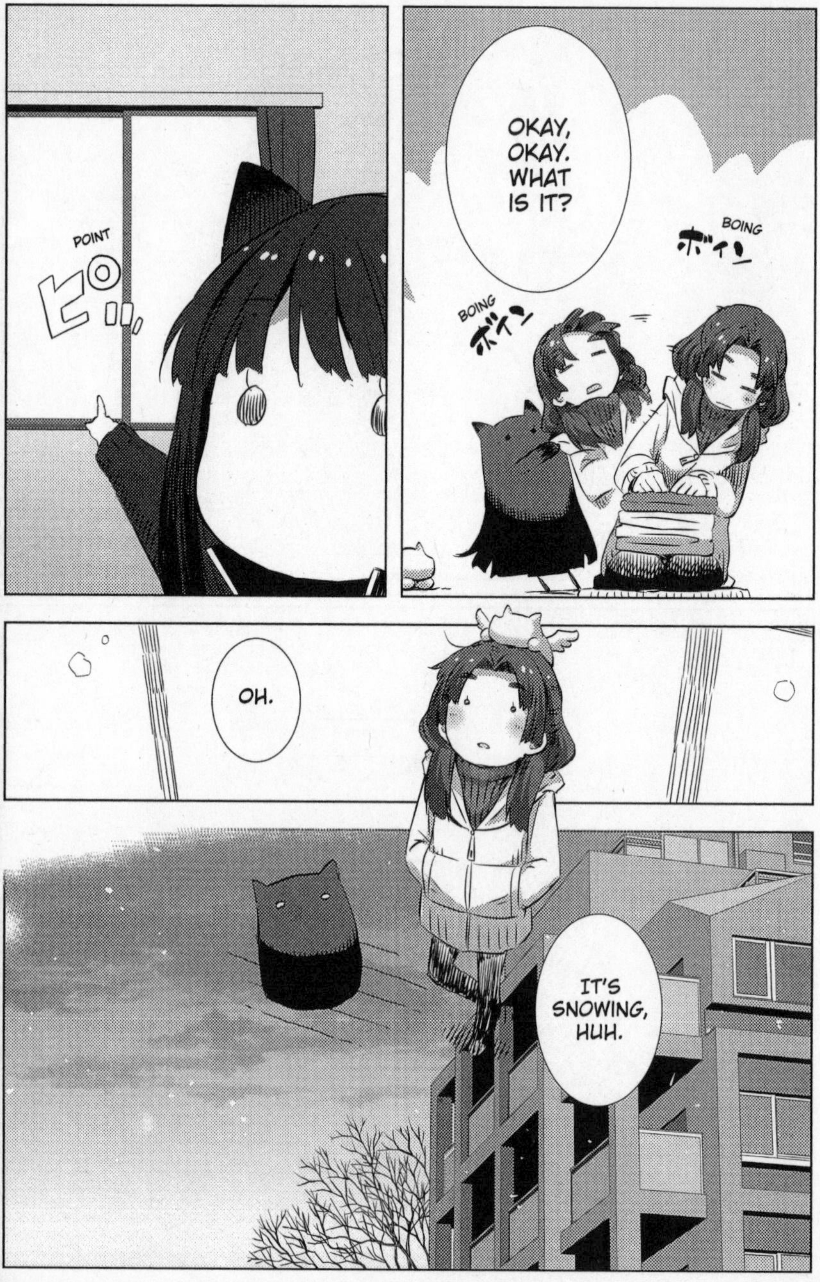
OKAY, OKAY. WHAT IS IT?
BOING
ボイン
BOING
ボイン
POINT
OH.
IT'S SNOWING, HUH.

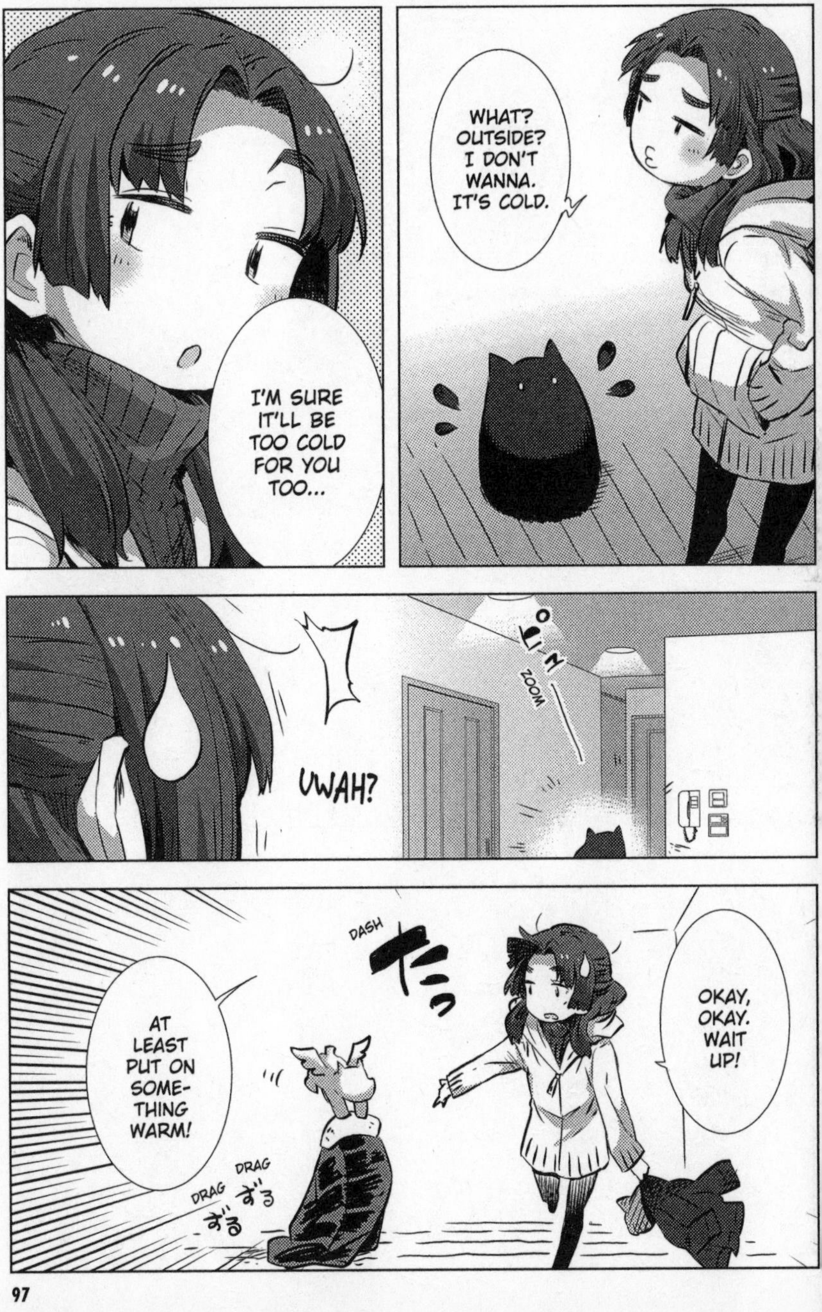
WHAT? OUTSIDE? I DON'T WANNA. IT'S COLD.
I'M SURE IT'LL BE TOO COLD FOR YOU TOO...
ZOOM
UWAH?
OKAY, OKAY. WAIT UP!
DASH
AT LEAST PUT ON SOME-THING WARM!
DRAG
ずる
DRAG
ずる

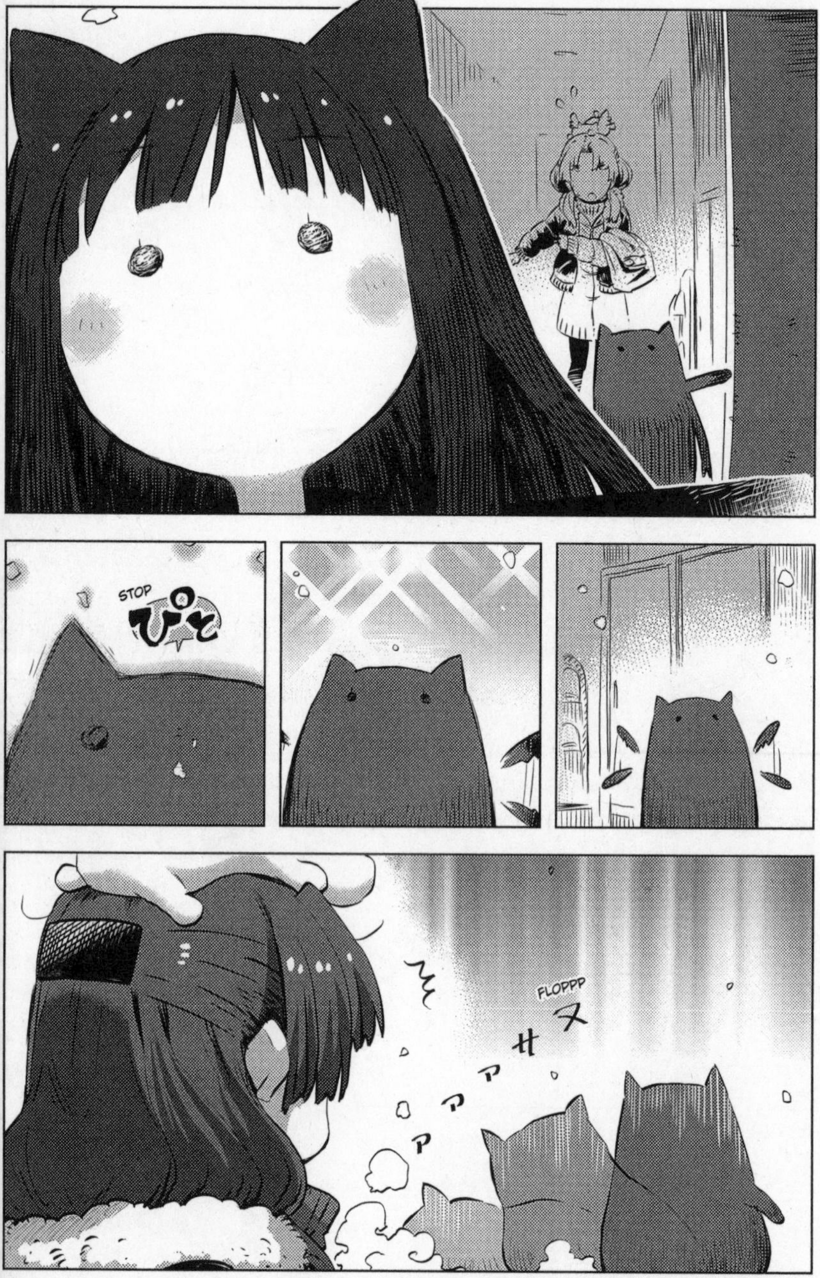
STOP
ぴと
FLOPPP
アァァサヌ

......

HYA-HA! WHAT A FRESH NEW WAY TO KICK THE BUCKET!

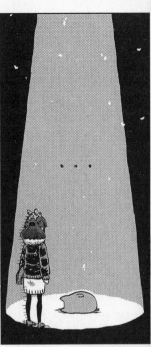

· · ·

I TOLD YOU IT WAS COLD!!!

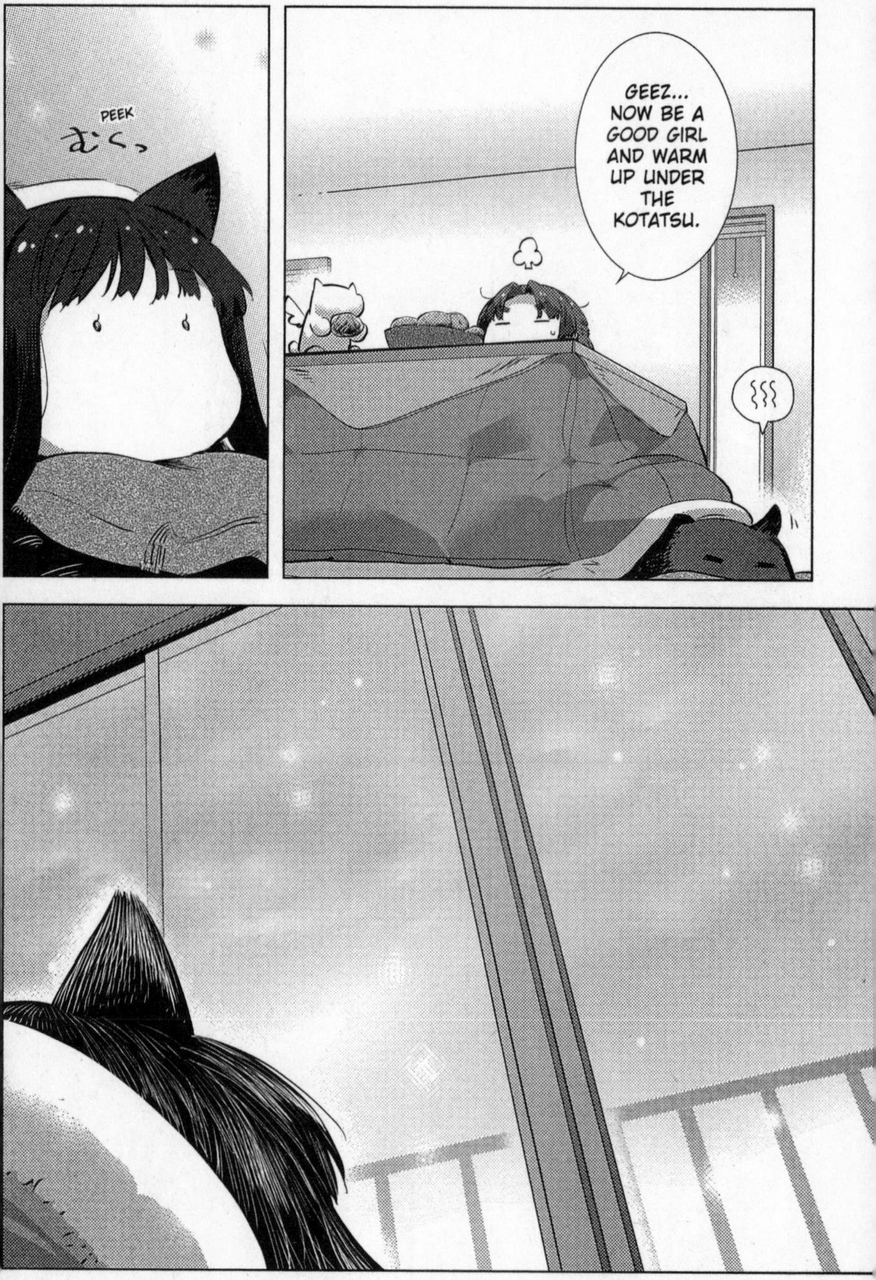
GEEZ... NOW BE A GOOD GIRL AND WARM UP UNDER THE KOTATSU.
PEEK
むくっ

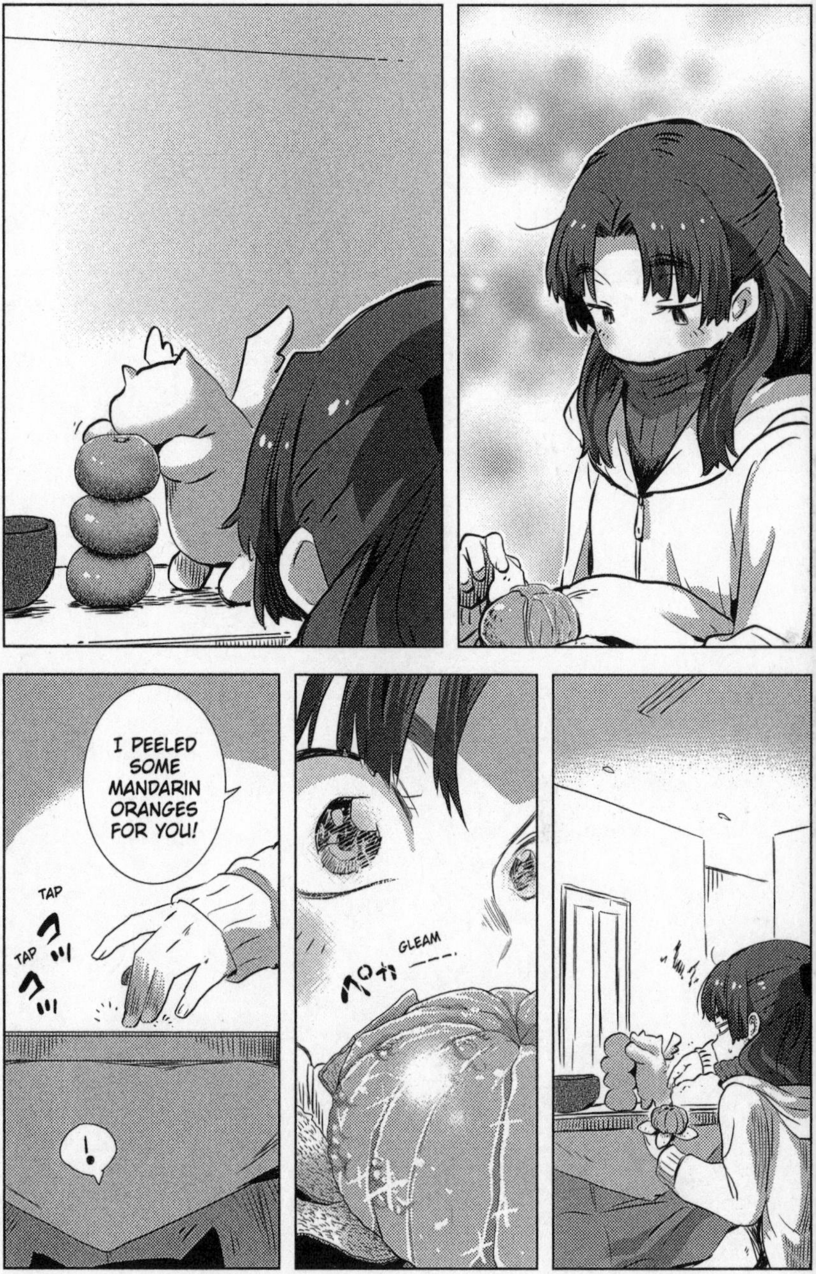
GLEAM
I PEELED SOME MANDARIN ORANGES FOR YOU!
TAP
TAP
!

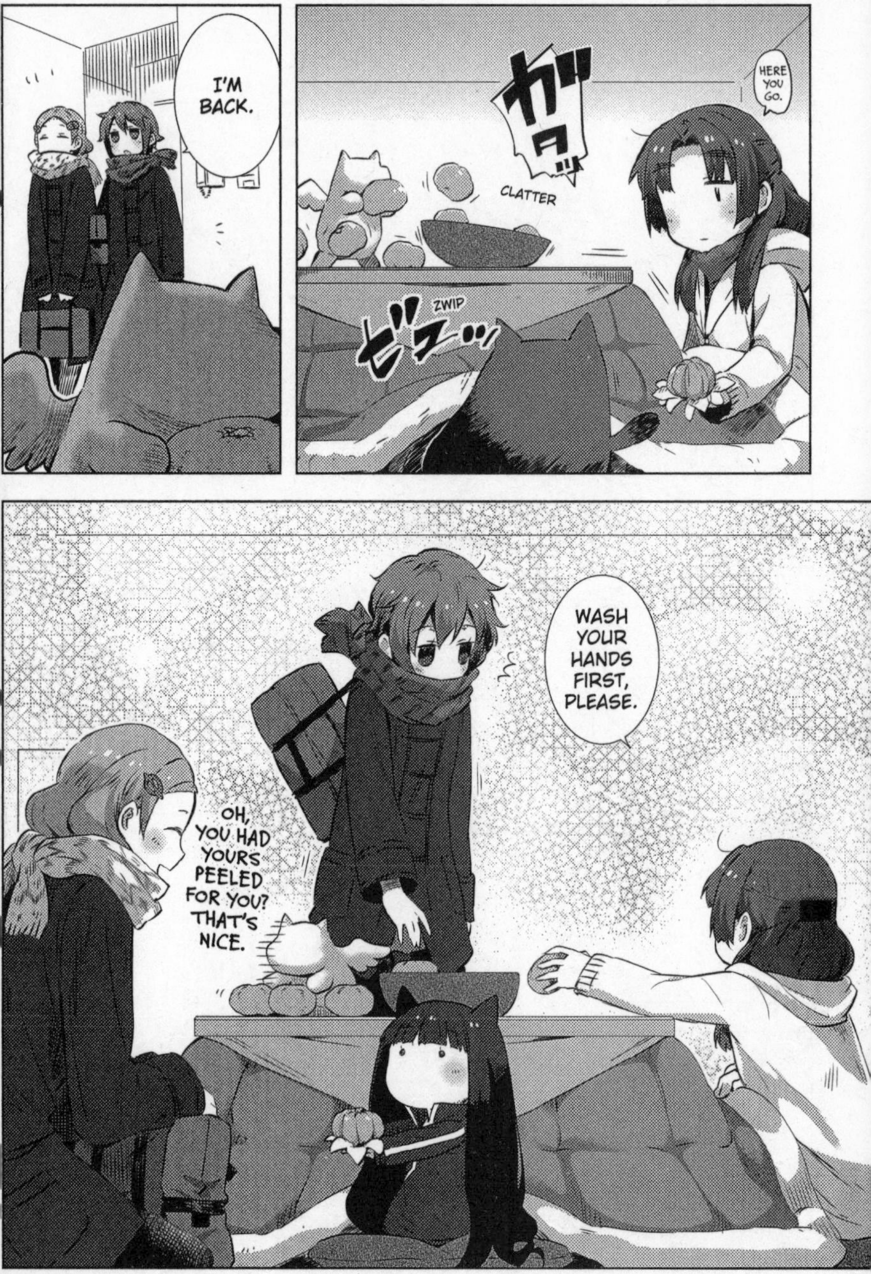
HERE YOU GO.
CLATTER
ZWIP
I'M BACK.
WASH YOUR HANDS FIRST, PLEASE.
OH, YOU HAD YOURS PEELED FOR YOU? THAT'S NICE.

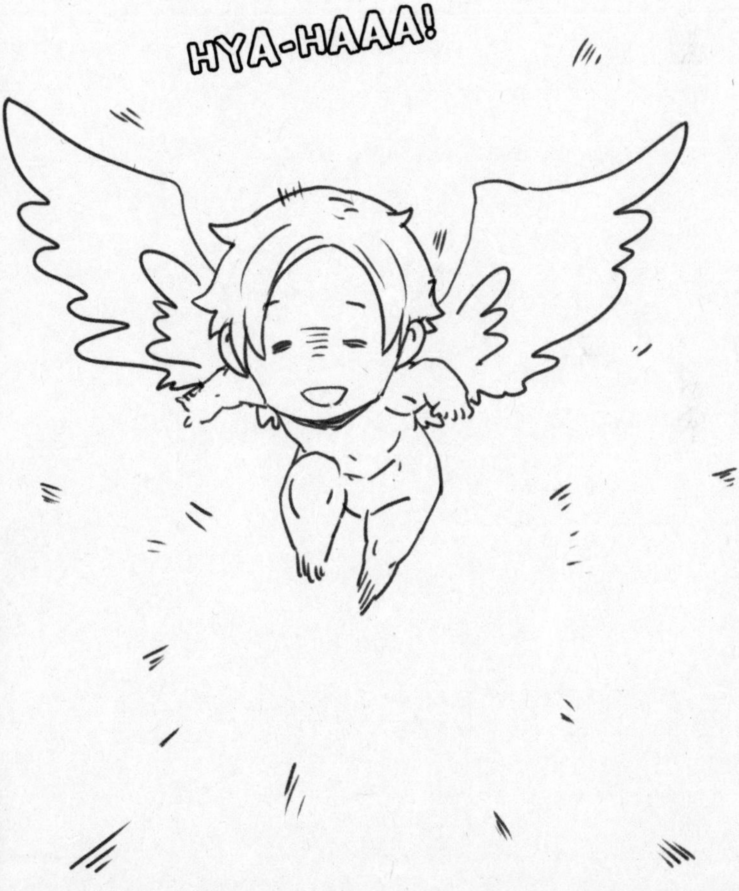
HYA-HAAA!

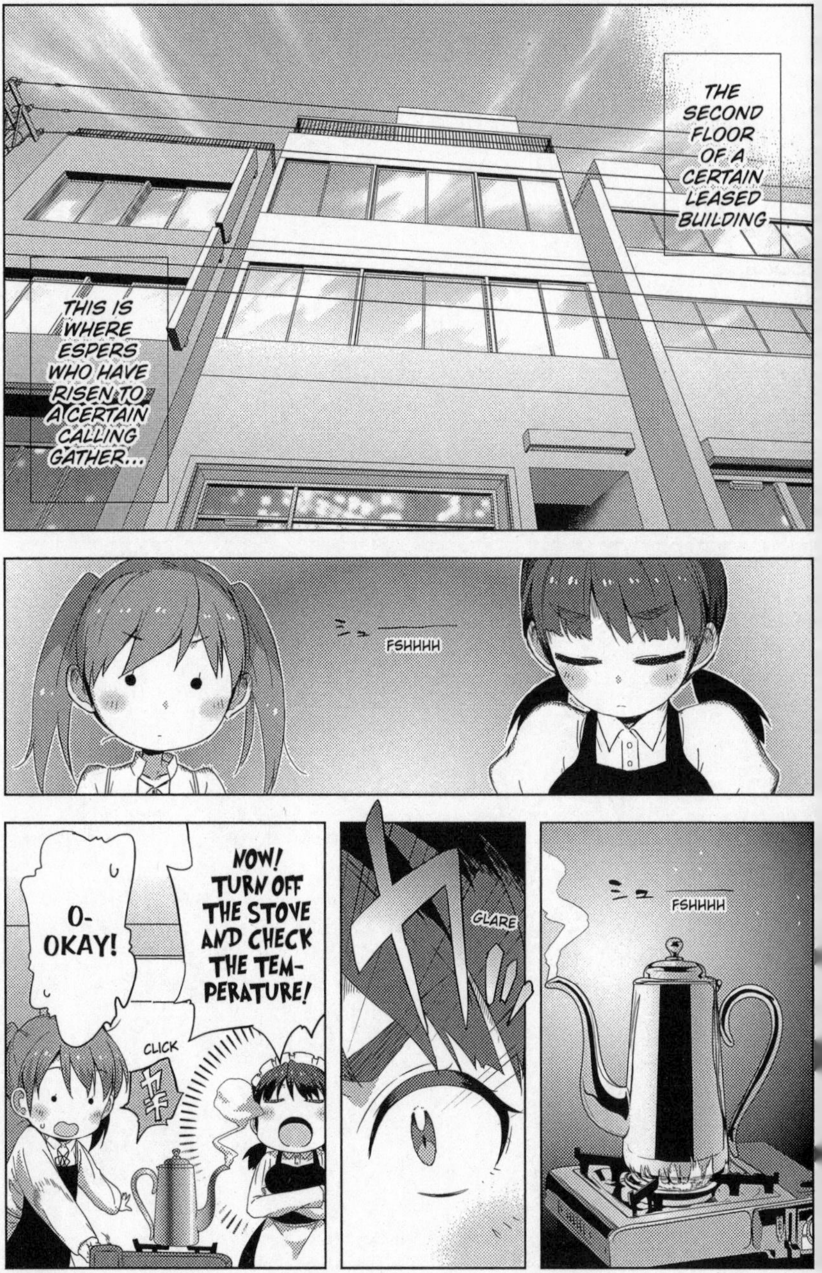
THE SECOND FLOOR OF A CERTAIN LEASED BUILDING
THIS IS WHERE ESPERS WHO HAVE RISEN TO A CERTAIN CALLING GATHER...
FSHHHH
FSHHHH
GLARE
NOW! TURN OFF THE STOVE AND CHECK THE TEM-PERATURE!
O-OKAY!
CLICK

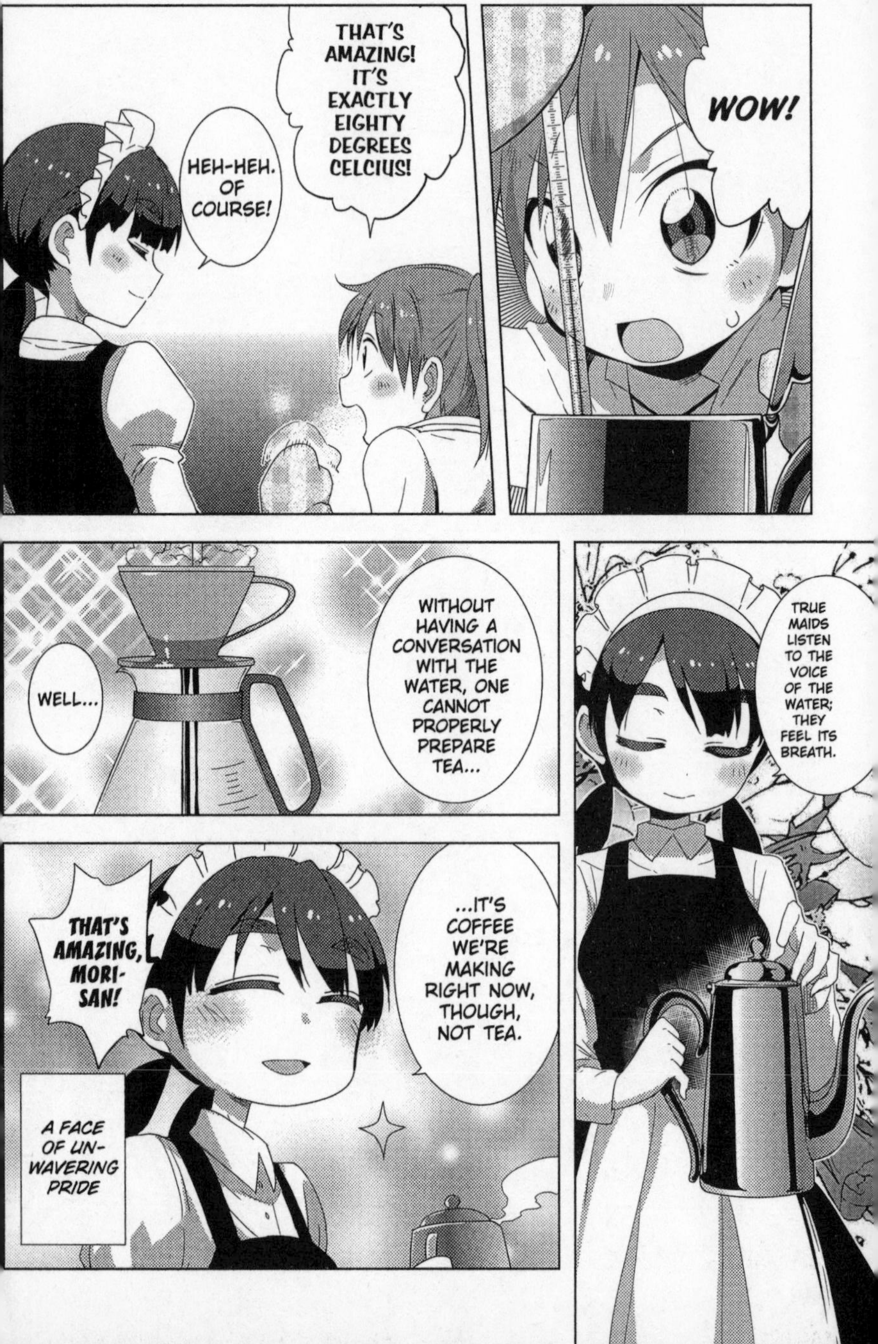
WOW!
THAT'S AMAZING! IT'S EXACTLY EIGHTY DEGREES CELCIUS!
HEH-HEH. OF COURSE!
TRUE MAIDS LISTEN TO THE VOICE OF THE WATER; THEY FEEL ITS BREATH.
WITHOUT HAVING A CONVERSATION WITH THE WATER, ONE CANNOT PROPERLY PREPARE TEA...
WELL...
...IT'S COFFEE WE'RE MAKING RIGHT NOW, THOUGH, NOT TEA.
THAT'S AMAZING, MORI-SAN!
A FACE OF UN-WAVERING PRIDE

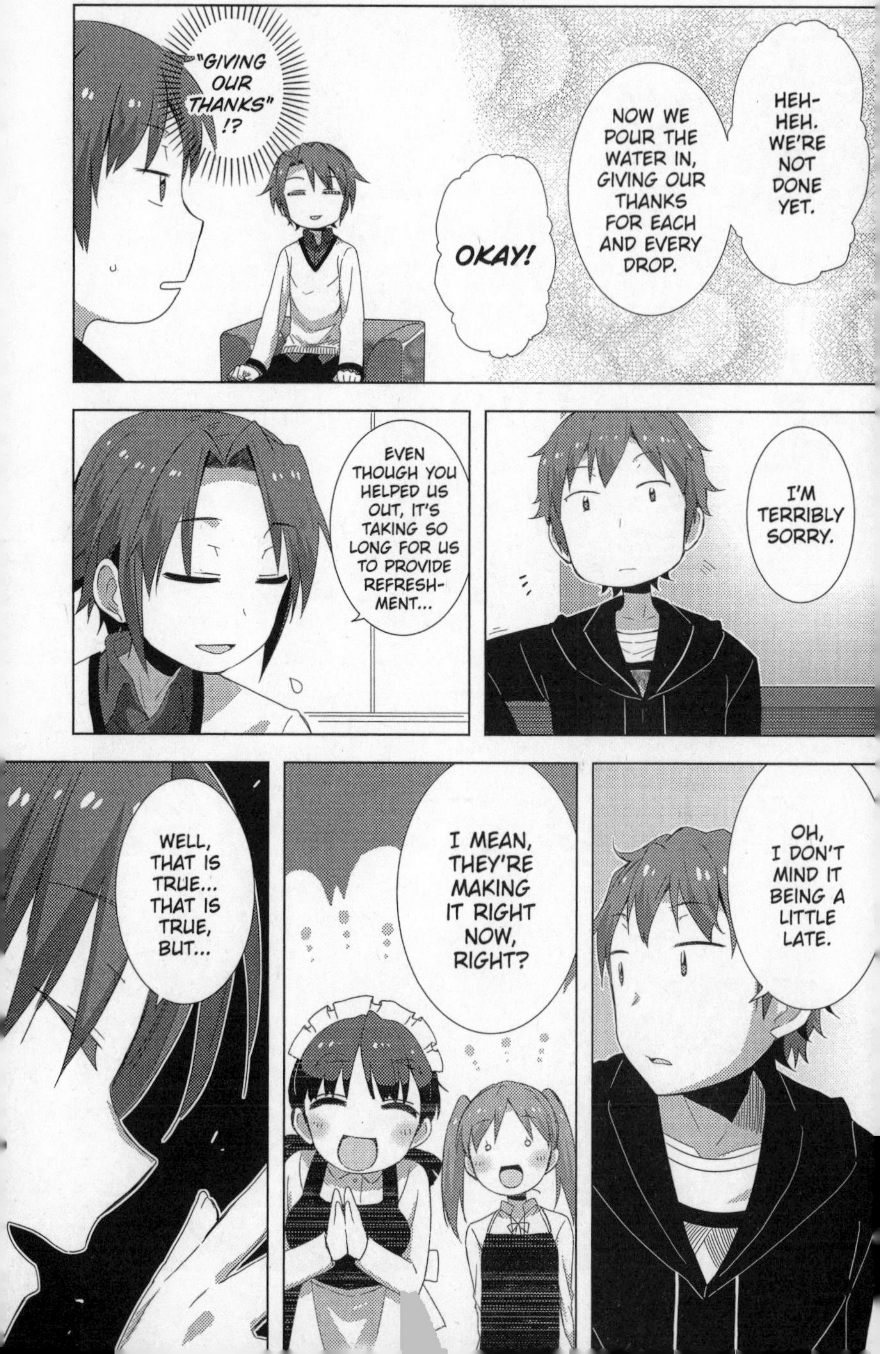
HEH-HEH. WE'RE NOT DONE YET.
NOW WE POUR THE WATER IN, GIVING OUR THANKS FOR EACH AND EVERY DROP.
OKAY!
"GIVING OUR THANKS"!?
I'M TERRIBLY SORRY.
EVEN THOUGH YOU HELPED US OUT, IT'S TAKING SO LONG FOR US TO PROVIDE REFRESHMENT...
OH, I DON'T MIND IT BEING A LITTLE LATE.
I MEAN, THEY'RE MAKING IT RIGHT NOW, RIGHT?
WELL, THAT IS TRUE... THAT IS TRUE, BUT...

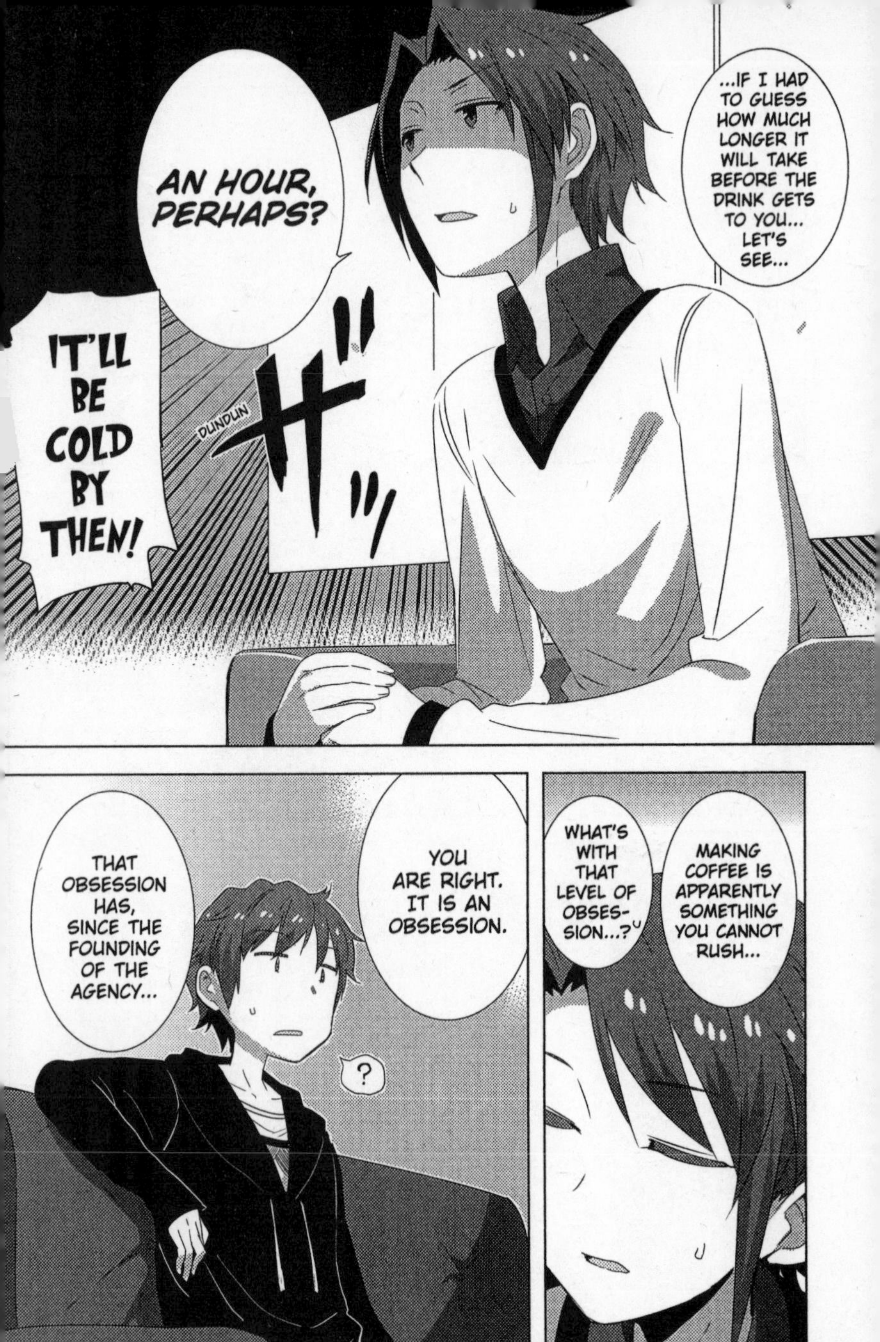
...IF I HAD TO GUESS HOW MUCH LONGER IT WILL TAKE BEFORE THE DRINK GETS TO YOU... LET'S SEE...
AN HOUR, PERHAPS?
DUNDUN
IT'LL BE COLD BY THEN!
MAKING COFFEE IS APPARENTLY SOMETHING YOU CANNOT RUSH...
WHAT'S WITH THAT LEVEL OF OBSES-SION...?
YOU ARE RIGHT. IT IS AN OBSESSION.
THAT OBSESSION HAS, SINCE THE FOUNDING OF THE AGENCY...
?

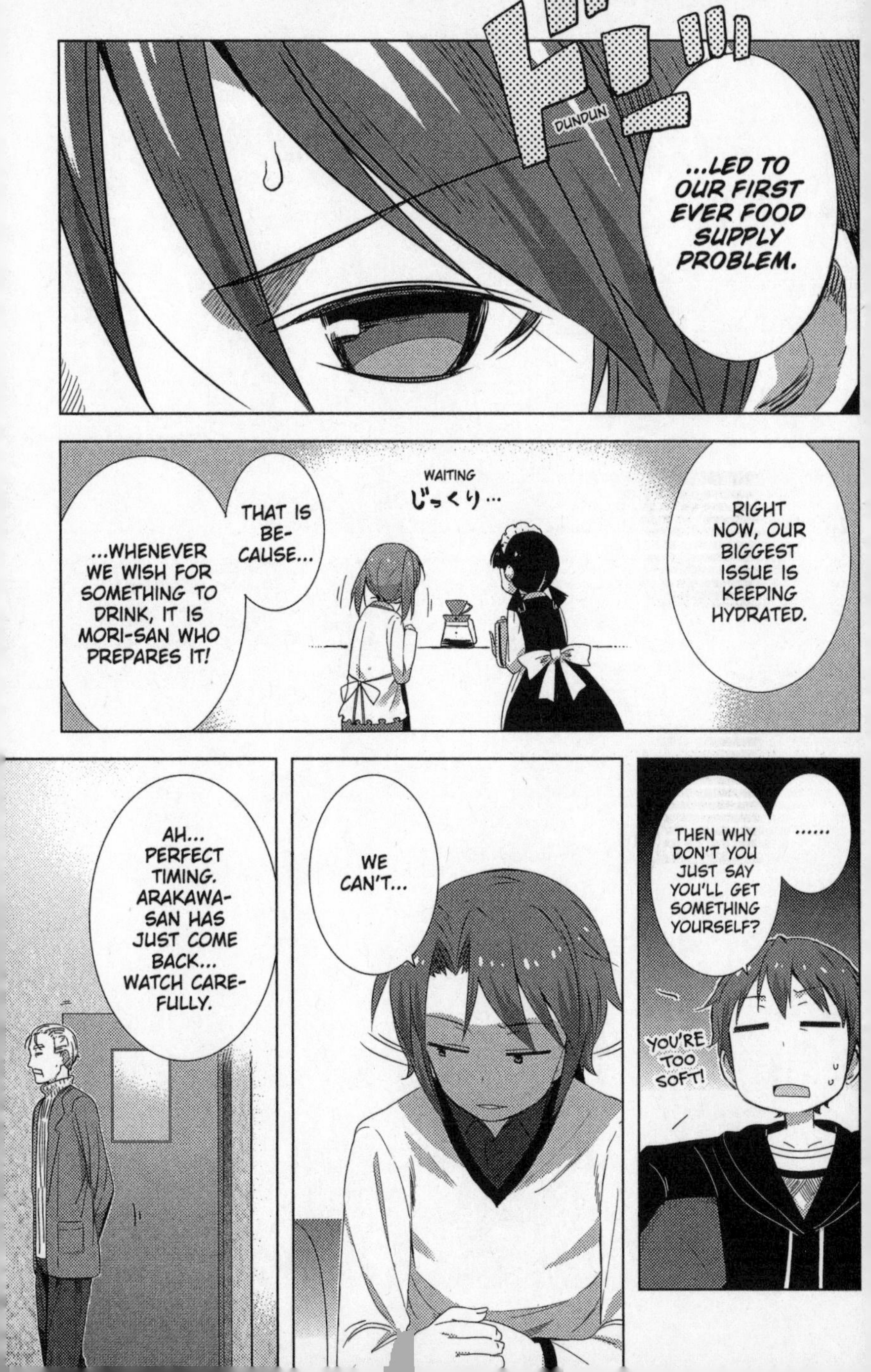
DUNDUN
...LED TO OUR FIRST EVER FOOD SUPPLY PROBLEM.
RIGHT NOW, OUR BIGGEST ISSUE IS KEEPING HYDRATED.
WAITING
じっくり…
THAT IS BE-CAUSE...
...WHENEVER WE WISH FOR SOMETHING TO DRINK, IT IS MORI-SAN WHO PREPARES IT!
......
THEN WHY DON'T YOU JUST SAY YOU'LL GET SOMETHING YOURSELF?
YOU'RE TOO SOFT!
WE CAN'T...
AH... PERFECT TIMING. ARAKAWA-SAN HAS JUST COME BACK... WATCH CARE-FULLY.

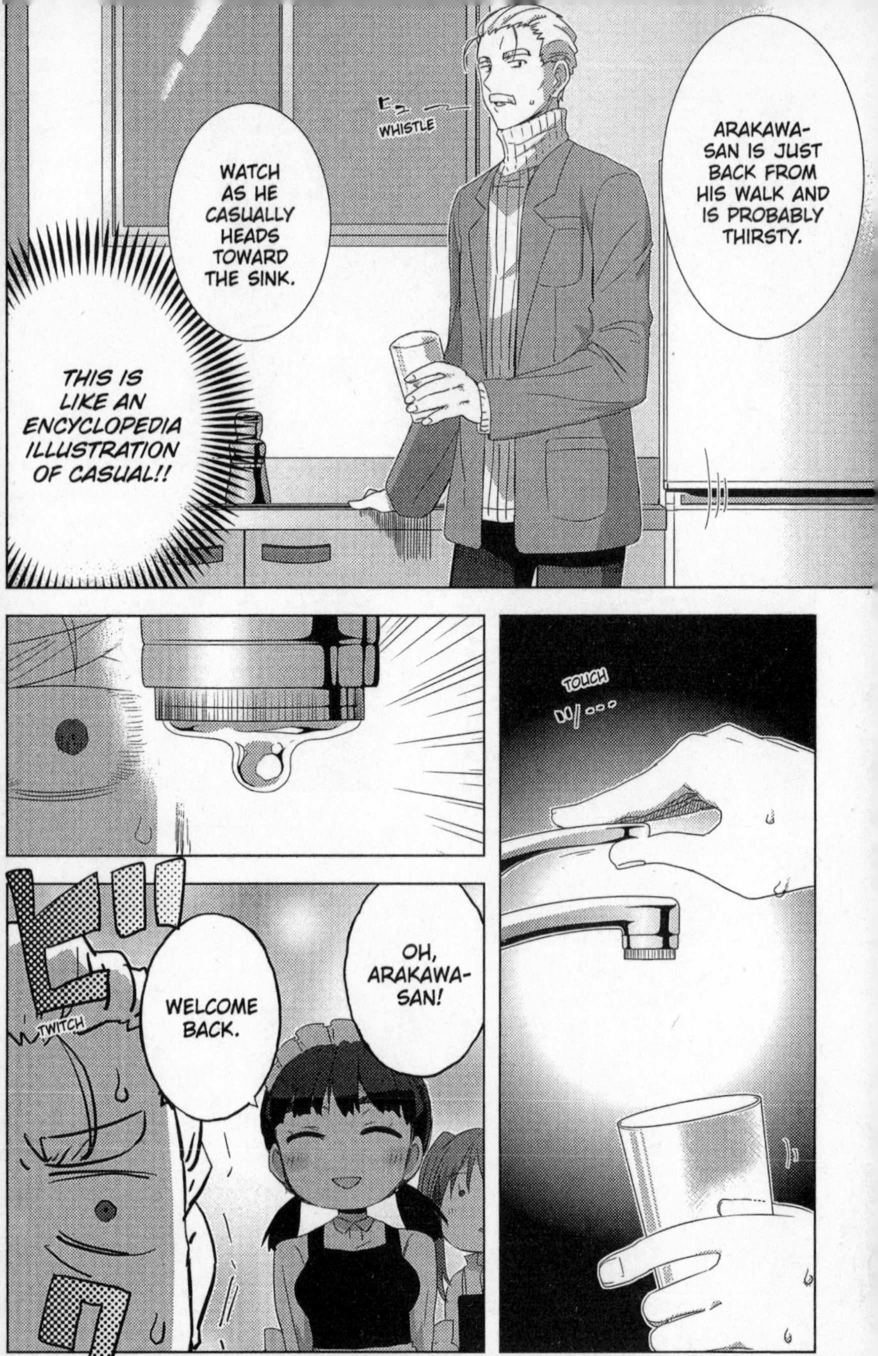
ARAKAWA-SAN IS JUST BACK FROM HIS WALK AND IS PROBABLY THIRSTY.
WHISTLE
WATCH AS HE CASUALLY HEADS TOWARD THE SINK.
THIS IS LIKE AN ENCYCLOPEDIA ILLUSTRATION OF CASUAL!!
TOUCH
OH, ARAKAWA-SAN!
WELCOME BACK.
TWITCH

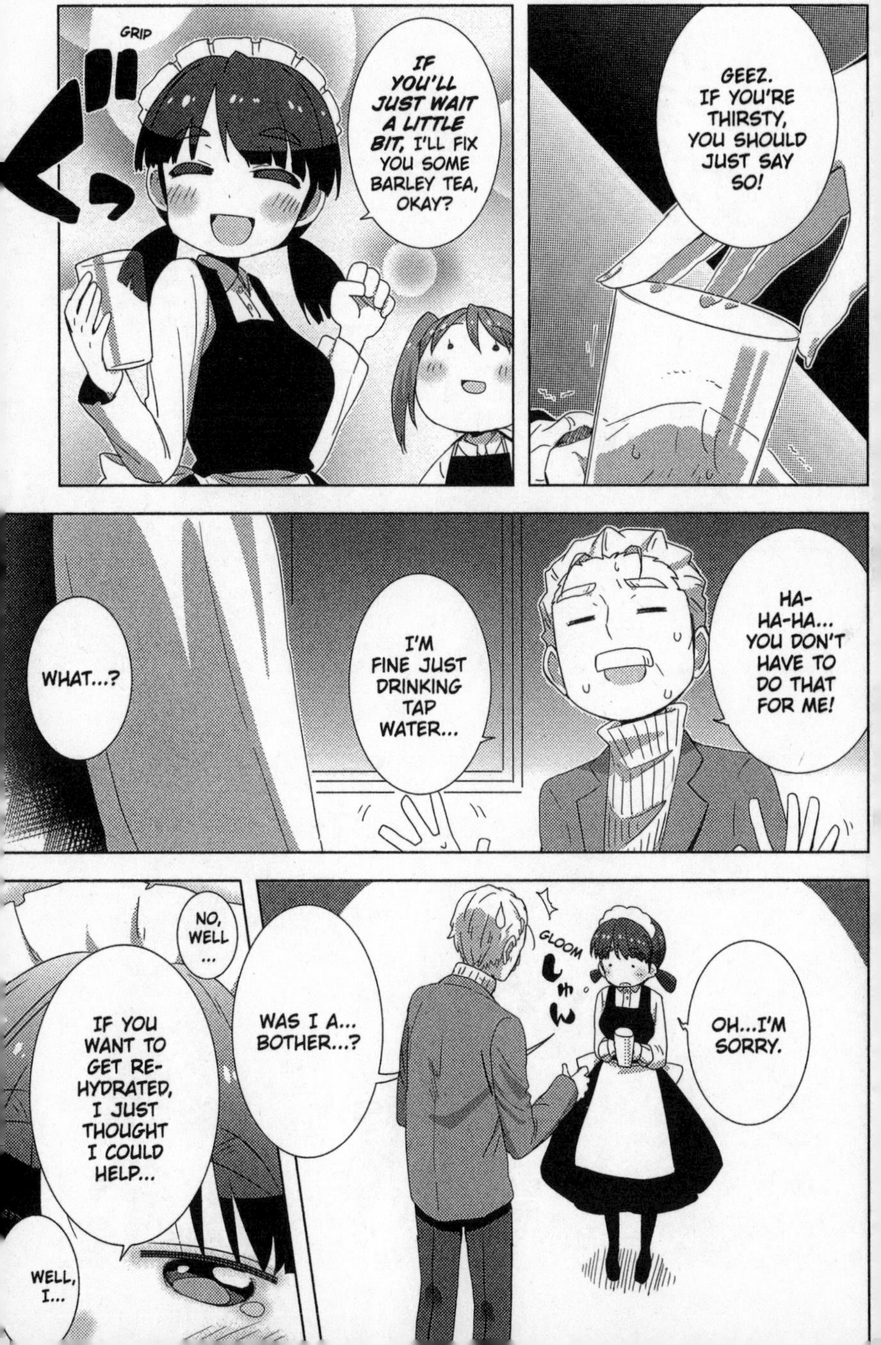
GEEZ. IF YOU'RE THIRSTY, YOU SHOULD JUST SAY SO!
IF YOU'LL JUST WAIT A LITTLE BIT, I'LL FIX YOU SOME BARLEY TEA, OKAY?
GRIP
HA-HA-HA... YOU DON'T HAVE TO DO THAT FOR ME!
I'M FINE JUST DRINKING TAP WATER...
WHAT...?
OH...I'M SORRY.
GLOOM
WAS I A... BOTHER...?
NO, WELL ...
IF YOU WANT TO GET RE-HYDRATED, I JUST THOUGHT I COULD HELP...
WELL, I...

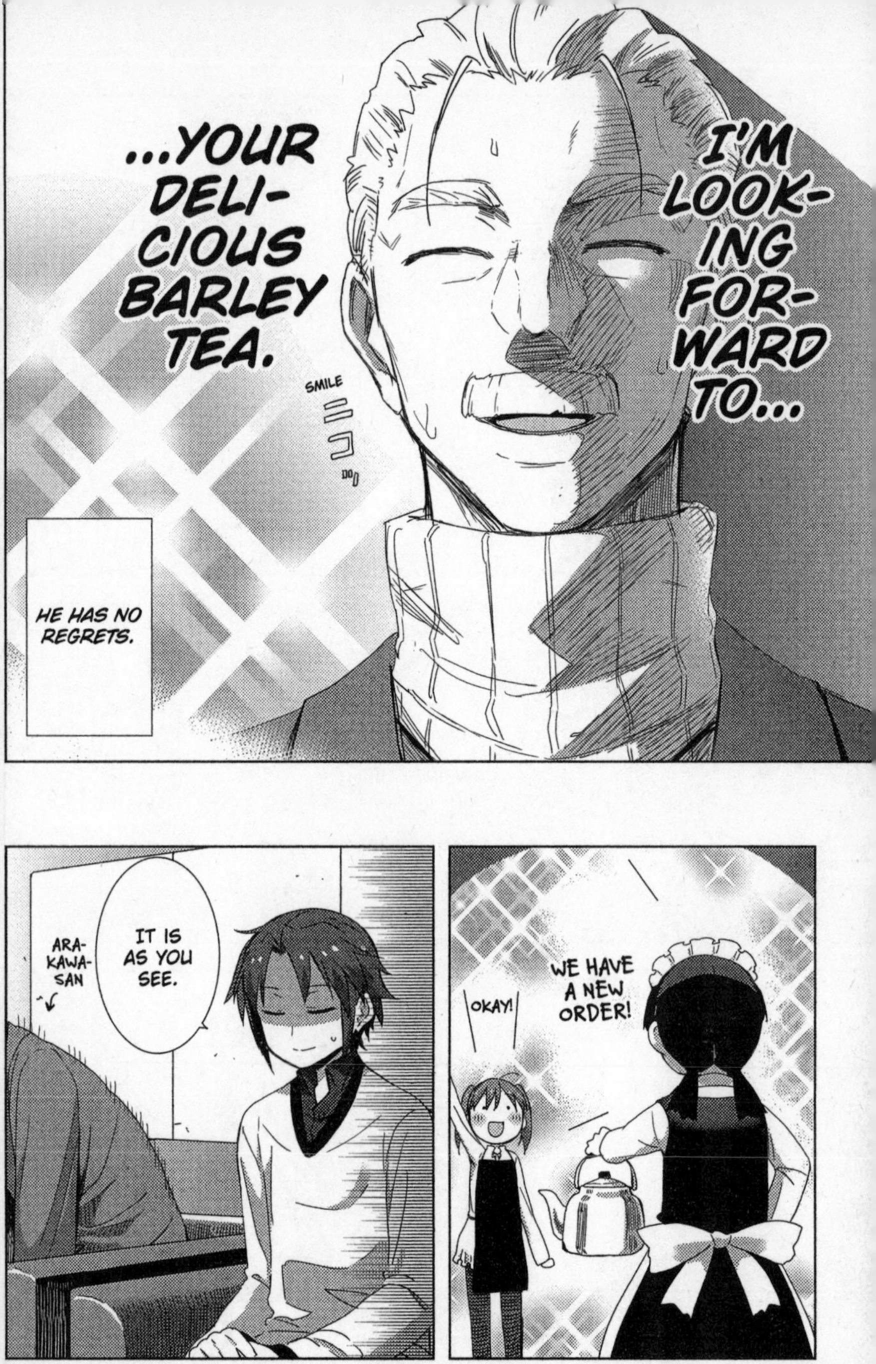
I'M LOOK-ING FOR-WARD TO...
...YOUR DELI-CIOUS BARLEY TEA.
SMILE
HE HAS NO REGRETS.
WE HAVE A NEW ORDER!
OKAY!
IT IS AS YOU SEE.
ARA-KAWA-SAN

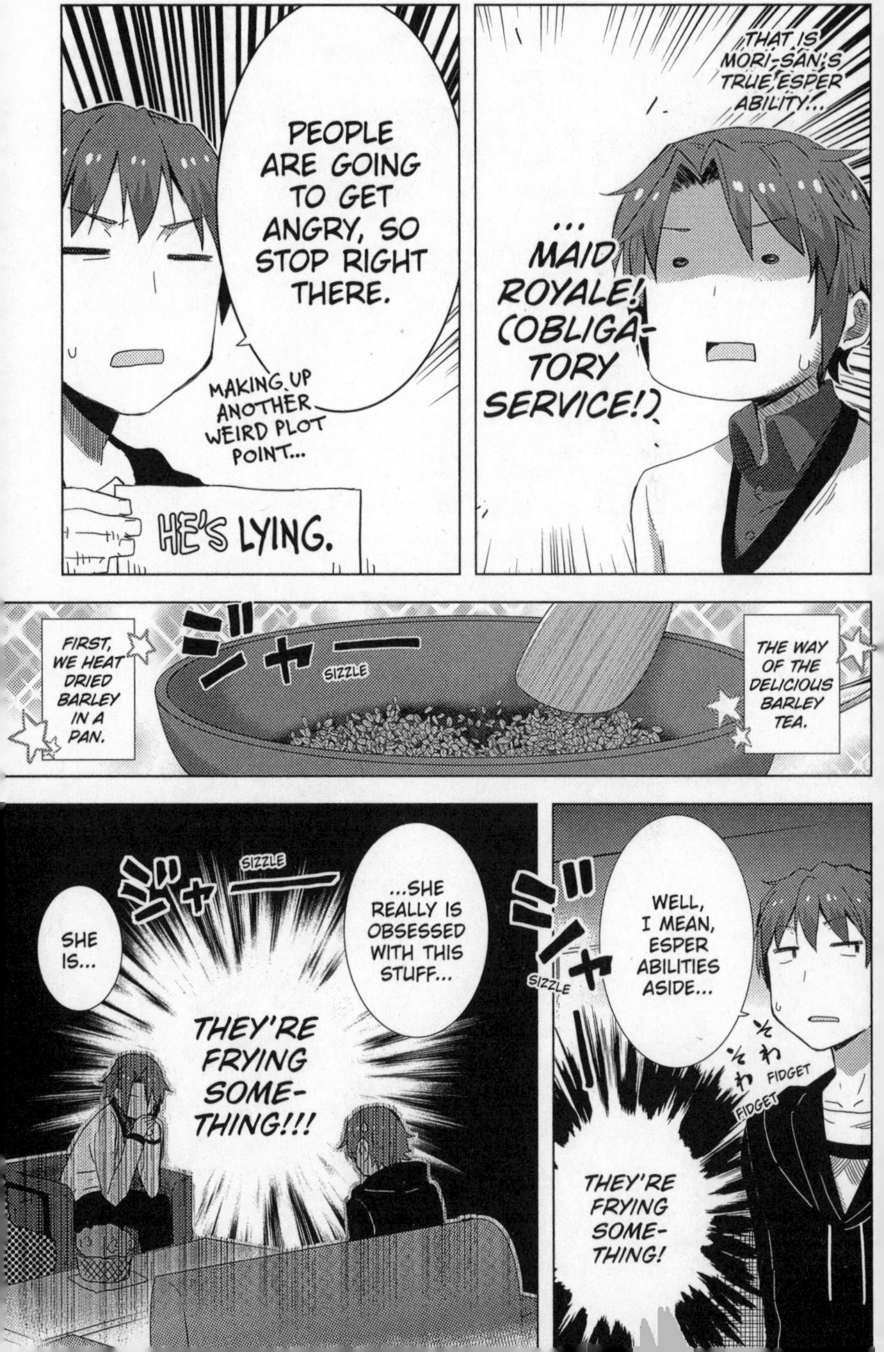
THAT IS MORI-SAN'S TRUE ESPER ABILITY...
...MAID ROYALE! (OBLIGATORY SERVICE!)
PEOPLE ARE GOING TO GET ANGRY, SO STOP RIGHT THERE.
MAKING UP ANOTHER WEIRD PLOT POINT...
HE'S LYING.
THE WAY OF THE DELICIOUS BARLEY TEA.
ジャー
SIZZLE
FIRST, WE HEAT DRIED BARLEY IN A PAN.
ジャー
SIZZLE
WELL, I MEAN, ESPER ABILITIES ASIDE...
そわそわ
FIDGET FIDGET
THEY'RE FRYING SOMETHING!
...SHE REALLY IS OBSESSED WITH THIS STUFF...
ジャー
SIZZLE
SHE IS...
THEY'RE FRYING SOMETHING!!!

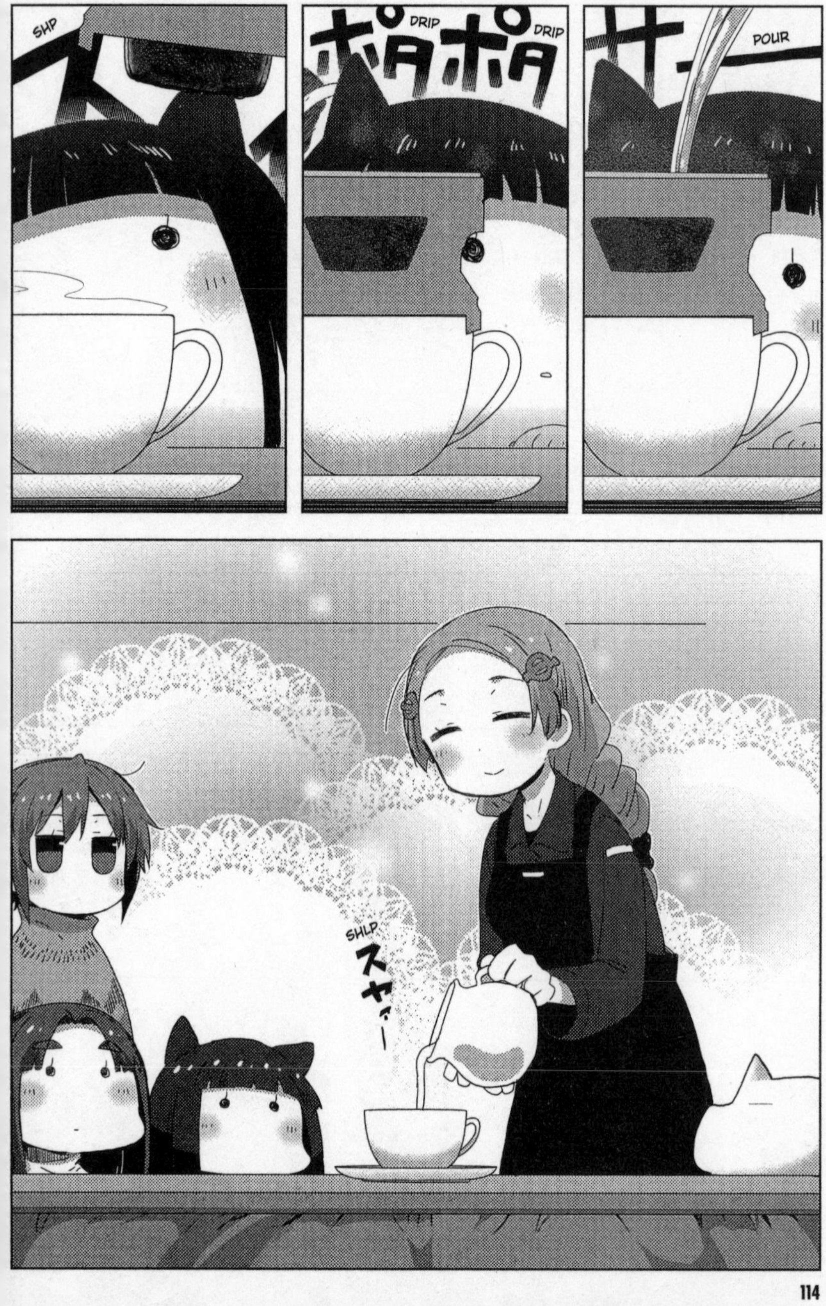
サー
POUR
ポタポタ
DRIP
DRIP
SHP
SHLP
スャァー

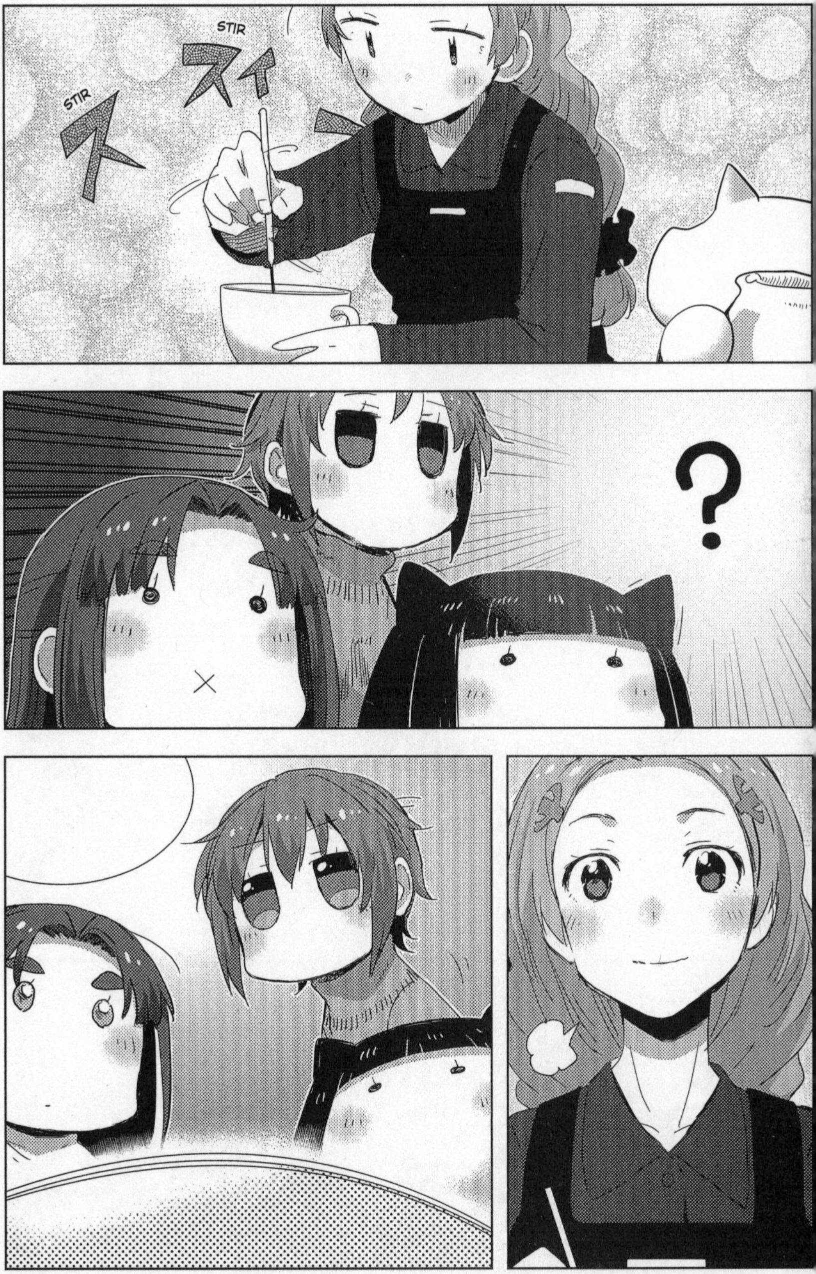
STIR
STIR
?

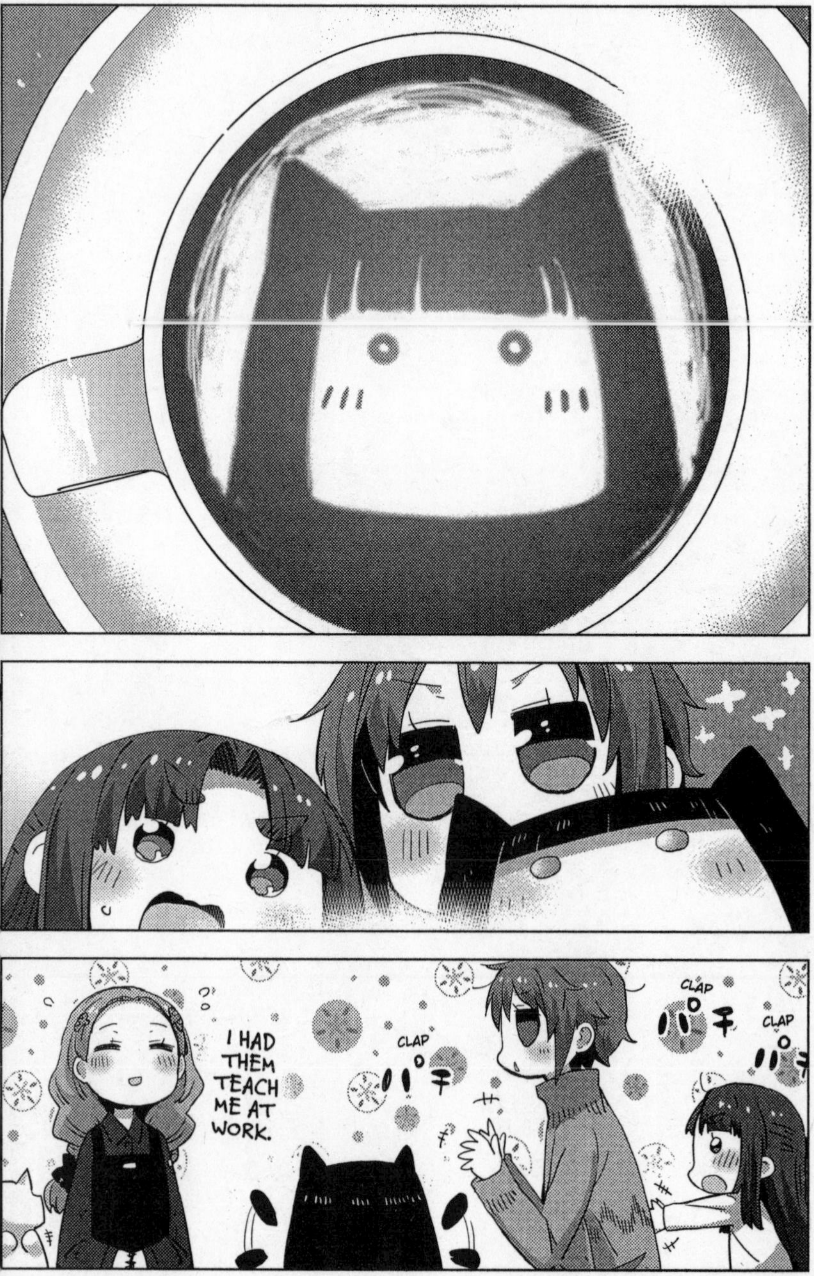
CLAP
CLAP
CLAP
I HAD THEM TEACH ME AT WORK.

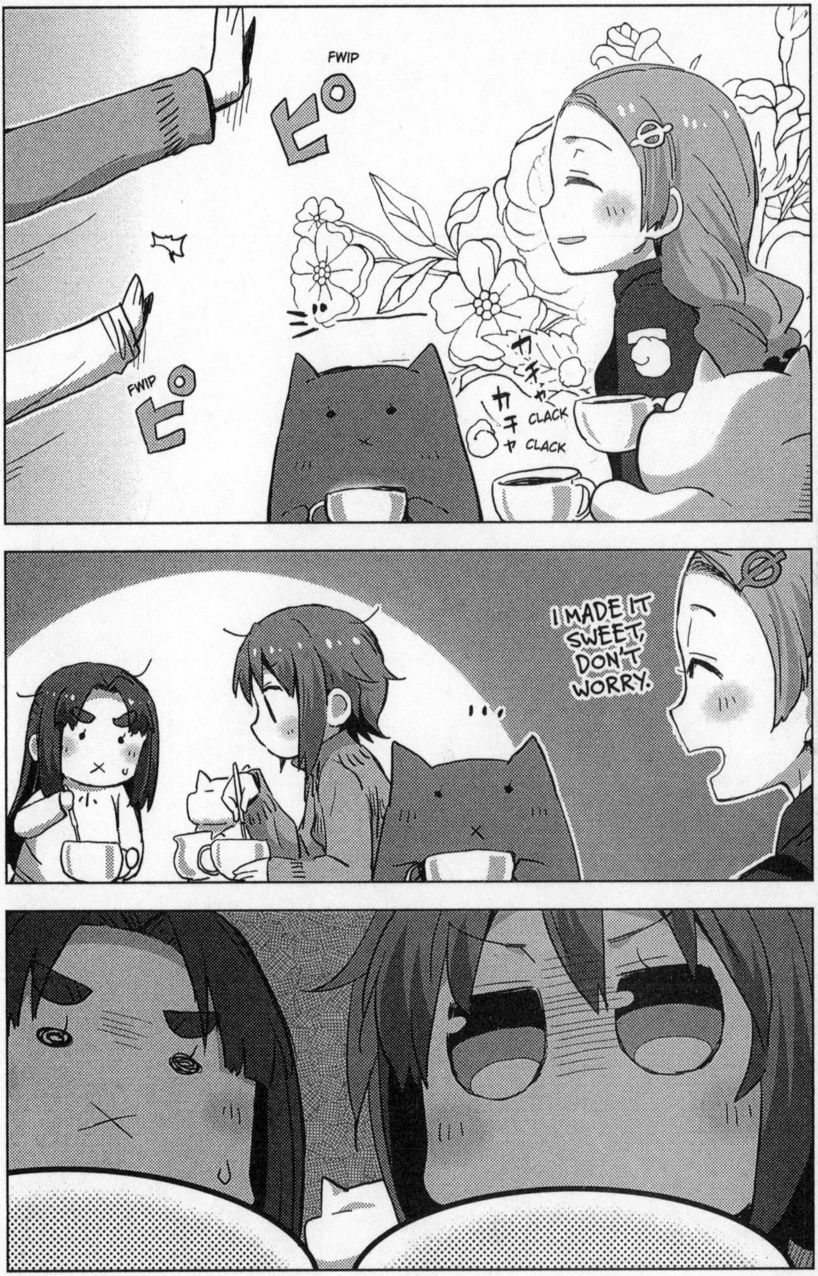
FWIP
ピ
FWIP
ピ
カチャ
CLACK
カチャ
CLACK
I MADE IT SWEET, DON'T WORRY.
...

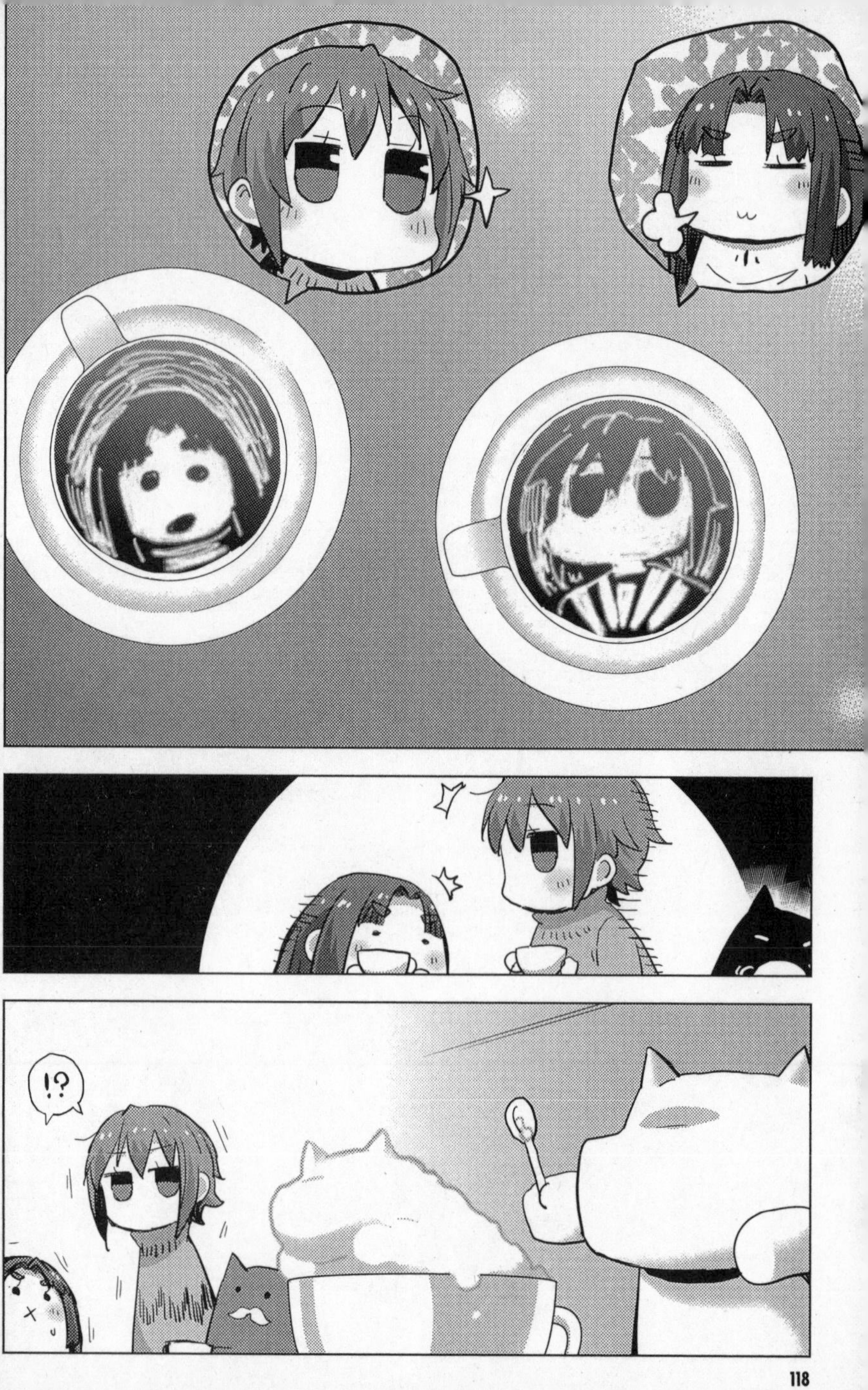
!?

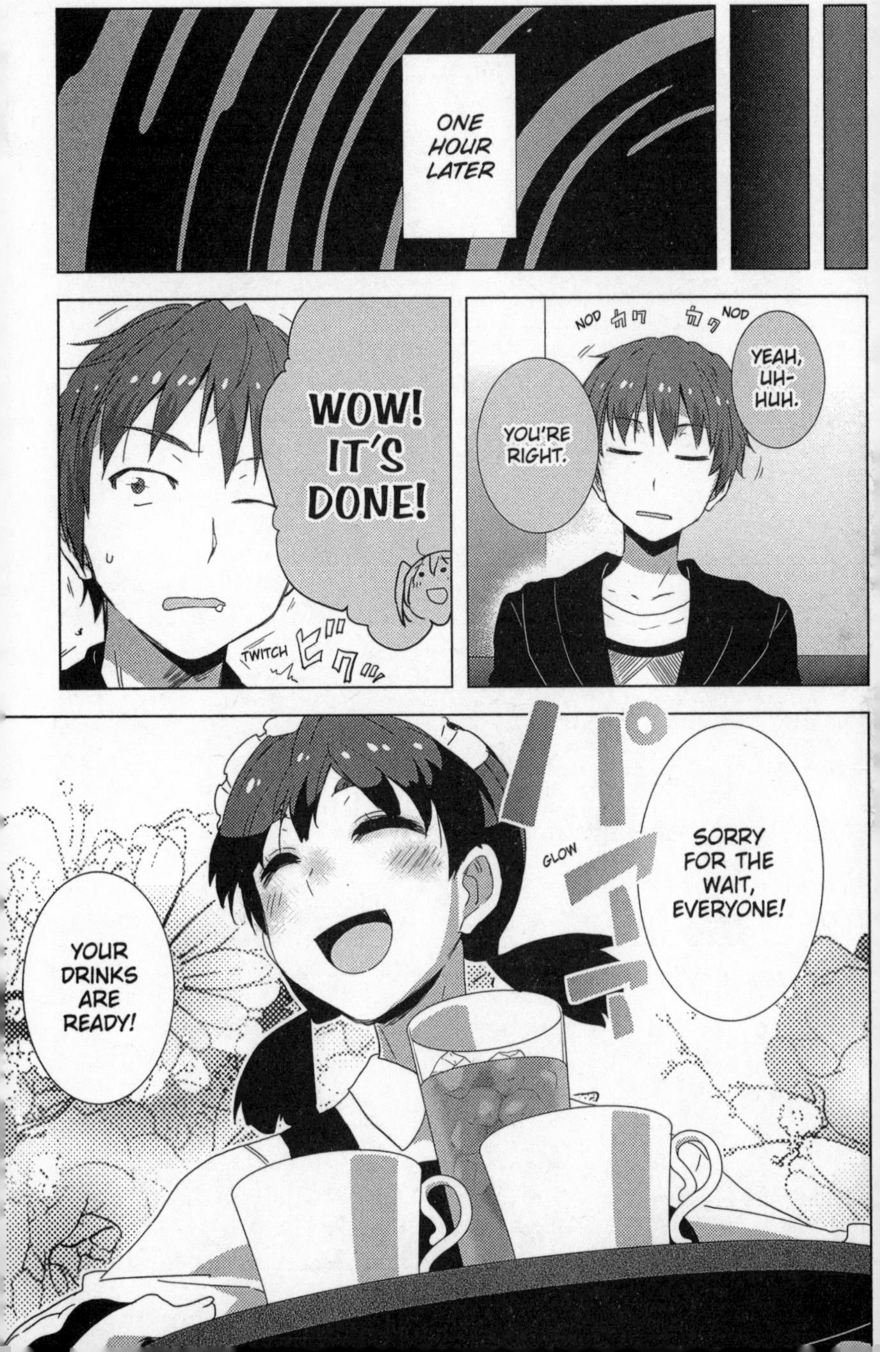
ONE HOUR LATER
NOD
NOD
YEAH, UH-HUH.
YOU'RE RIGHT.
WOW! IT'S DONE!
TWITCH
SORRY FOR THE WAIT, EVERYONE!
GLOW
YOUR DRINKS ARE READY!

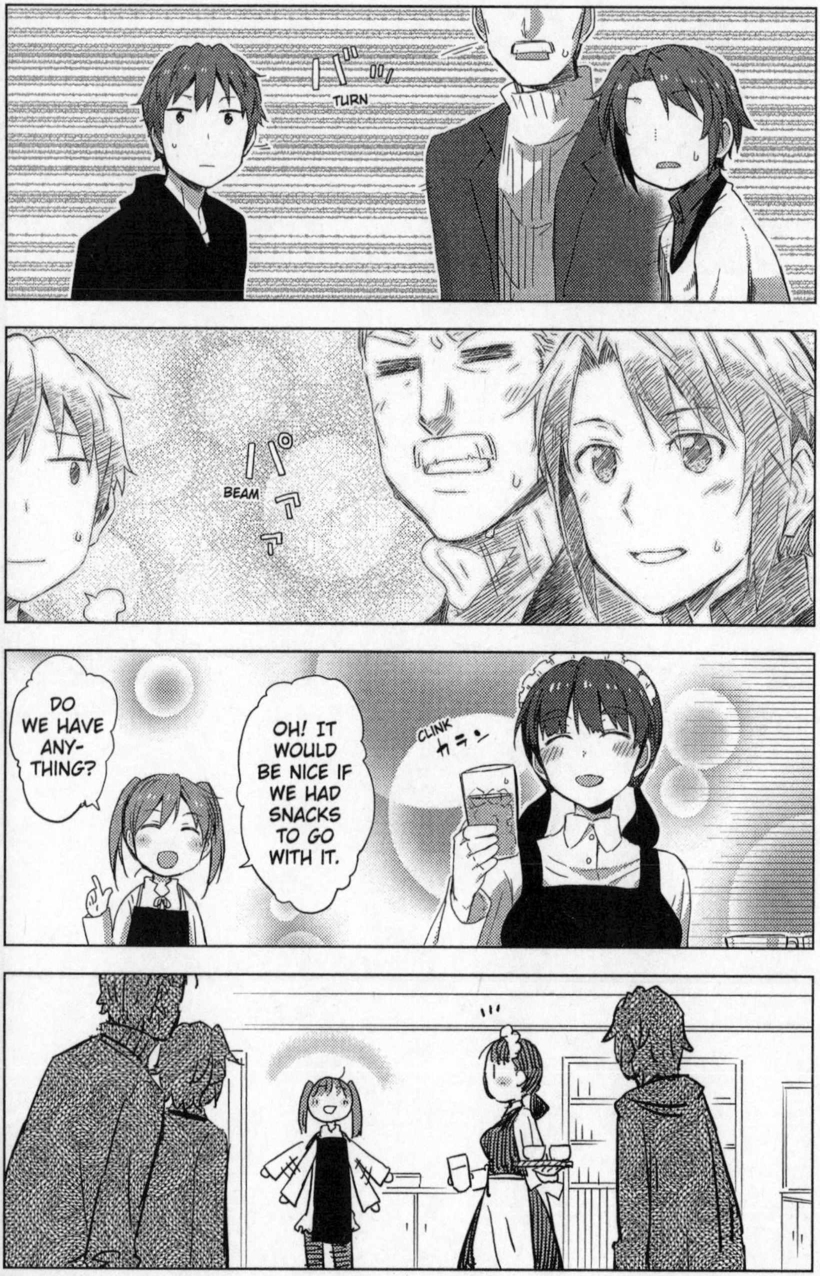
TURN
BEAM
CLINK
OH! IT WOULD BE NICE IF WE HAD SNACKS TO GO WITH IT.
DO WE HAVE ANYTHING?

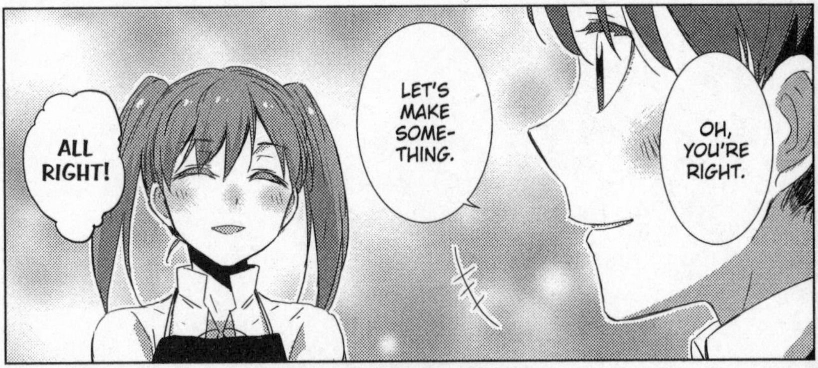
OH, YOU'RE RIGHT.
LET'S MAKE SOME-THING.
ALL RIGHT!

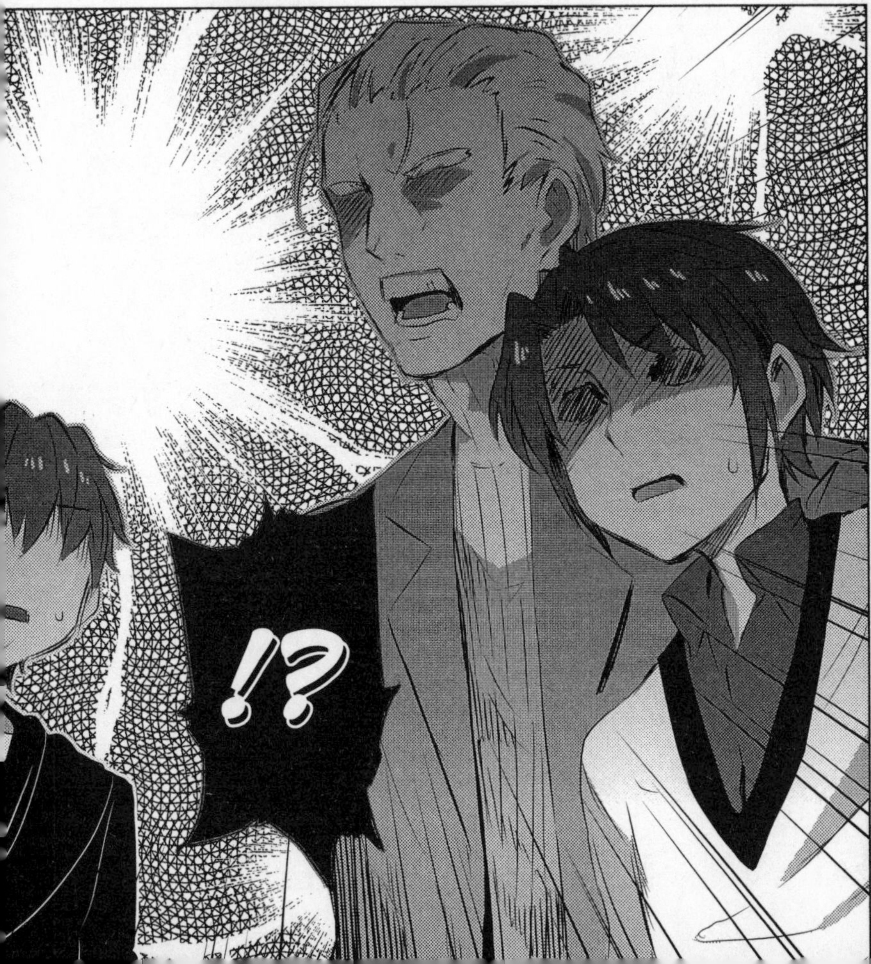
!?

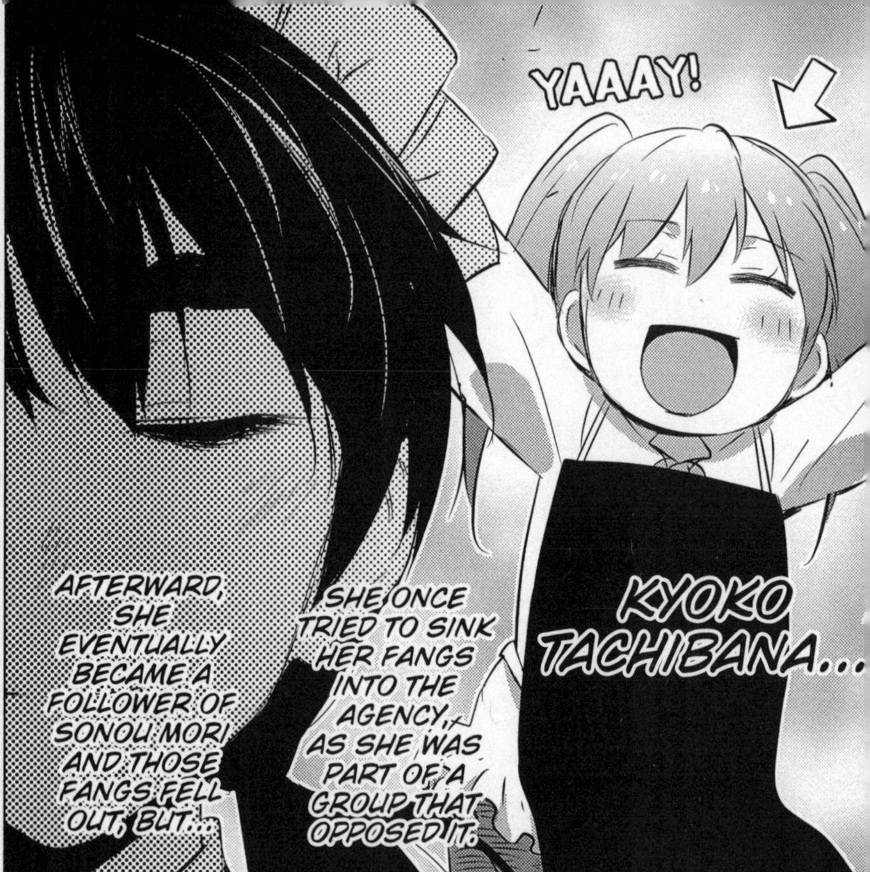
YAAAY!
KYOKO TACHIBANA...
SHE ONCE TRIED TO SINK HER FANGS INTO THE AGENCY, AS SHE WAS PART OF A GROUP THAT OPPOSED IT.
AFTERWARD, SHE EVENTUALLY BECAME A FOLLOWER OF SONOU MORI AND THOSE FANGS FELL OUT, BUT...

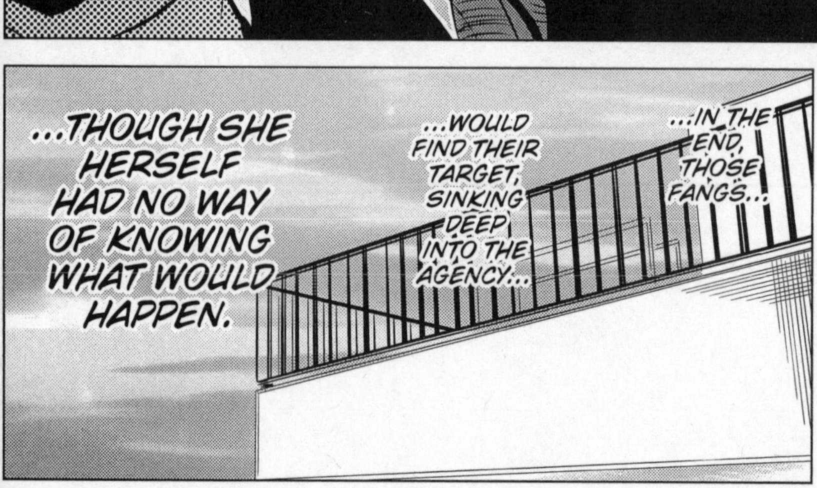
...IN THE END, THOSE FANGS...
...WOULD FIND THEIR TARGET, SINKING DEEP INTO THE AGENCY...
...THOUGH SHE HERSELF HAD NO WAY OF KNOWING WHAT WOULD HAPPEN.

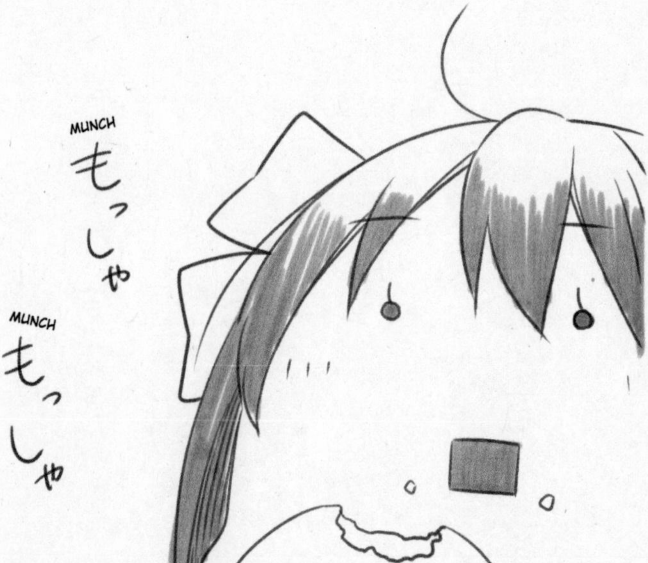
MUNCH
もっしゃ
MUNCH
もっしゃ

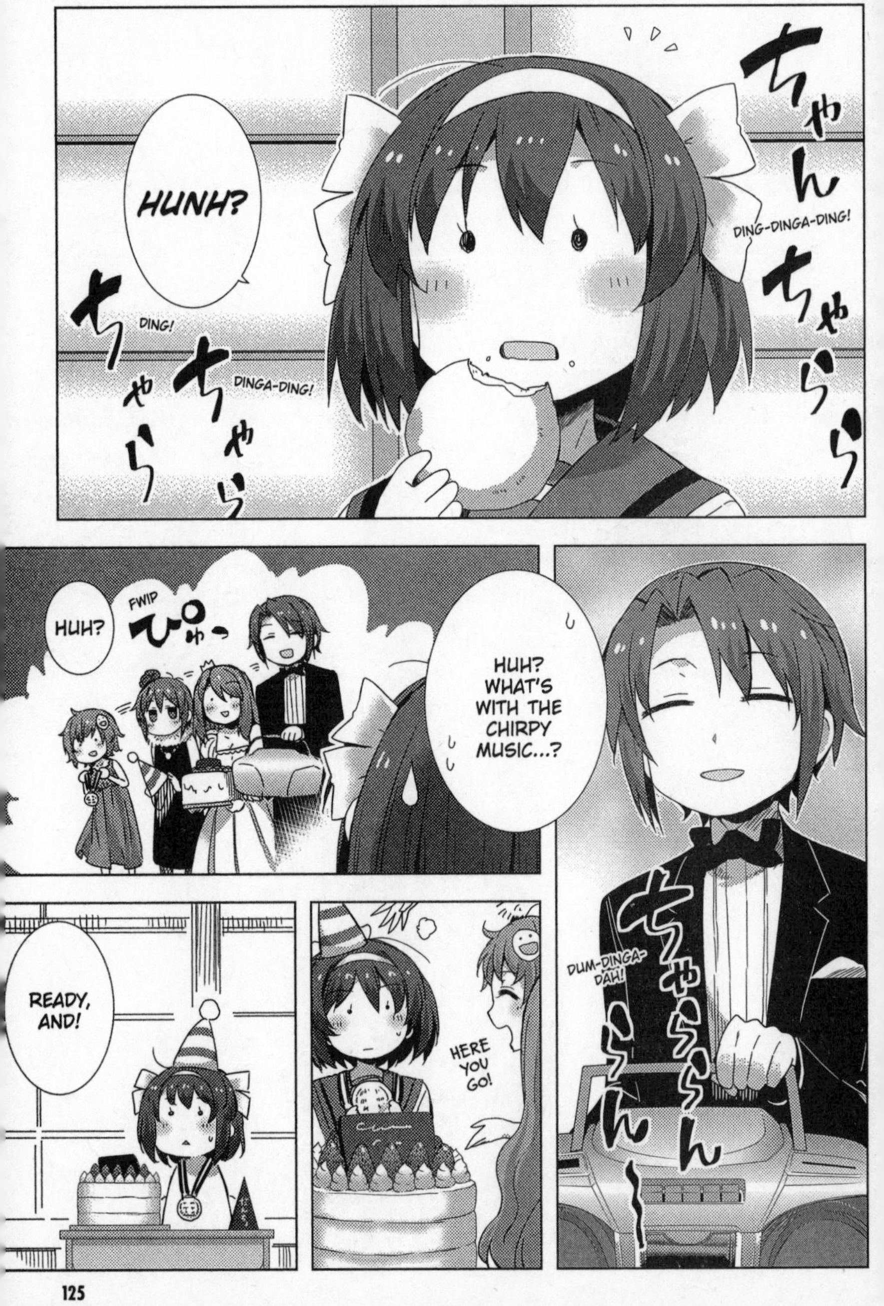
ちゃんちゃらら
DING-DINGA-DING!
HUNH?
ちゃらちゃら
DINGA-DING!
ちゃら
DING!
ちゃらら〜ん〜
DUM-DINGA-DAH!
HUH? WHAT'S WITH THE CHIRPY MUSIC...?
FWIP
ぴゅっ
HUH?
HERE YOU GO!
READY, AND!

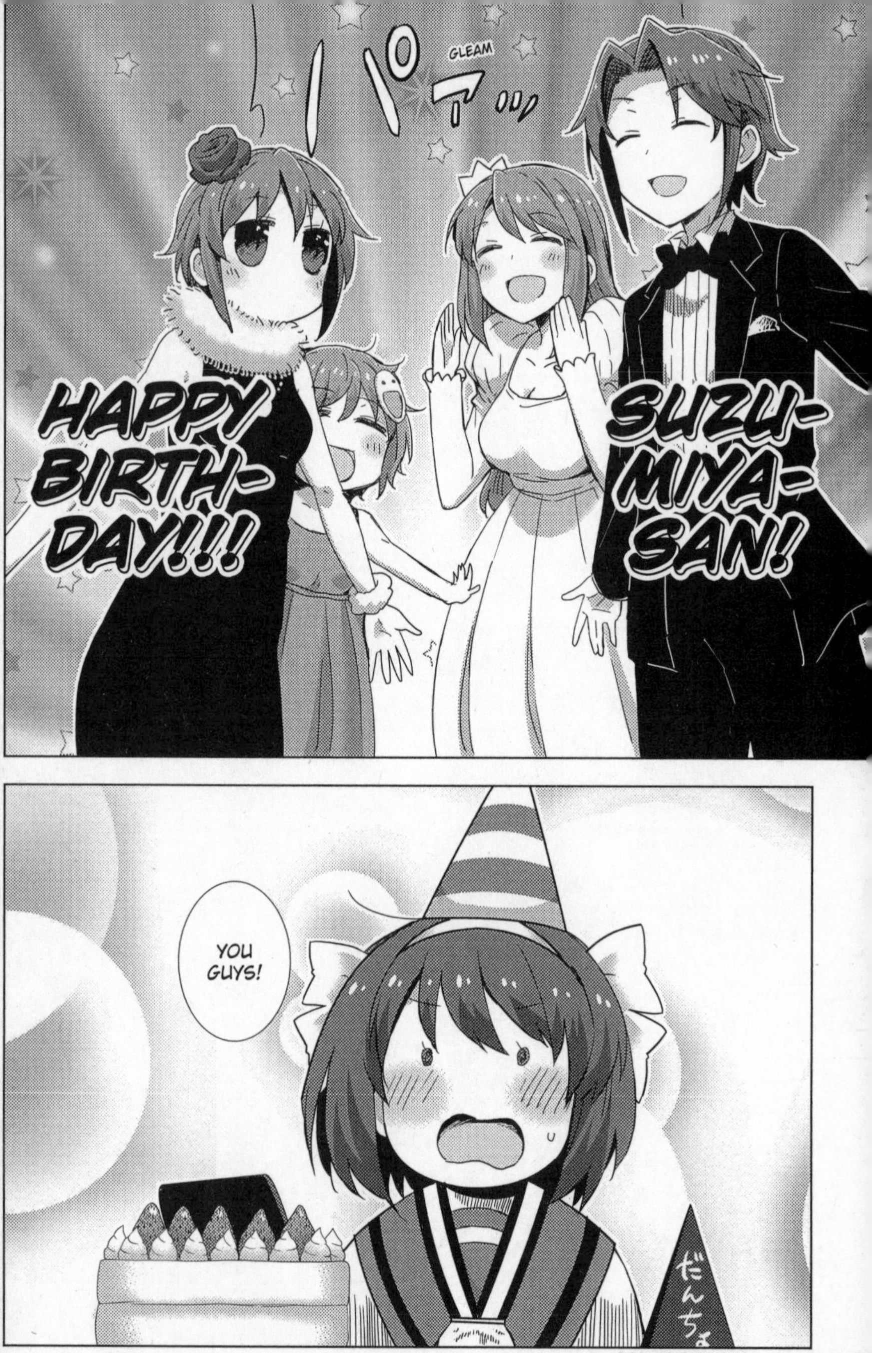
パァッ
GLEAM
SUZU-MIYA-SAN!
HAPPY BIRTH-DAY!!!
YOU GUYS!
だんちょ

SIGN: BRIGADE CHIEF

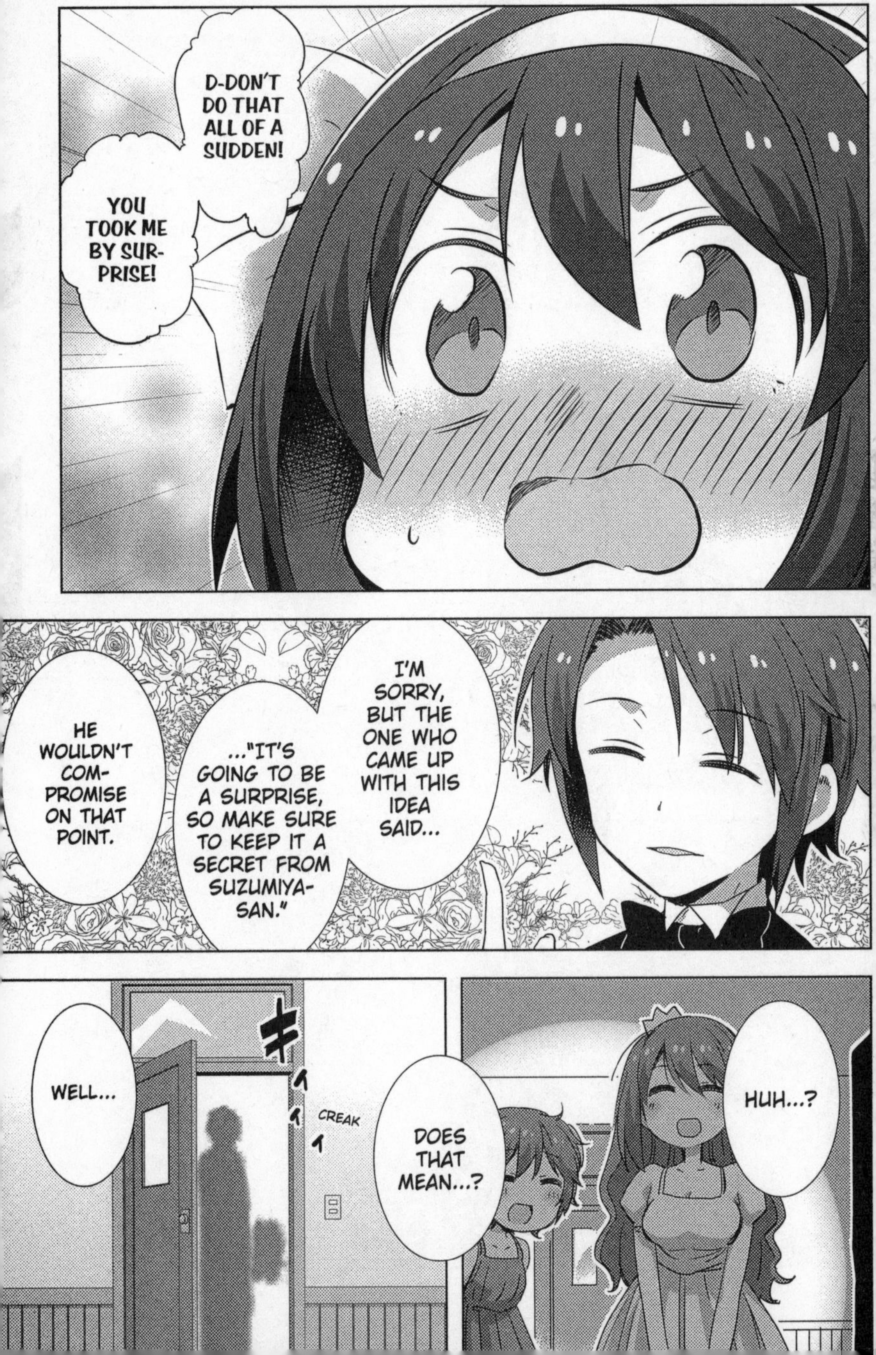
D-DON'T DO THAT ALL OF A SUDDEN!
YOU TOOK ME BY SURPRISE!
I'M SORRY, BUT THE ONE WHO CAME UP WITH THIS IDEA SAID...
..."IT'S GOING TO BE A SURPRISE, SO MAKE SURE TO KEEP IT A SECRET FROM SUZUMIYA-SAN."
HE WOULDN'T COMPROMISE ON THAT POINT.
HUH...?
DOES THAT MEAN...?
CREAK
WELL...

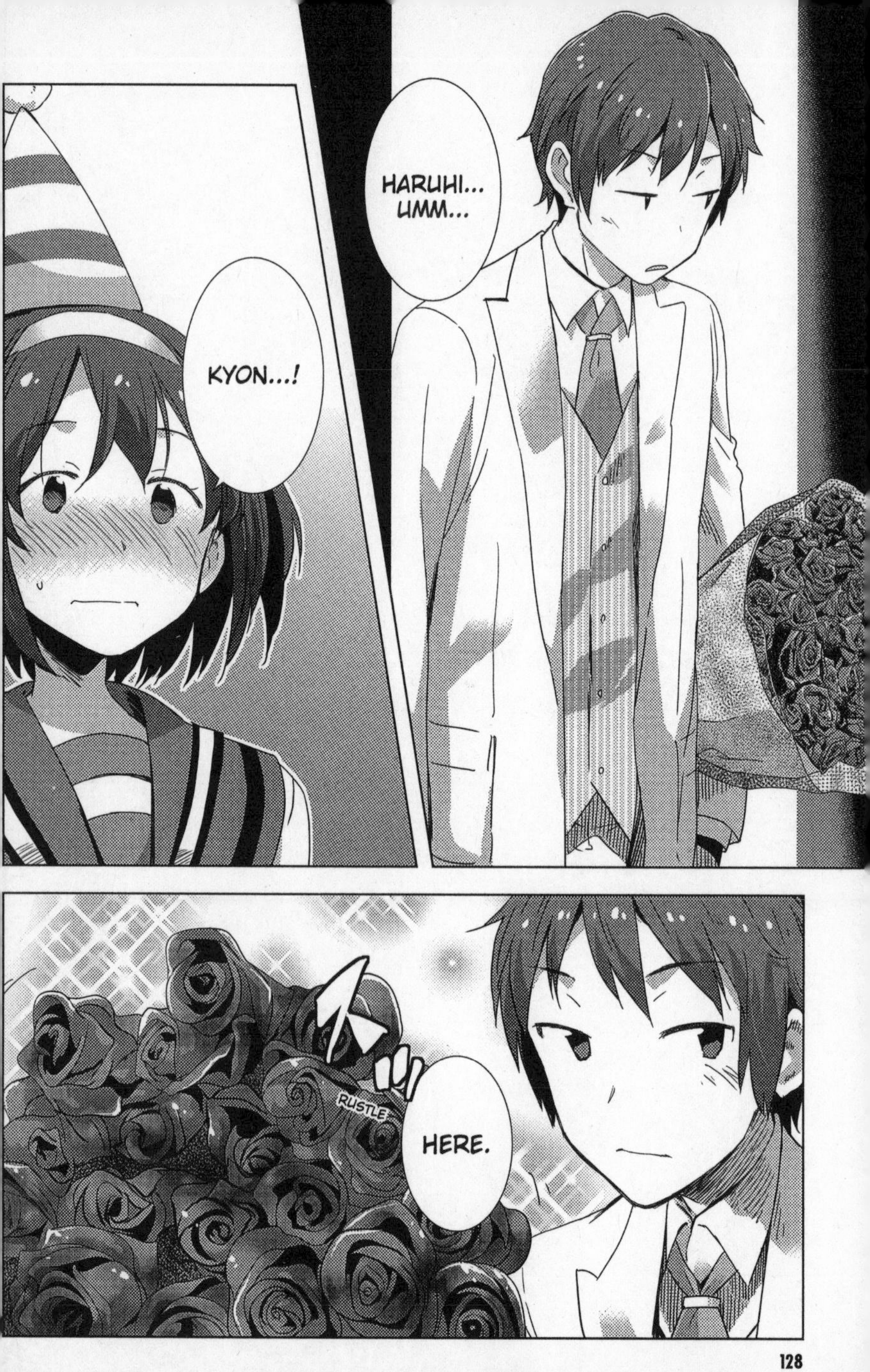
HARUHI... UMM...
KYON...!
RUSTLE
HERE.

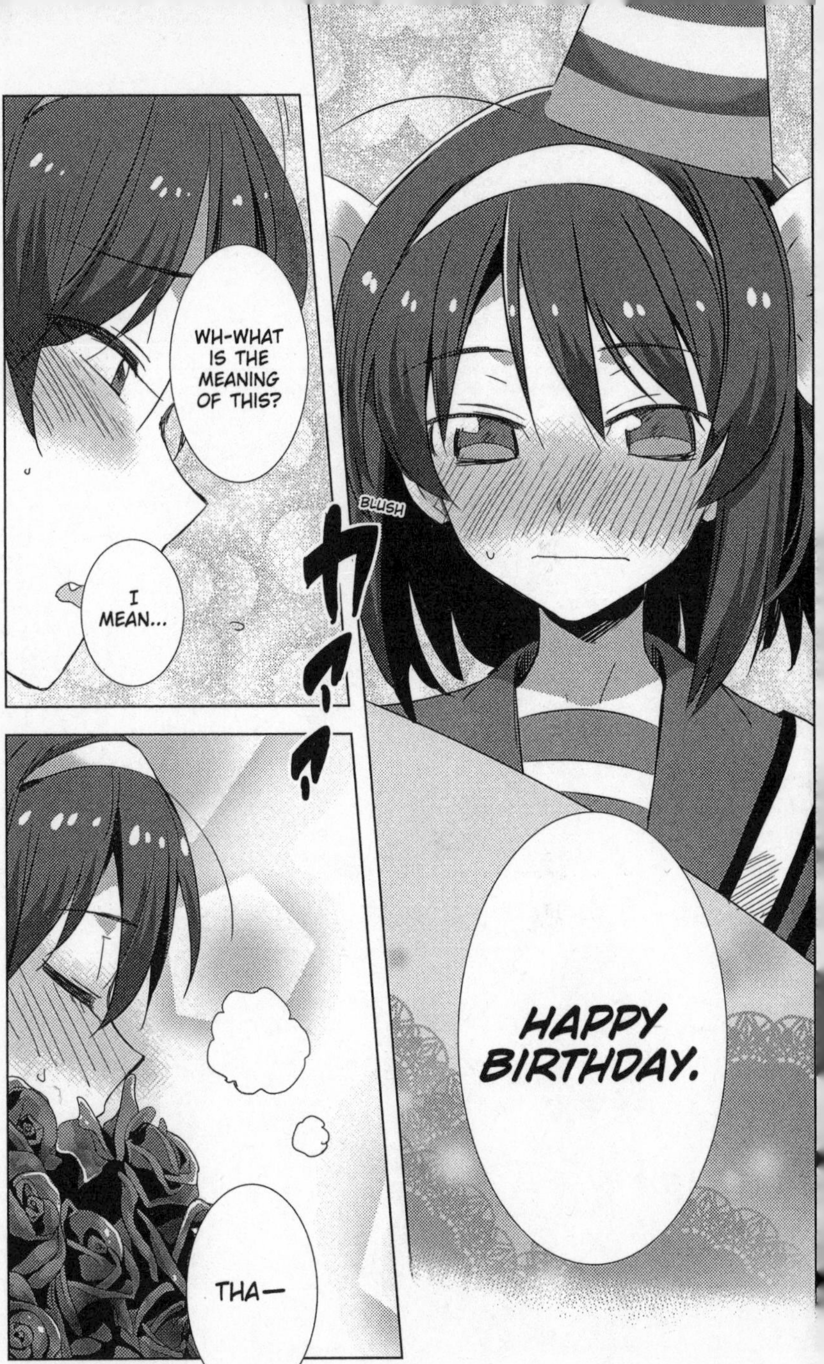
BLUSH
HAPPY BIRTHDAY.
WH-WHAT IS THE MEANING OF THIS?
I MEAN...
THA—

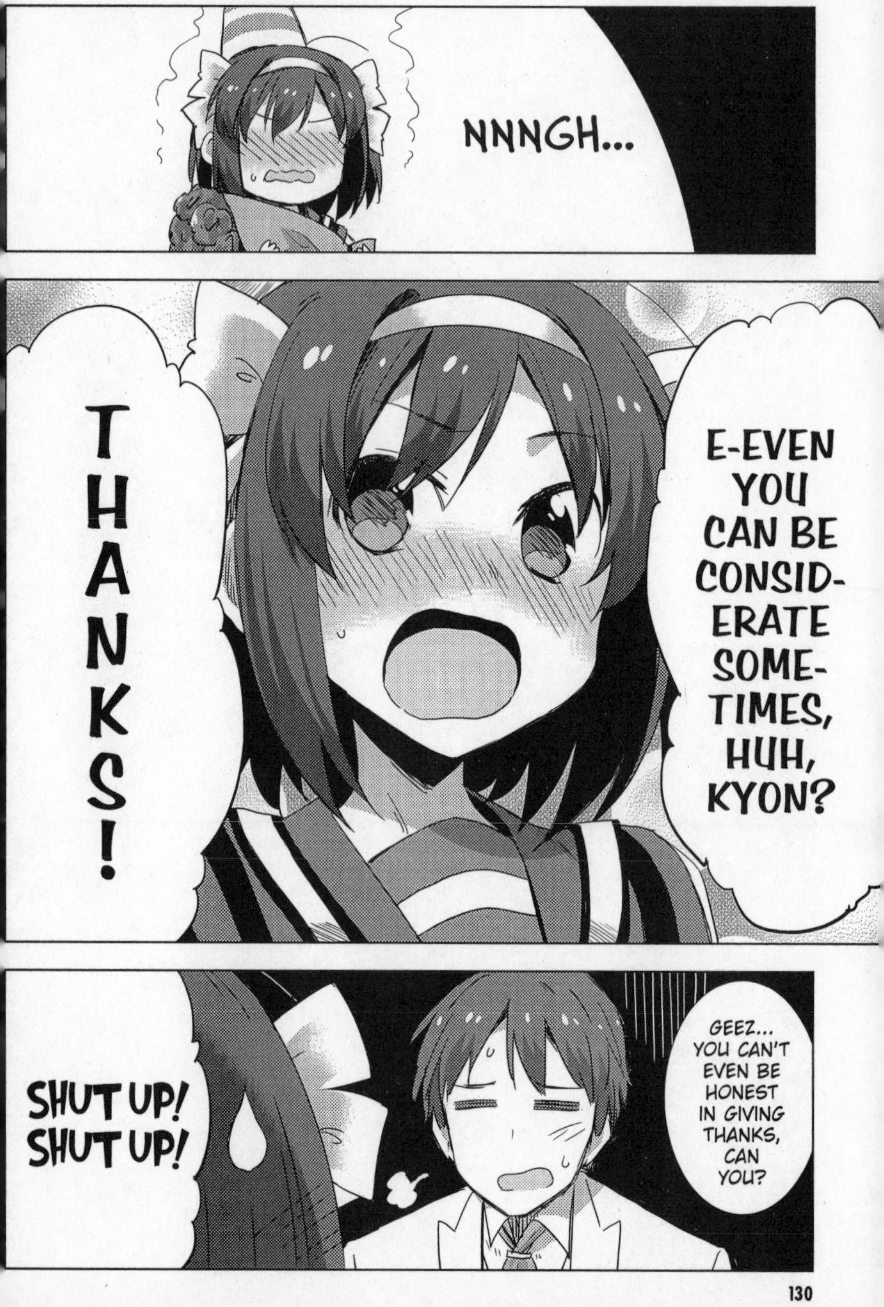
NNNGH...
E-EVEN YOU CAN BE CONSID-ERATE SOME-TIMES, HUH, KYON?
THANKS!
GEEZ... YOU CAN'T EVEN BE HONEST IN GIVING THANKS, CAN YOU?
SHUT UP! SHUT UP!

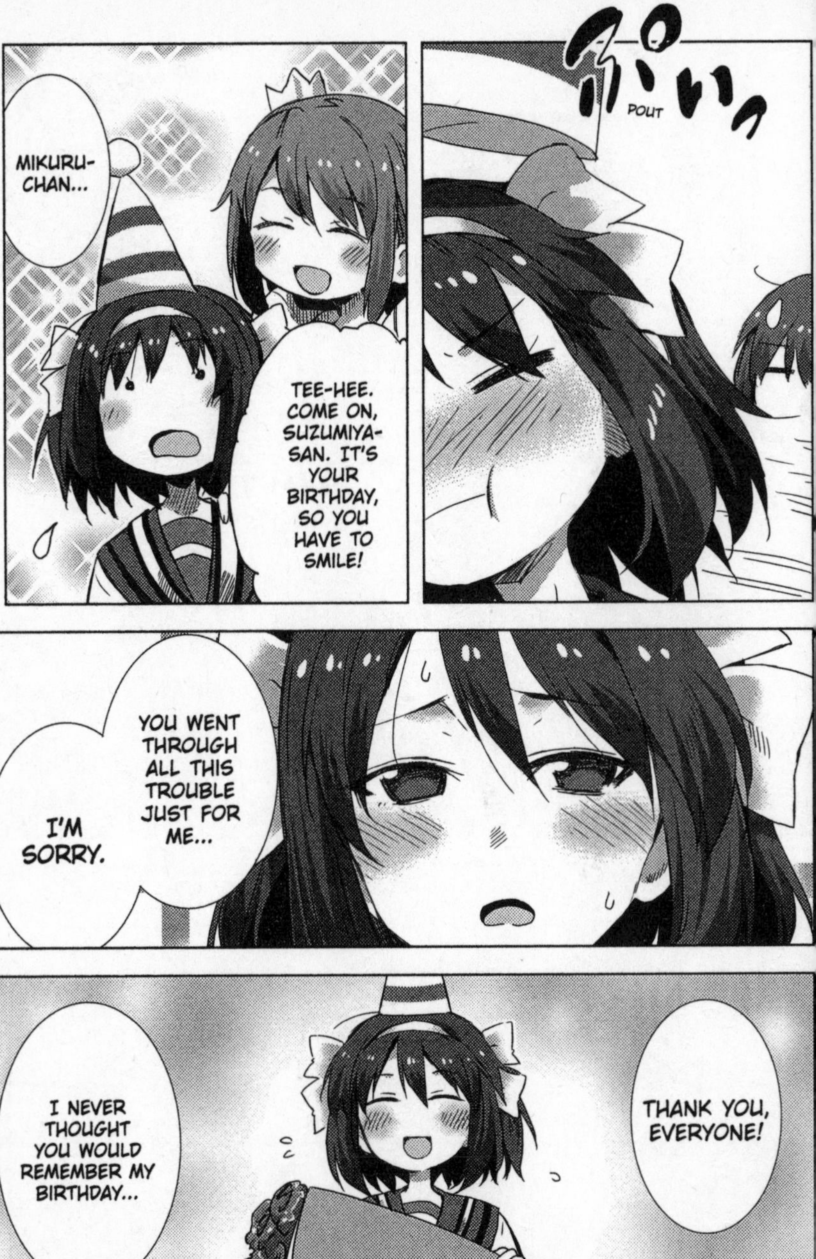
ぷいっ
POUT
TEE-HEE. COME ON, SUZUMIYA-SAN. IT'S YOUR BIRTHDAY, SO YOU HAVE TO SMILE!
MIKURU-CHAN...
YOU WENT THROUGH ALL THIS TROUBLE JUST FOR ME...
I'M SORRY.
THANK YOU, EVERYONE!
I NEVER THOUGHT YOU WOULD REMEMBER MY BIRTHDAY...

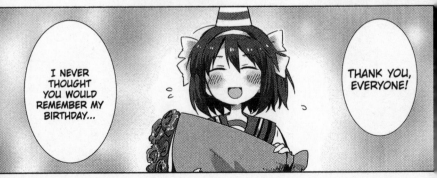

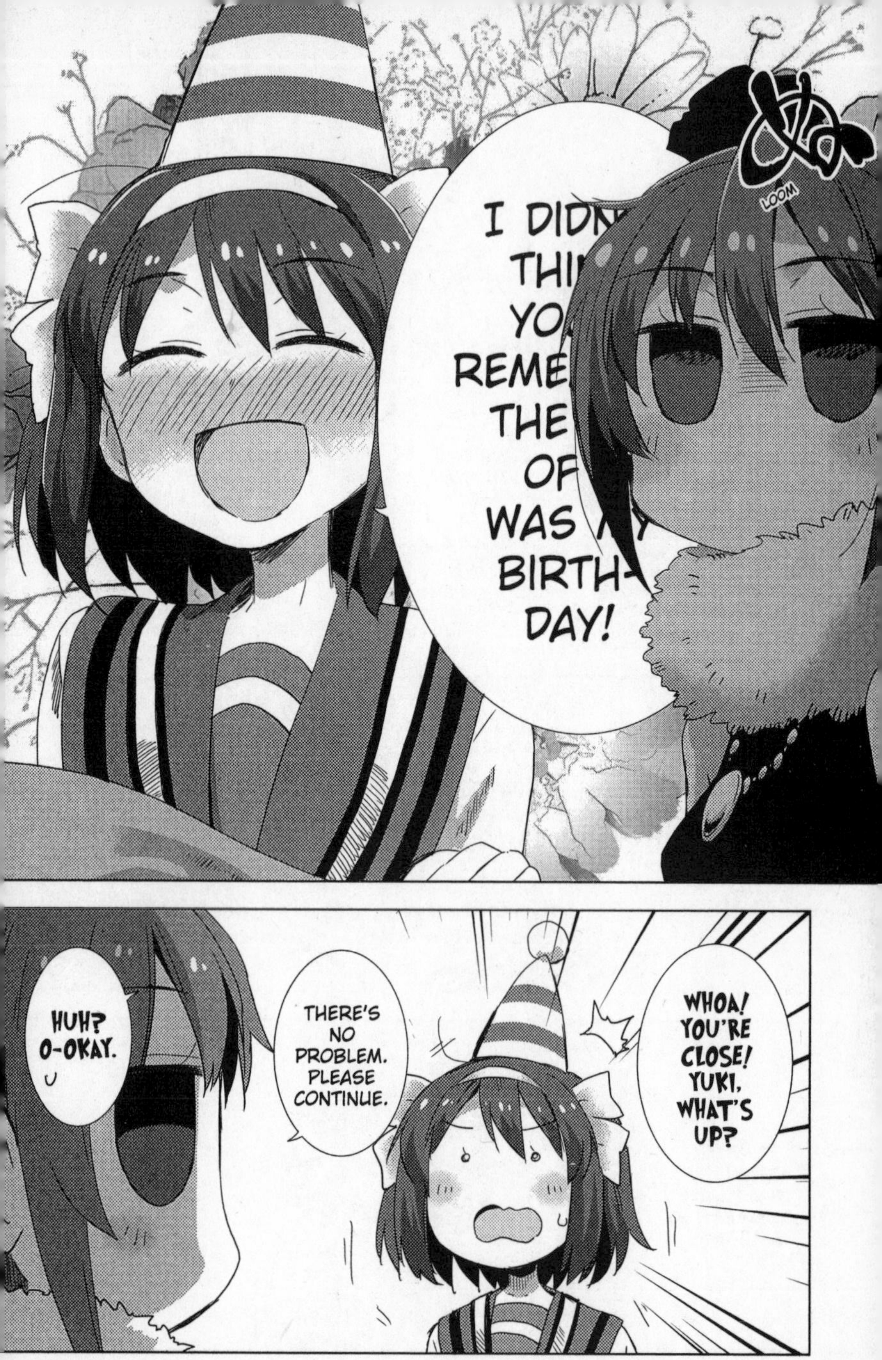
LOOM
I DIDN THI YO REME THE OF WAS BIRTH-DAY!
WHOA! YOU'RE CLOSE! YUKI, WHAT'S UP?
THERE'S NO PROBLEM. PLEASE CONTINUE.
HUH? O-OKAY.

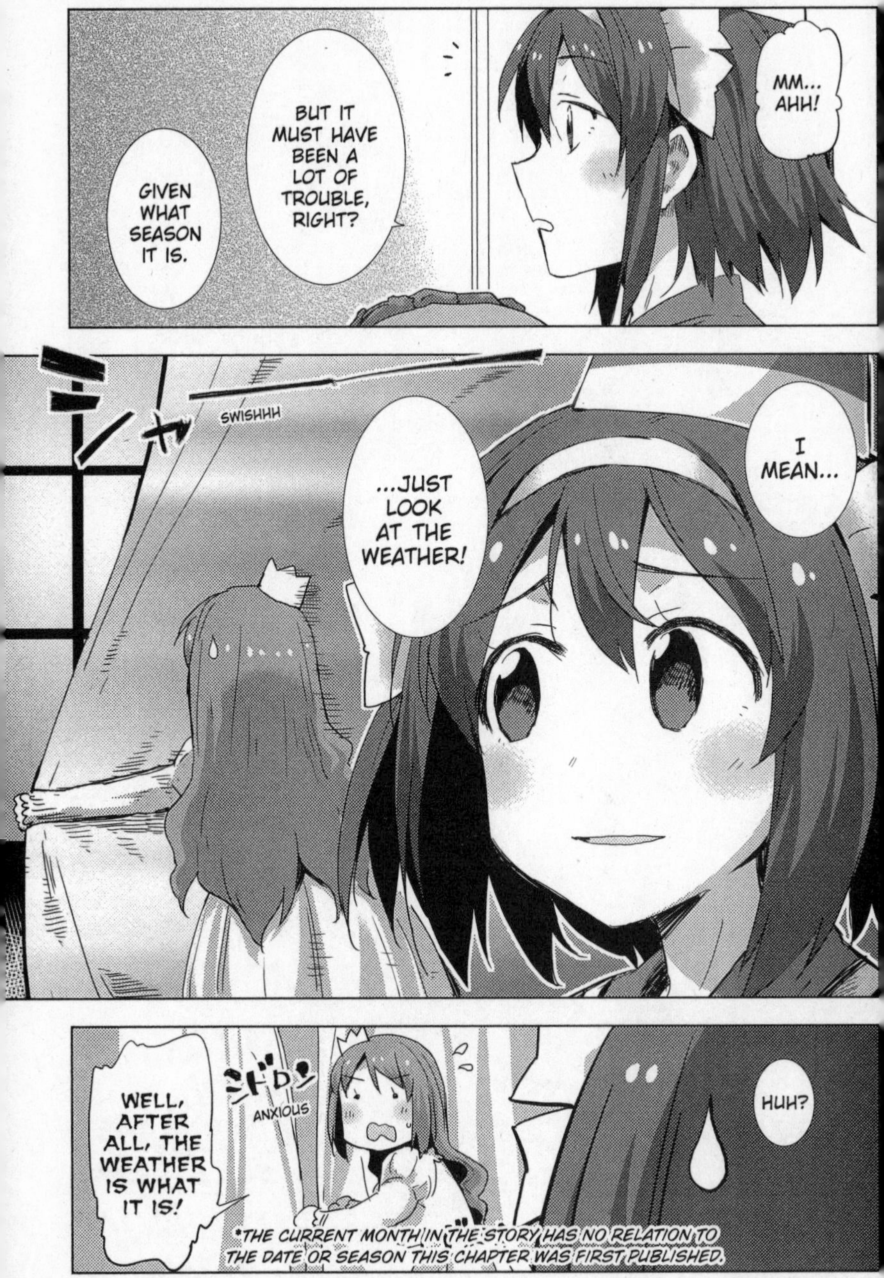

MM... AHH!
BUT IT MUST HAVE BEEN A LOT OF TROUBLE, RIGHT?
GIVEN WHAT SEASON IT IS.
I MEAN...
...JUST LOOK AT THE WEATHER!
SWISHHH
HUH?
ANXIOUS
WELL, AFTER ALL, THE WEATHER IS WHAT IT IS!
*THE CURRENT MONTH IN THE STORY HAS NO RELATION TO THE DATE OR SEASON THIS CHAPTER WAS FIRST PUBLISHED.

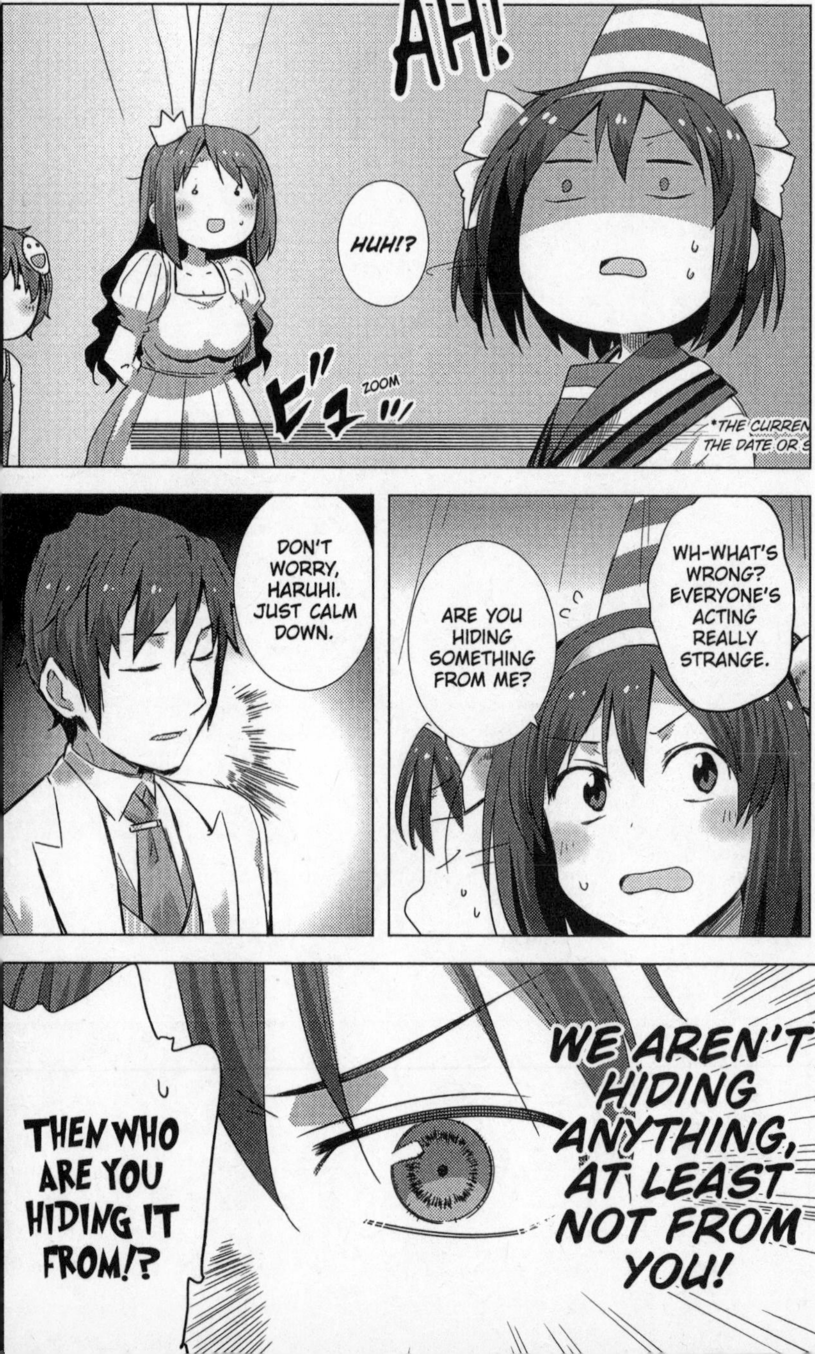
AH!
HUH!?
ZOOM
*THE CURREN
THE DATE OR S
WH-WHAT'S WRONG? EVERYONE'S ACTING REALLY STRANGE.
ARE YOU HIDING SOMETHING FROM ME?
DON'T WORRY, HARUHI. JUST CALM DOWN.
WE AREN'T HIDING ANYTHING, AT LEAST NOT FROM YOU!
THEN WHO ARE YOU HIDING IT FROM!?

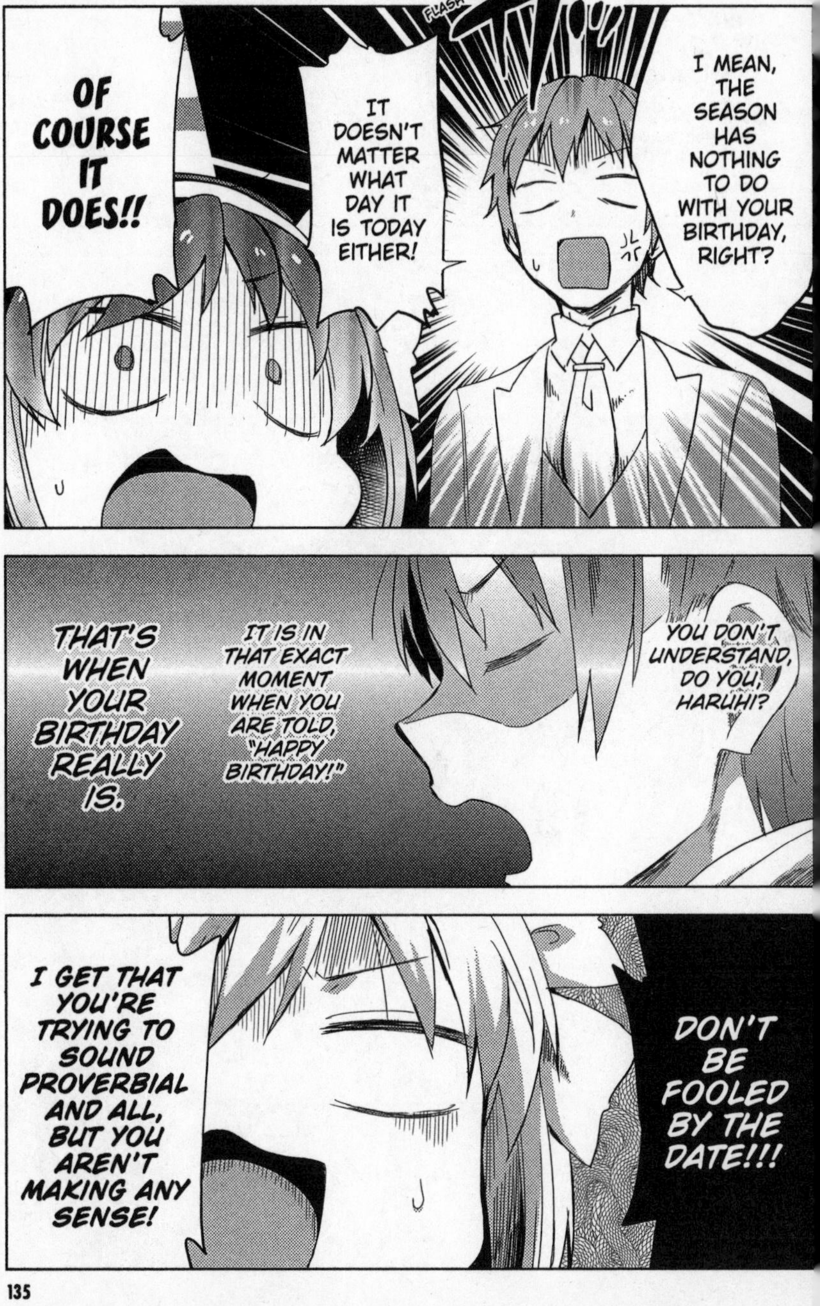
FLASH
I MEAN, THE SEASON HAS NOTHING TO DO WITH YOUR BIRTHDAY, RIGHT?
IT DOESN'T MATTER WHAT DAY IT IS TODAY EITHER!
OF COURSE IT DOES!!
YOU DON'T UNDERSTAND, DO YOU, HARUHI?
IT IS IN THAT EXACT MOMENT WHEN YOU ARE TOLD, "HAPPY BIRTHDAY!"
THAT'S WHEN YOUR BIRTHDAY REALLY IS.
DON'T BE FOOLED BY THE DATE!!!
I GET THAT YOU'RE TRYING TO SOUND PROVERBIAL AND ALL, BUT YOU AREN'T MAKING ANY SENSE!

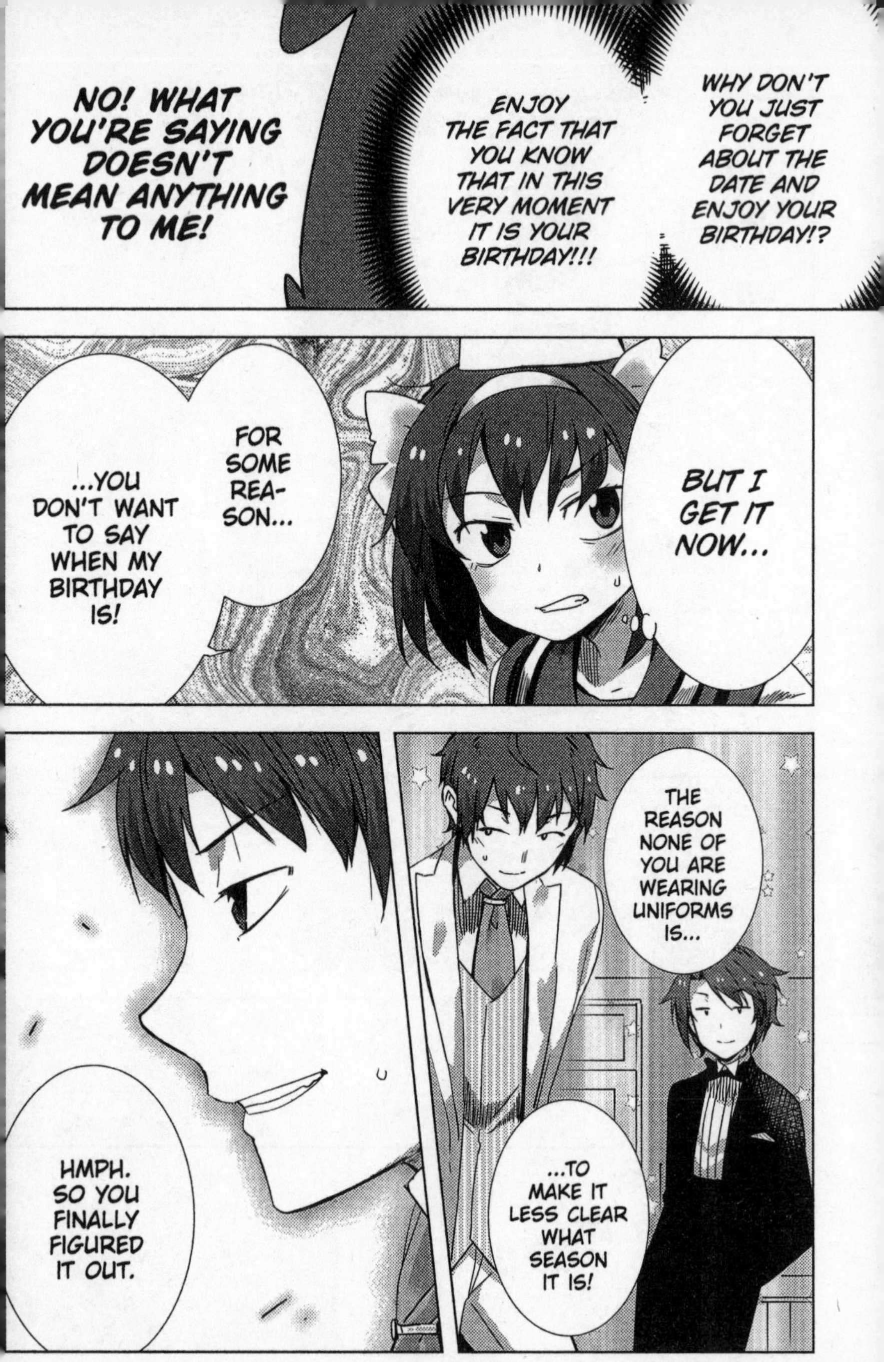
WHY DON'T YOU JUST FORGET ABOUT THE DATE AND ENJOY YOUR BIRTHDAY!?
ENJOY THE FACT THAT YOU KNOW THAT IN THIS VERY MOMENT IT IS YOUR BIRTHDAY!!!
NO! WHAT YOU'RE SAYING DOESN'T MEAN ANYTHING TO ME!
BUT I GET IT NOW...
FOR SOME REA-SON...
...YOU DON'T WANT TO SAY WHEN MY BIRTHDAY IS!
THE REASON NONE OF YOU ARE WEARING UNIFORMS IS...
...TO MAKE IT LESS CLEAR WHAT SEASON IT IS!
HMPH. SO YOU FINALLY FIGURED IT OUT.

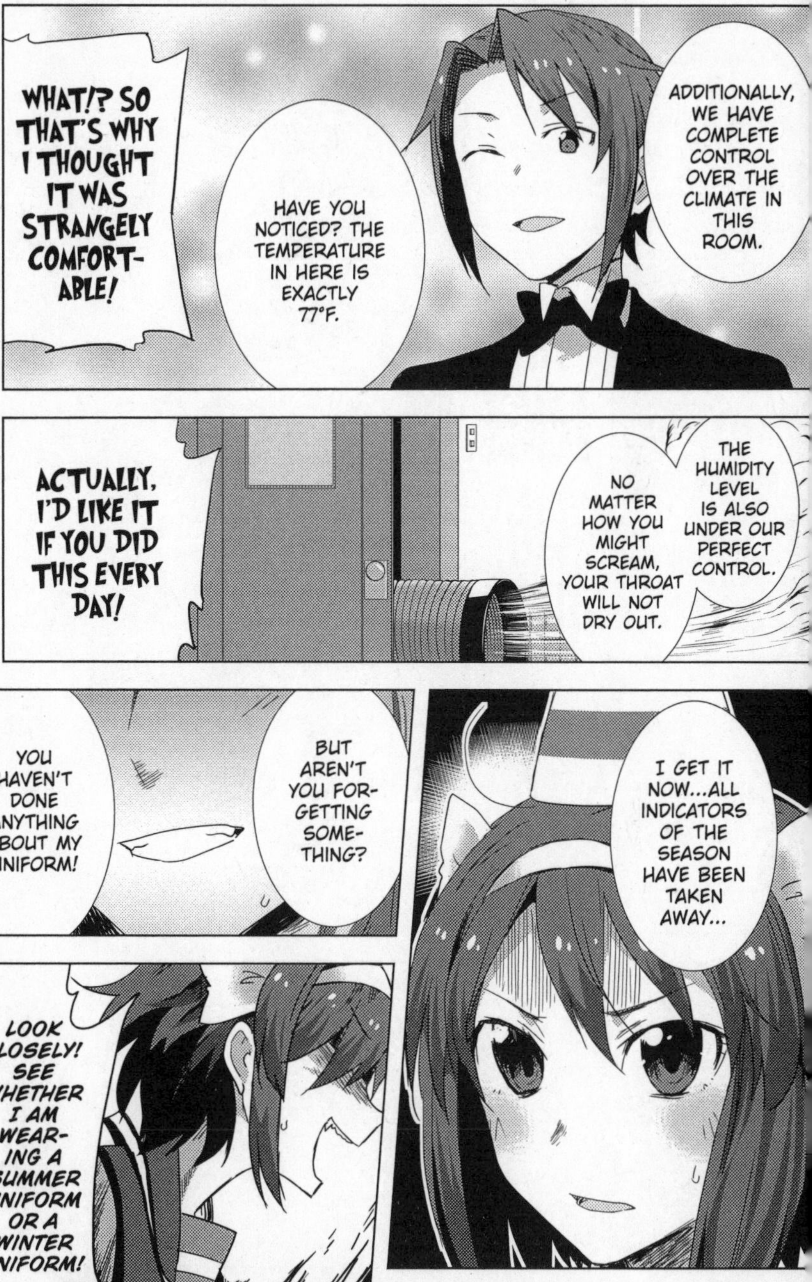
ADDITIONALLY, WE HAVE COMPLETE CONTROL OVER THE CLIMATE IN THIS ROOM.
HAVE YOU NOTICED? THE TEMPERATURE IN HERE IS EXACTLY 77°F.
WHAT!? SO THAT'S WHY I THOUGHT IT WAS STRANGELY COMFORT-ABLE!
THE HUMIDITY LEVEL IS ALSO UNDER OUR PERFECT CONTROL.
NO MATTER HOW YOU MIGHT SCREAM, YOUR THROAT WILL NOT DRY OUT.
ACTUALLY, I'D LIKE IT IF YOU DID THIS EVERY DAY!
I GET IT NOW...ALL INDICATORS OF THE SEASON HAVE BEEN TAKEN AWAY...
BUT AREN'T YOU FOR-GETTING SOME-THING?
YOU HAVEN'T DONE ANYTHING ABOUT MY UNIFORM!
LOOK CLOSELY! SEE WHETHER I AM WEAR-ING A SUMMER UNIFORM OR A WINTER UNIFORM!

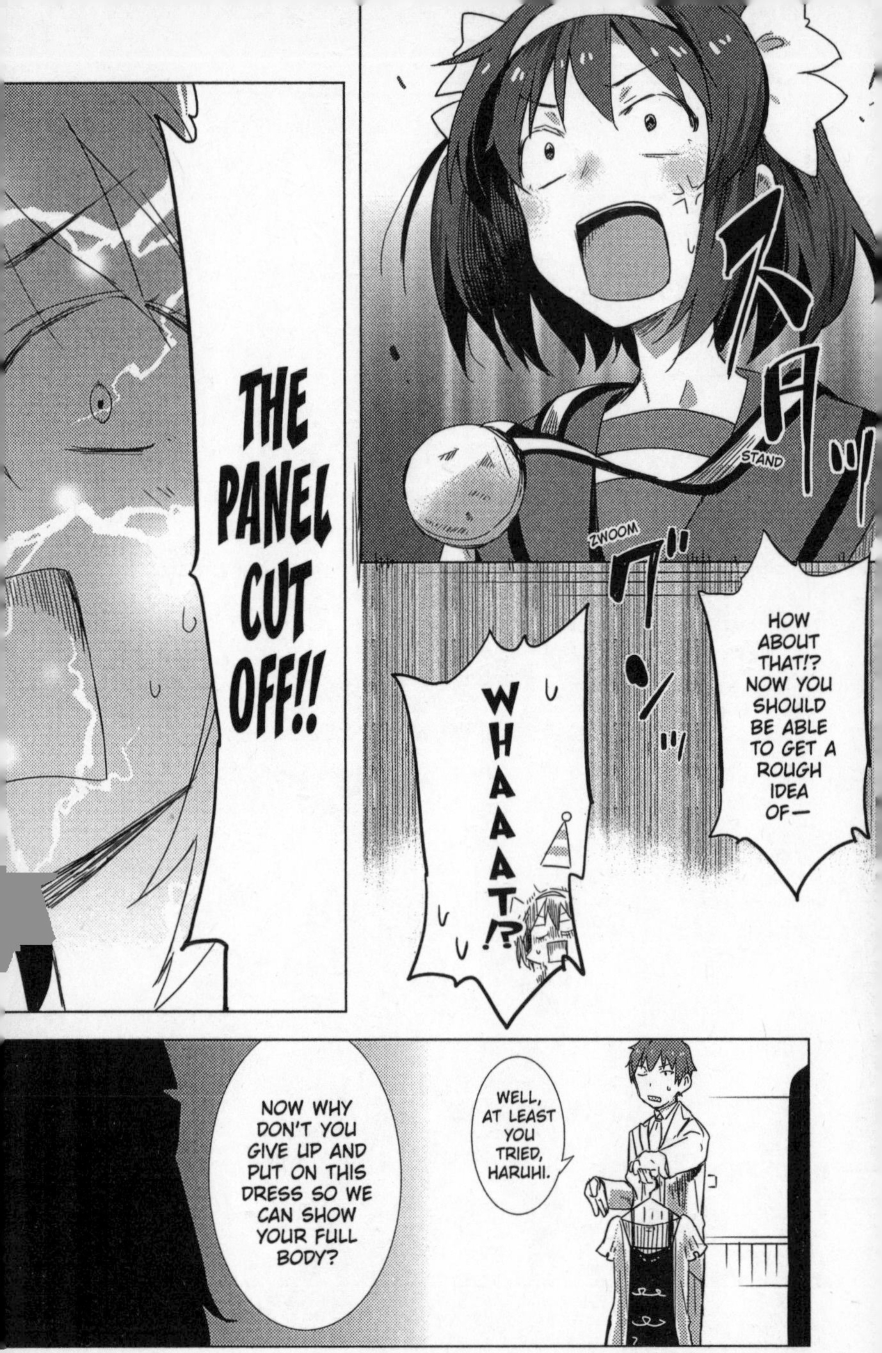
STAND
ZWOOM
HOW ABOUT THAT!? NOW YOU SHOULD BE ABLE TO GET A ROUGH IDEA OF—
WHAAAAT!?
THE PANEL CUT OFF!!
WELL, AT LEAST YOU TRIED, HARUHI.
NOW WHY DON'T YOU GIVE UP AND PUT ON THIS DRESS SO WE CAN SHOW YOUR FULL BODY?

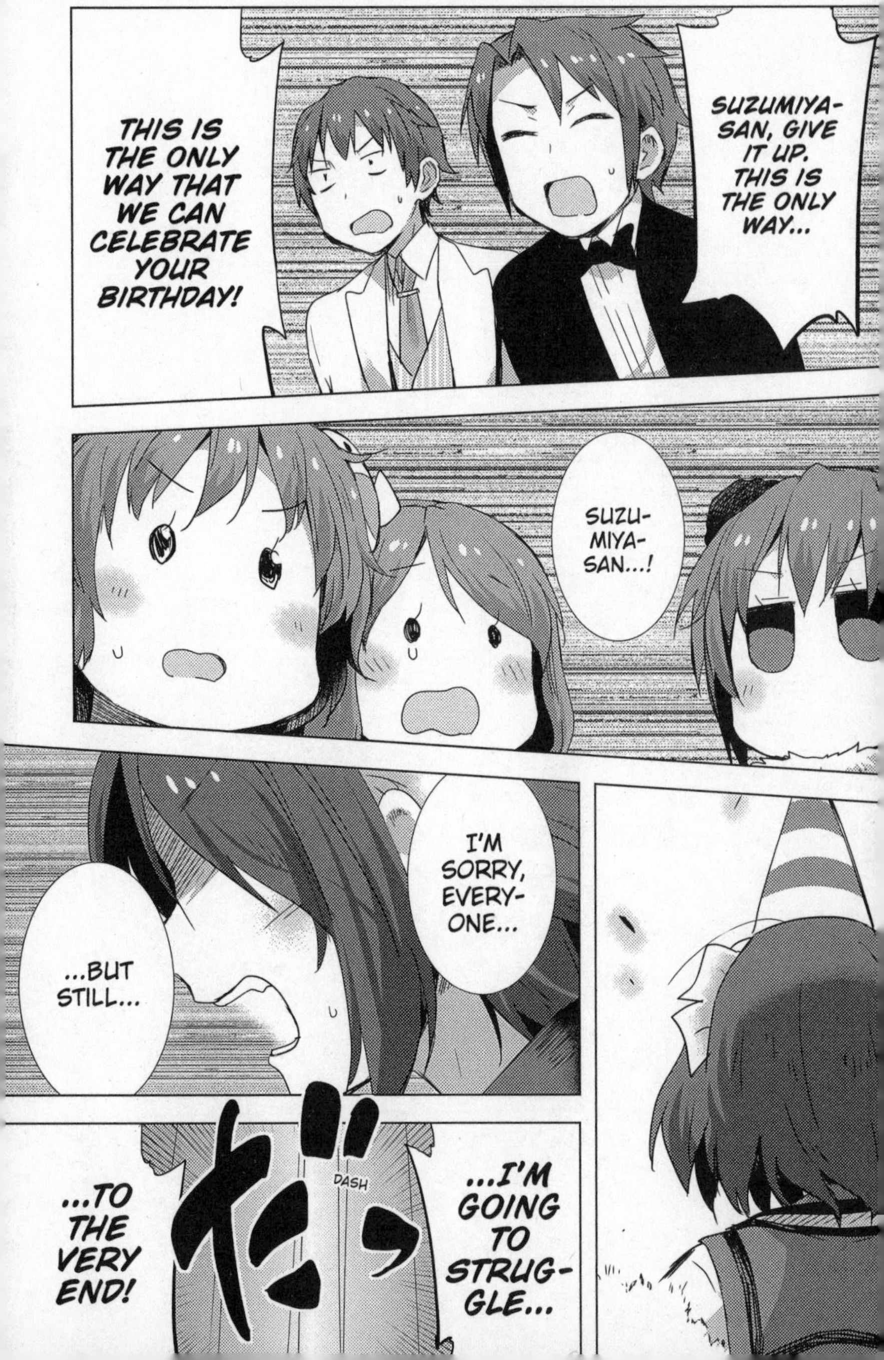
SUZUMIYA-SAN, GIVE IT UP. THIS IS THE ONLY WAY...
THIS IS THE ONLY WAY THAT WE CAN CELEBRATE YOUR BIRTHDAY!
SUZU-MIYA-SAN...!
I'M SORRY, EVERY-ONE...
...BUT STILL...
...I'M GOING TO STRUG-GLE...
DASH
...TO THE VERY END!

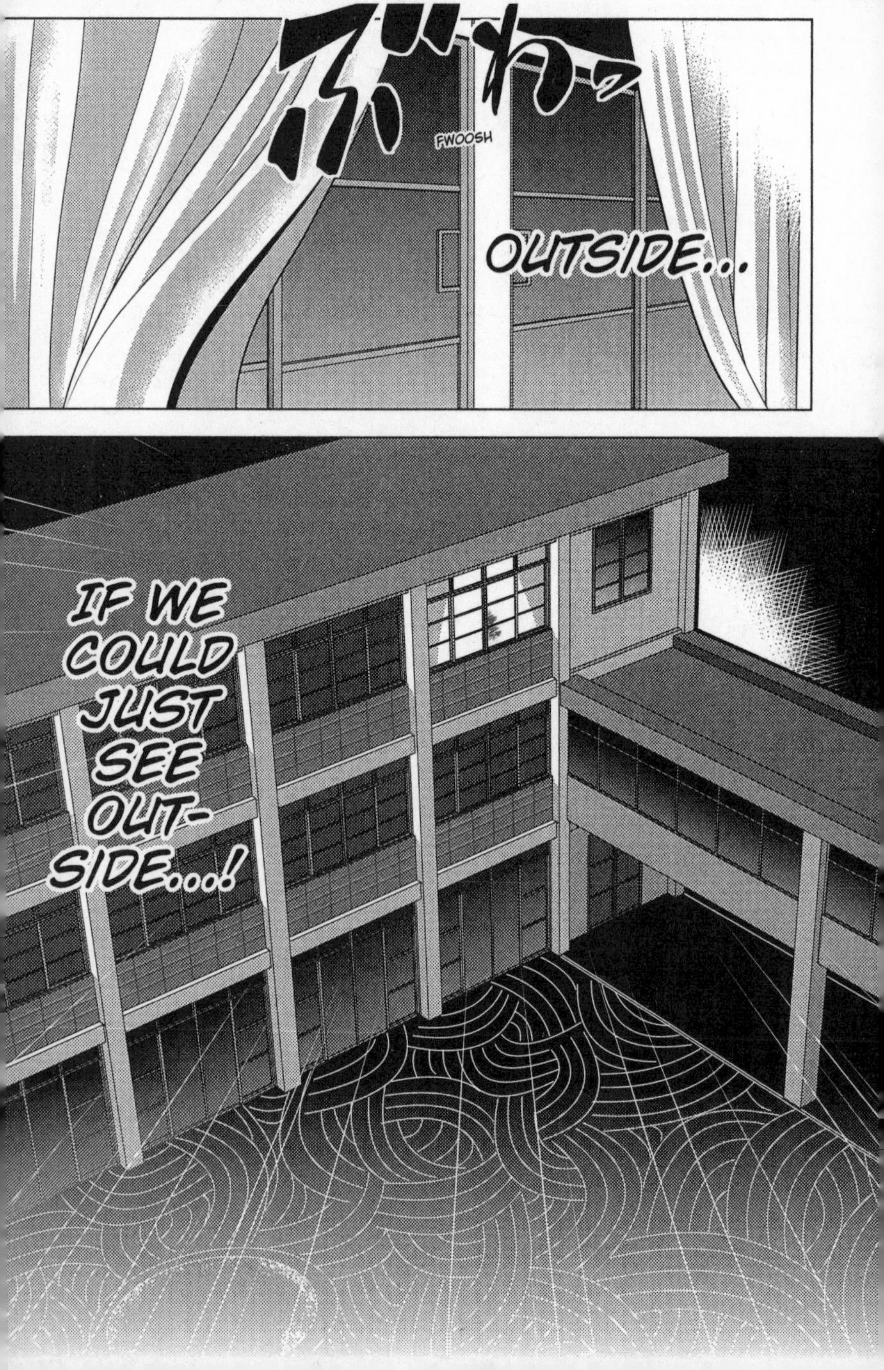
ぶわっ
FWOOSH
OUTSIDE...
IF WE COULD JUST SEE OUT-SIDE...!

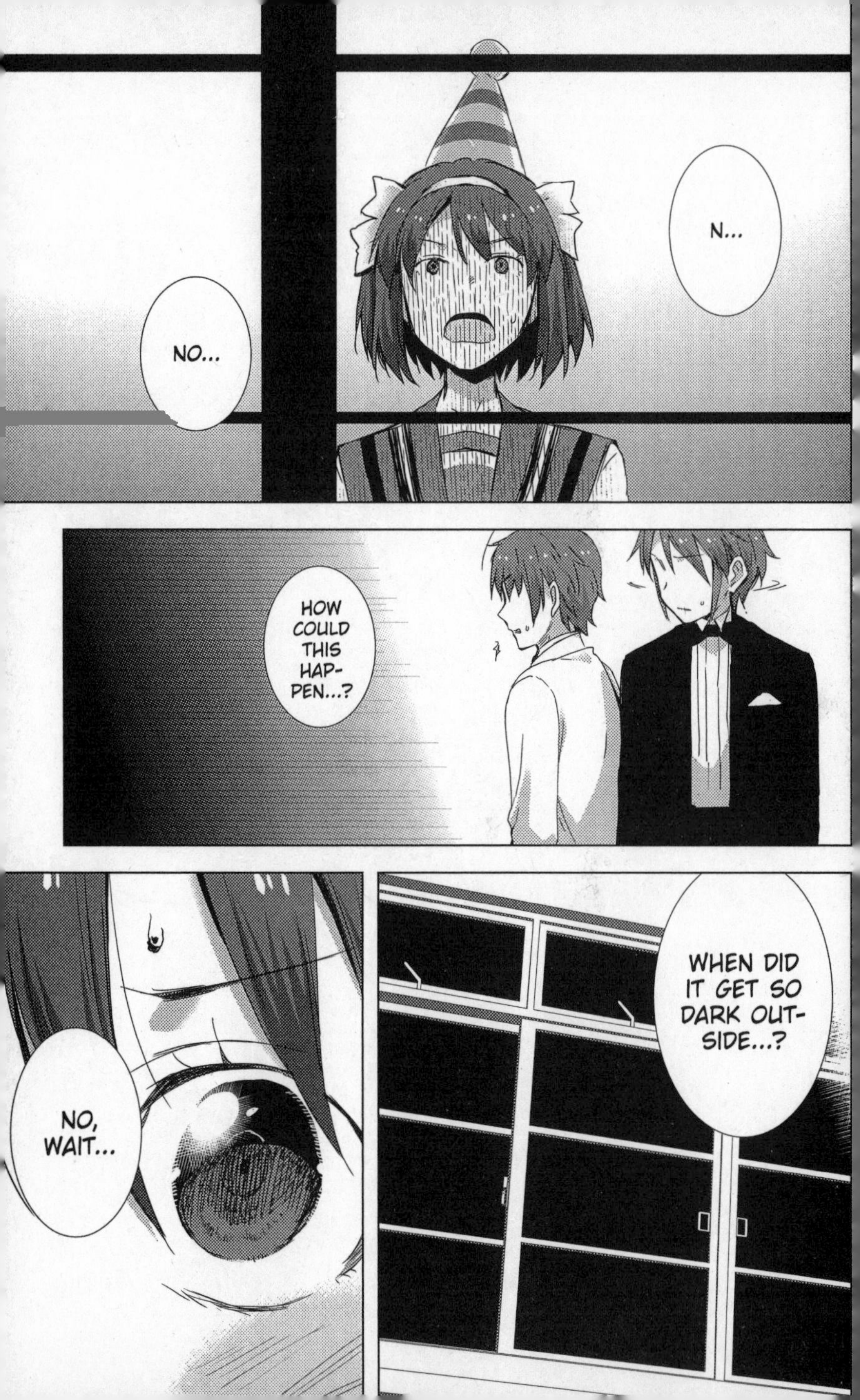
N...
NO...
HOW COULD THIS HAP-PEN...?
WHEN DID IT GET SO DARK OUT-SIDE...?
NO, WAIT...

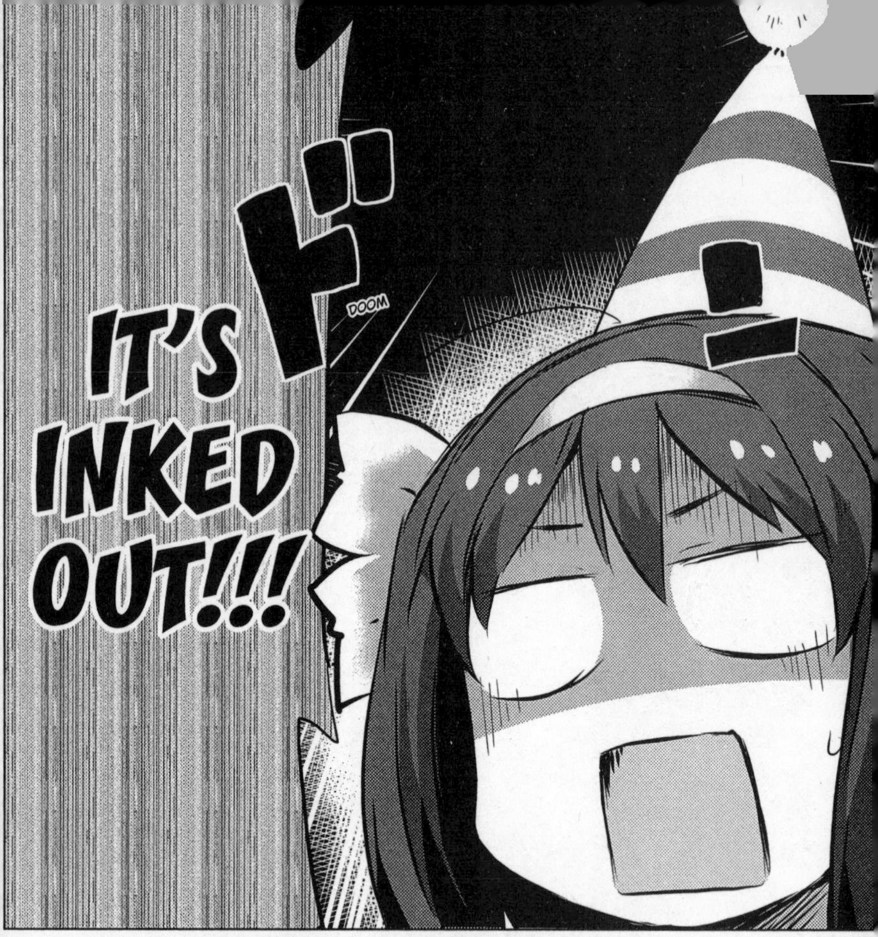
ド
DOOM
IT'S INKED OUT!!!

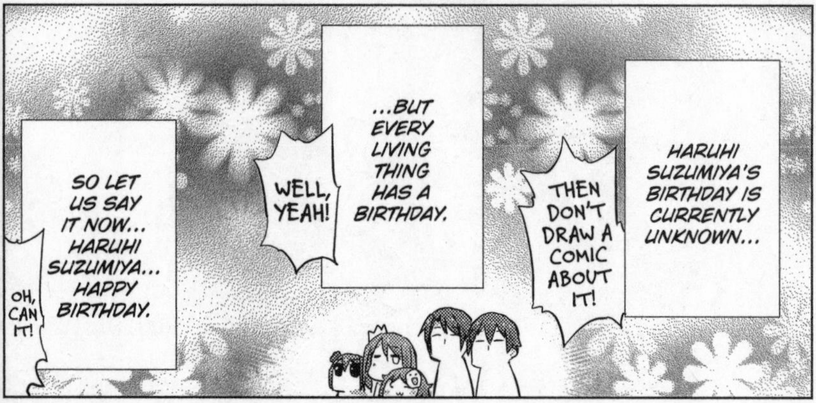
HARUHI SUZUMIYA'S BIRTHDAY IS CURRENTLY UNKNOWN...
THEN DON'T DRAW A COMIC ABOUT IT!
...BUT EVERY LIVING THING HAS A BIRTHDAY.
WELL, YEAH!
SO LET US SAY IT NOW... HARUHI SUZUMIYA... HAPPY BIRTHDAY.
OH, CAN IT!

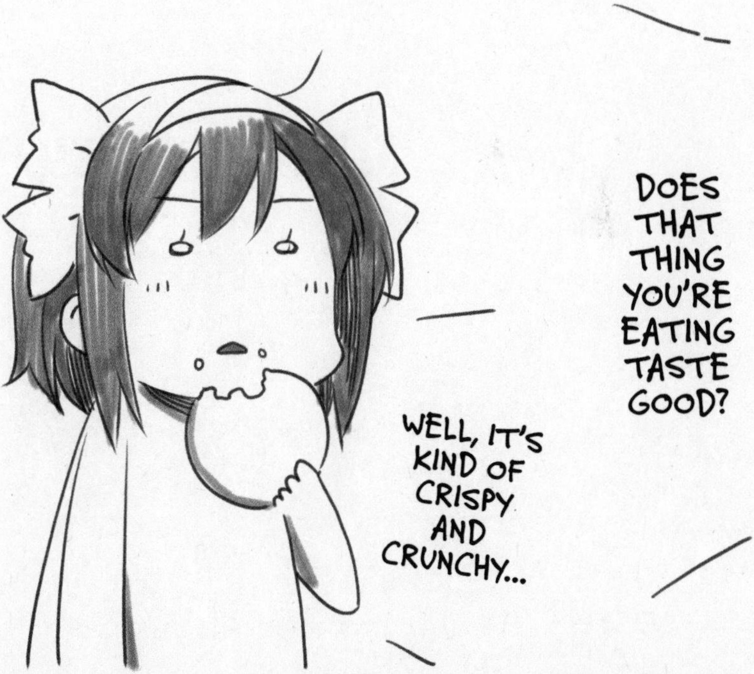
DOES THAT THING YOU'RE EATING TASTE GOOD?
WELL, IT'S KIND OF CRISPY AND CRUNCHY...

DON'T SPEND A WHOLE YEAR
GETTING TO THE SECOND HALF...

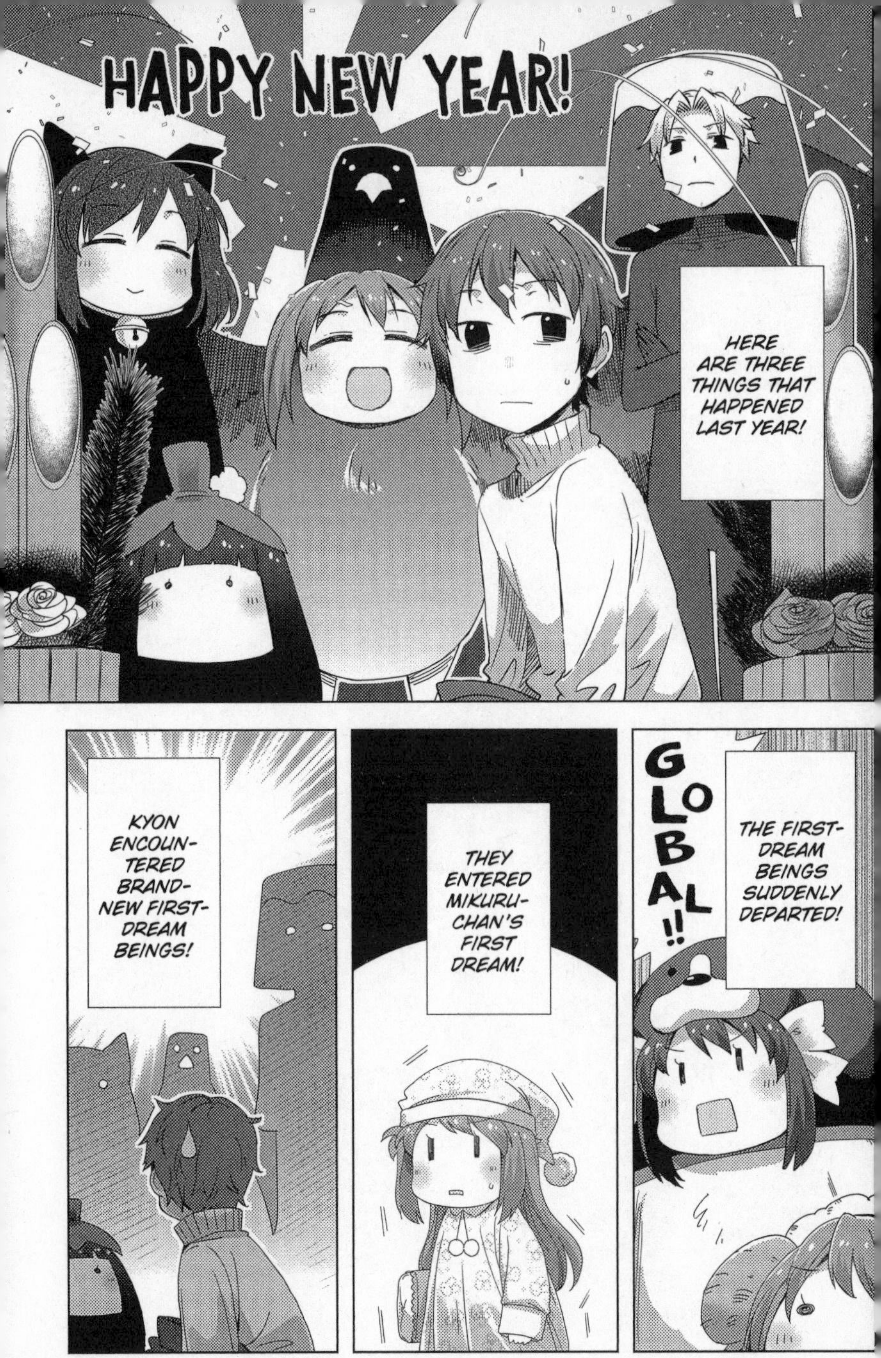
HAPPY NEW YEAR!
HERE ARE THREE THINGS THAT HAPPENED LAST YEAR!
THE FIRST-DREAM BEINGS SUDDENLY DEPARTED!
GLOBAL!!
THEY ENTERED MIKURU-CHAN'S FIRST DREAM!
KYON ENCOUNTERED BRAND-NEW FIRST-DREAM BEINGS!

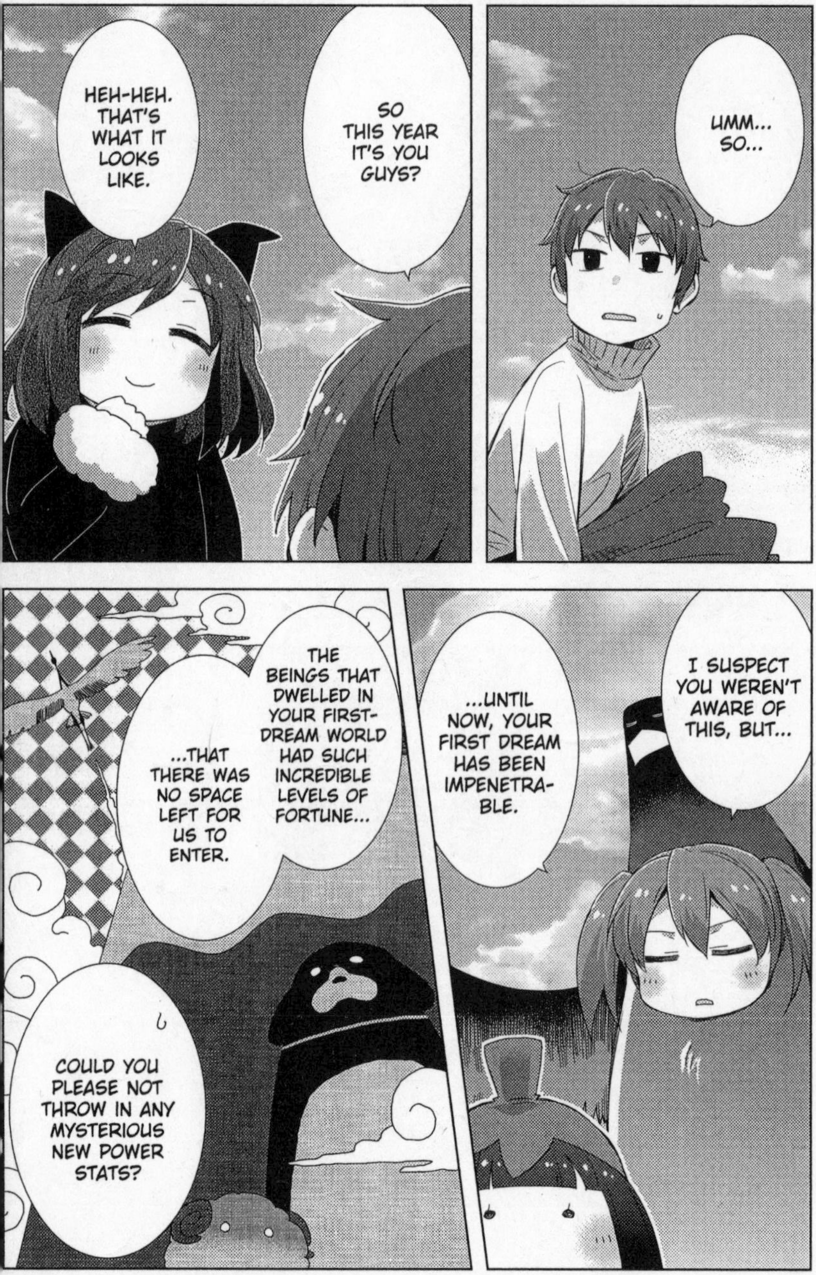
UMM... SO...
SO THIS YEAR IT'S YOU GUYS?
HEH-HEH. THAT'S WHAT IT LOOKS LIKE.
I SUSPECT YOU WEREN'T AWARE OF THIS, BUT...
...UNTIL NOW, YOUR FIRST DREAM HAS BEEN IMPENETRA-BLE.
THE BEINGS THAT DWELLED IN YOUR FIRST-DREAM WORLD HAD SUCH INCREDIBLE LEVELS OF FORTUNE...
...THAT THERE WAS NO SPACE LEFT FOR US TO ENTER.
COULD YOU PLEASE NOT THROW IN ANY MYSTERIOUS NEW POWER STATS?

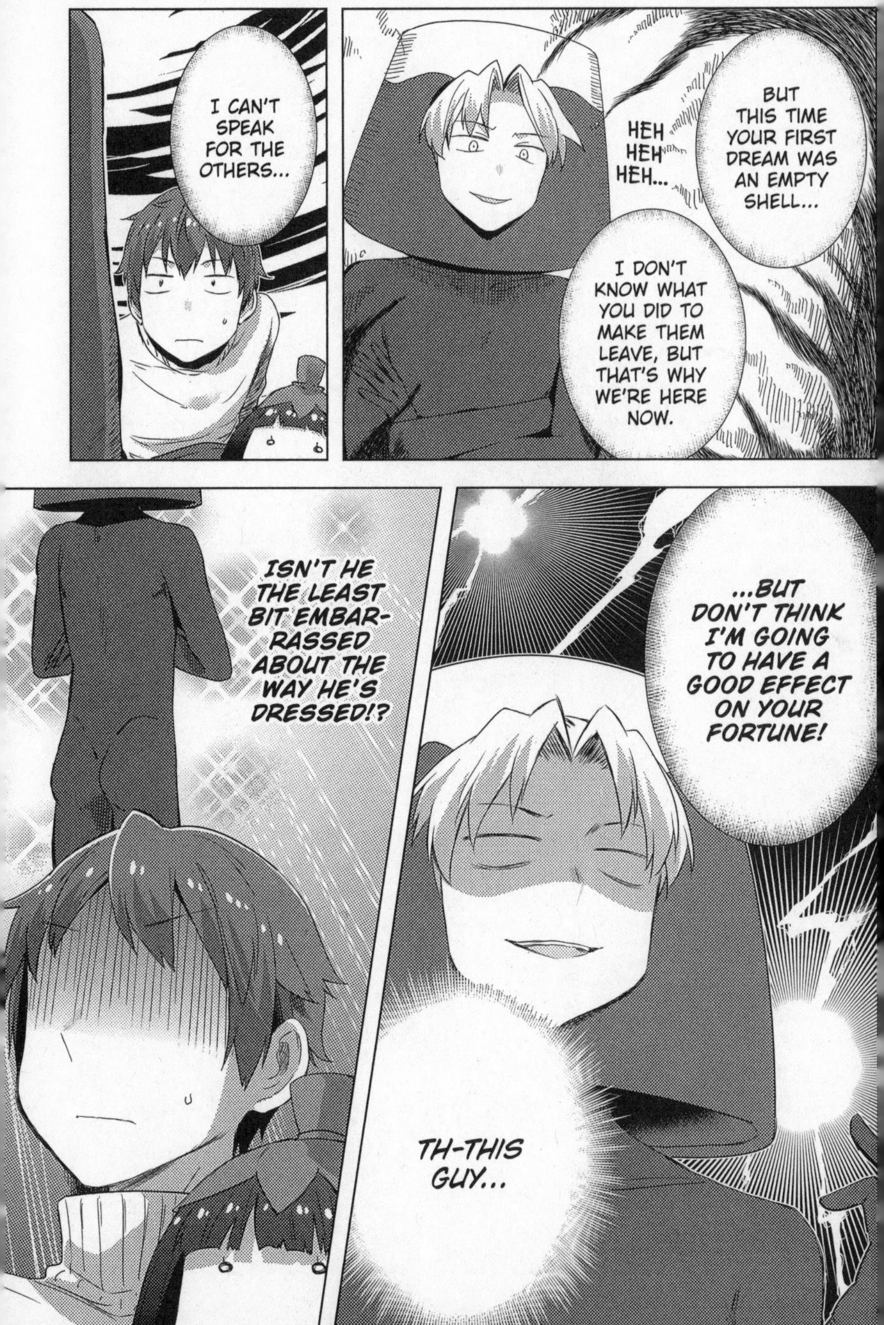
BUT THIS TIME YOUR FIRST DREAM WAS AN EMPTY SHELL...
HEH HEH HEH...
I DON'T KNOW WHAT YOU DID TO MAKE THEM LEAVE, BUT THAT'S WHY WE'RE HERE NOW.
I CAN'T SPEAK FOR THE OTHERS...
...BUT DON'T THINK I'M GOING TO HAVE A GOOD EFFECT ON YOUR FORTUNE!
TH-THIS GUY...
ISN'T HE THE LEAST BIT EMBAR-RASSED ABOUT THE WAY HE'S DRESSED!?

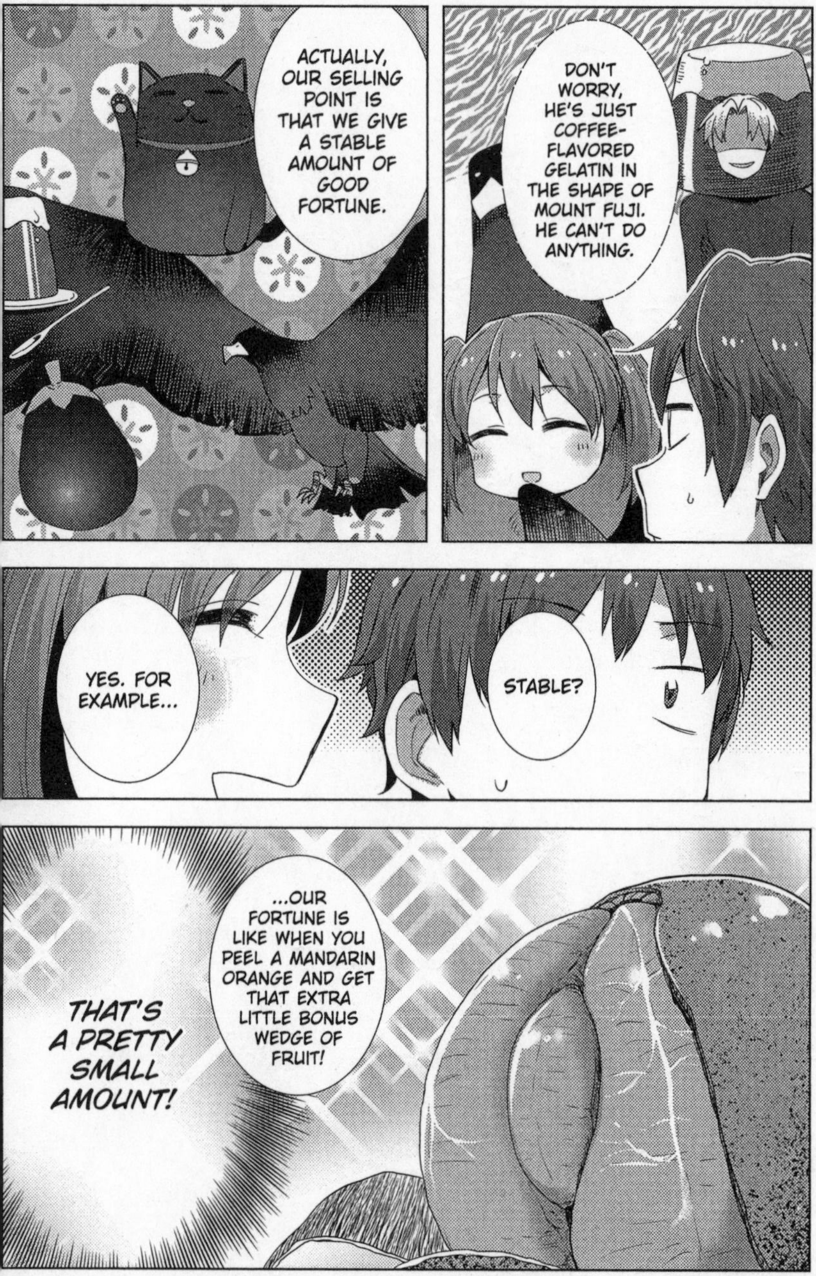
DON'T WORRY, HE'S JUST COFFEE-FLAVORED GELATIN IN THE SHAPE OF MOUNT FUJI. HE CAN'T DO ANYTHING.
ACTUALLY, OUR SELLING POINT IS THAT WE GIVE A STABLE AMOUNT OF GOOD FORTUNE.
STABLE?
YES. FOR EXAMPLE...
...OUR FORTUNE IS LIKE WHEN YOU PEEL A MANDARIN ORANGE AND GET THAT EXTRA LITTLE BONUS WEDGE OF FRUIT!
THAT'S A PRETTY SMALL AMOUNT!

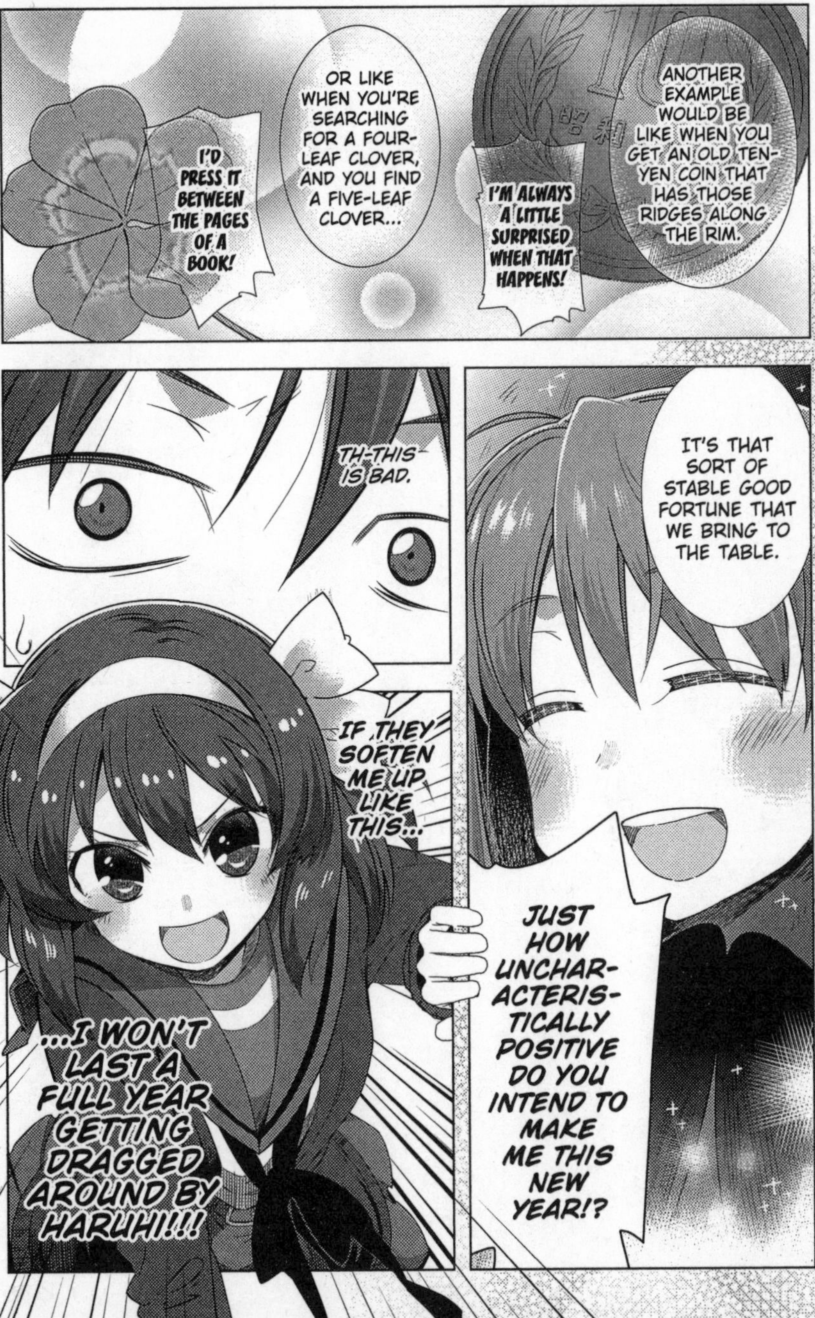
ANOTHER EXAMPLE WOULD BE LIKE WHEN YOU GET AN OLD TEN-YEN COIN THAT HAS THOSE RIDGES ALONG THE RIM.
I'M ALWAYS A LITTLE SURPRISED WHEN THAT HAPPENS!
OR LIKE WHEN YOU'RE SEARCHING FOR A FOUR-LEAF CLOVER, AND YOU FIND A FIVE-LEAF CLOVER...
I'D PRESS IT BETWEEN THE PAGES OF A BOOK!
IT'S THAT SORT OF STABLE GOOD FORTUNE THAT WE BRING TO THE TABLE.
JUST HOW UNCHARACTERISTICALLY POSITIVE DO YOU INTEND TO MAKE ME THIS NEW YEAR!?
TH-THIS IS BAD.
IF THEY SOFTEN ME UP LIKE THIS...
...I WON'T LAST A FULL YEAR GETTING DRAGGED AROUND BY HARUHI!!!

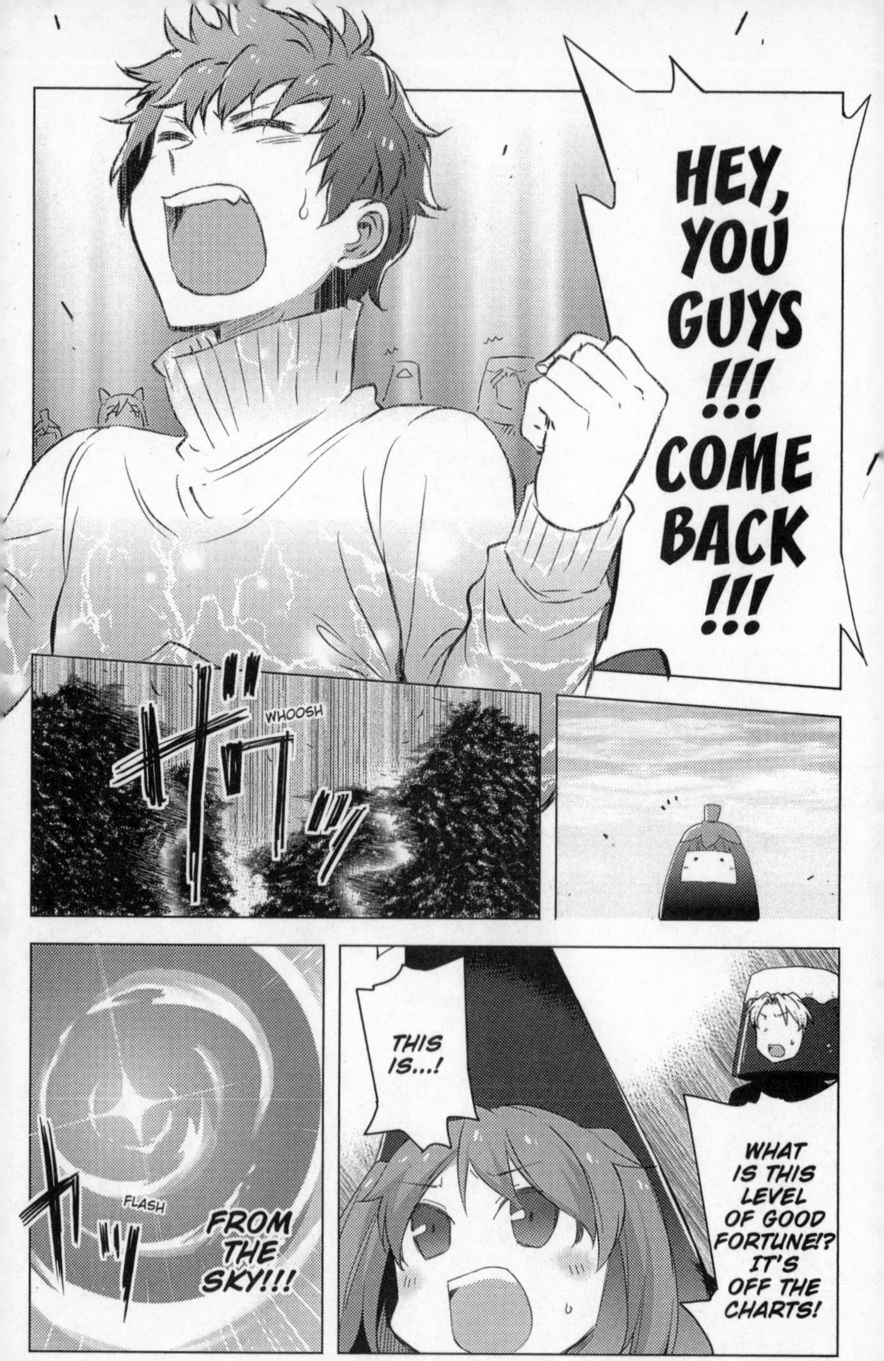
HEY, YOU GUYS!!! COME BACK!!!
WHOOSH
THIS IS...!
WHAT IS THIS LEVEL OF GOOD FORTUNE!? IT'S OFF THE CHARTS!
FLASH
FROM THE SKY!!!

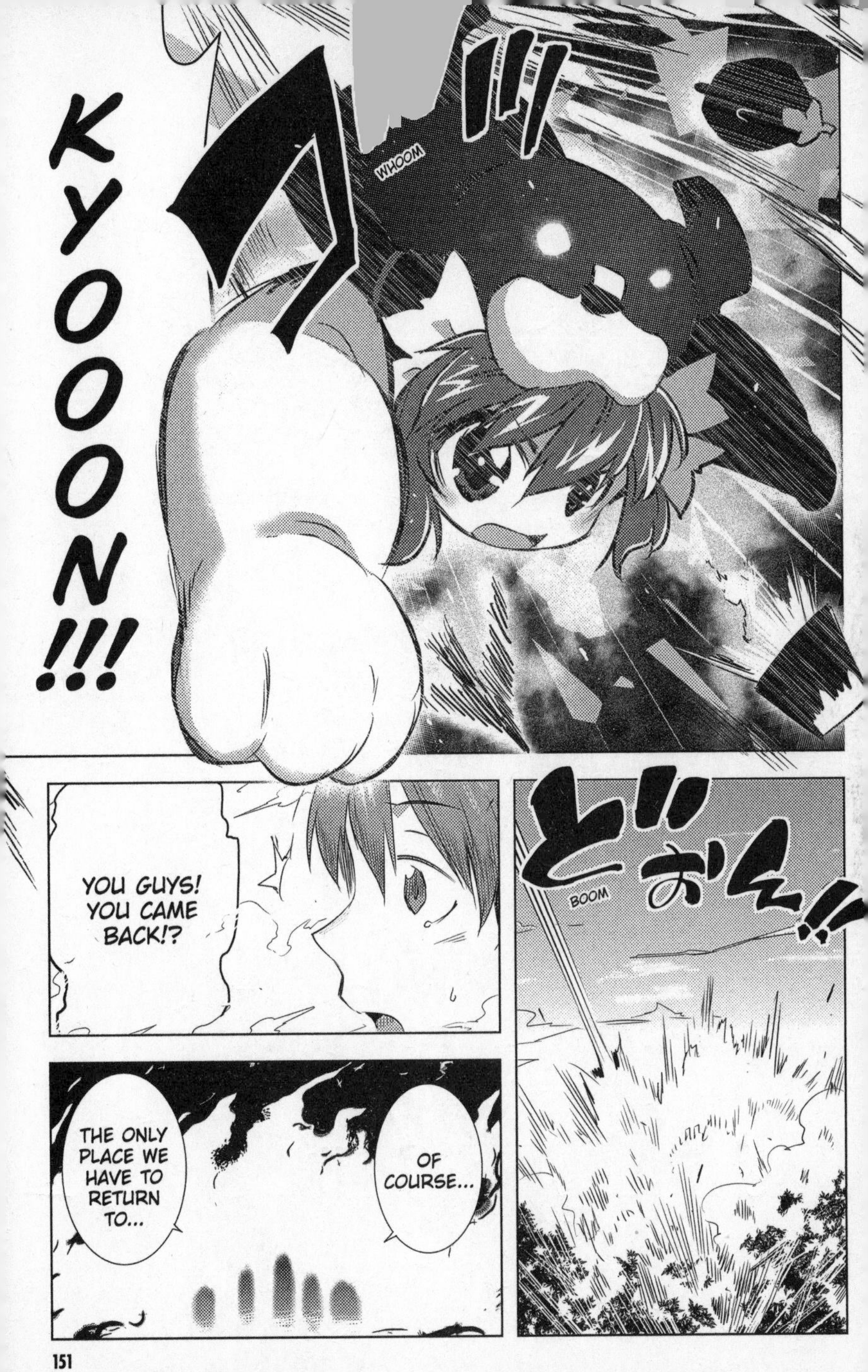
WHOOM
KYOOON!!!
どおん!!
BOOM
YOU GUYS! YOU CAME BACK!?
OF COURSE...
THE ONLY PLACE WE HAVE TO RETURN TO...

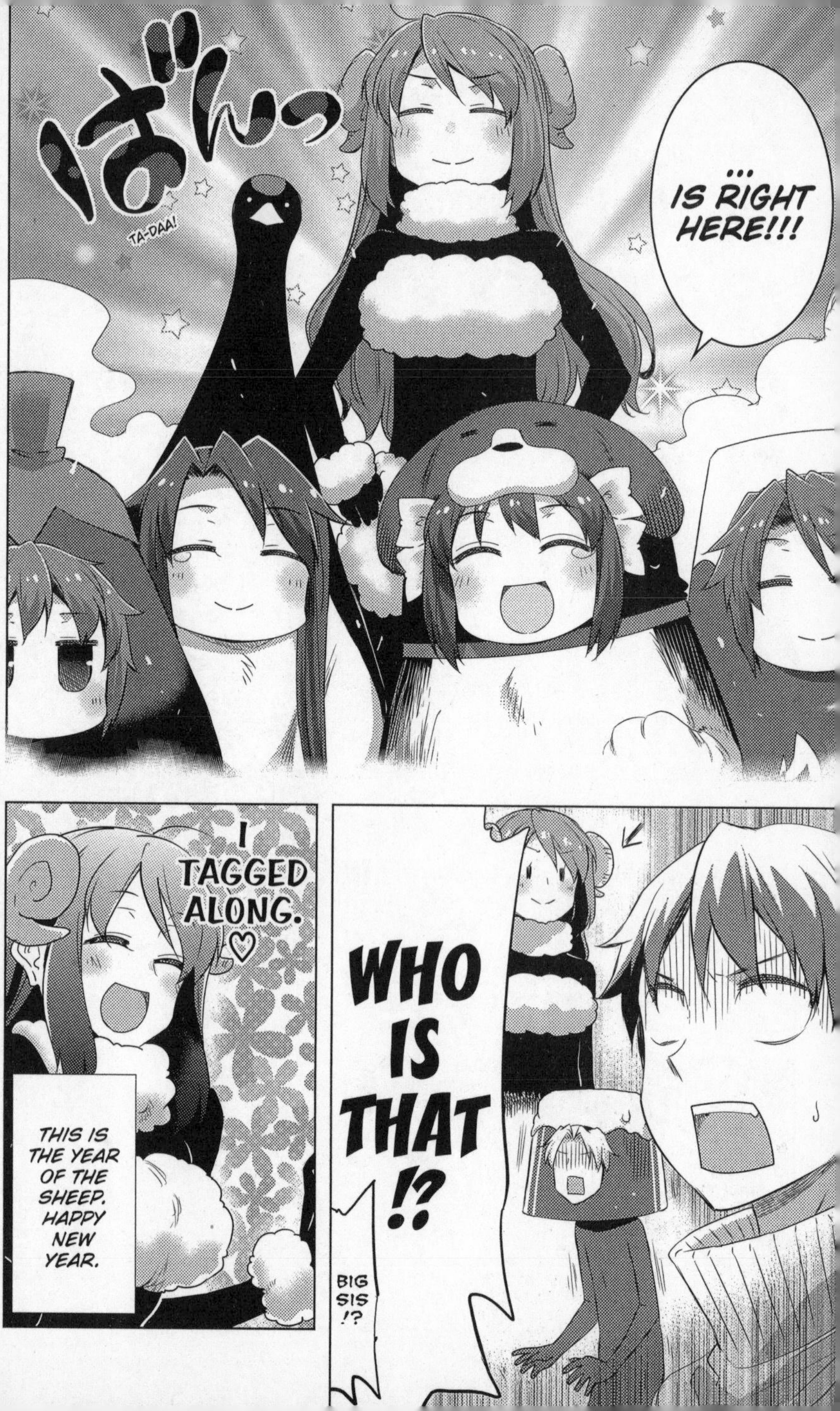
... IS RIGHT HERE!!!
ばんっ
TA-DAA!
WHO IS THAT !?
BIG SIS !?
I TAGGED ALONG. ♡
THIS IS THE YEAR OF THE SHEEP. HAPPY NEW YEAR.

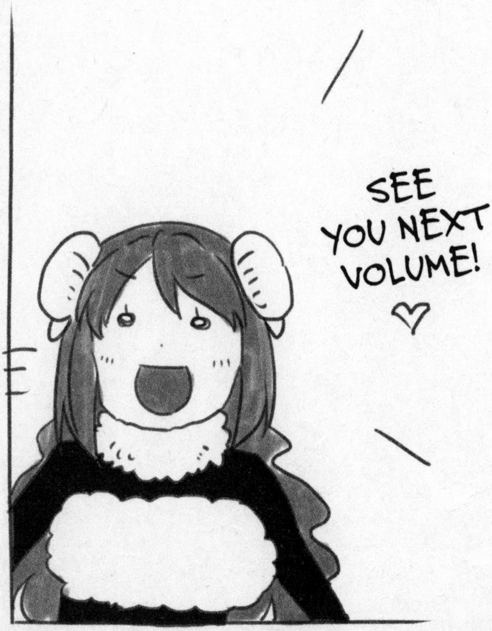
SEE YOU NEXT VOLUME! ♡

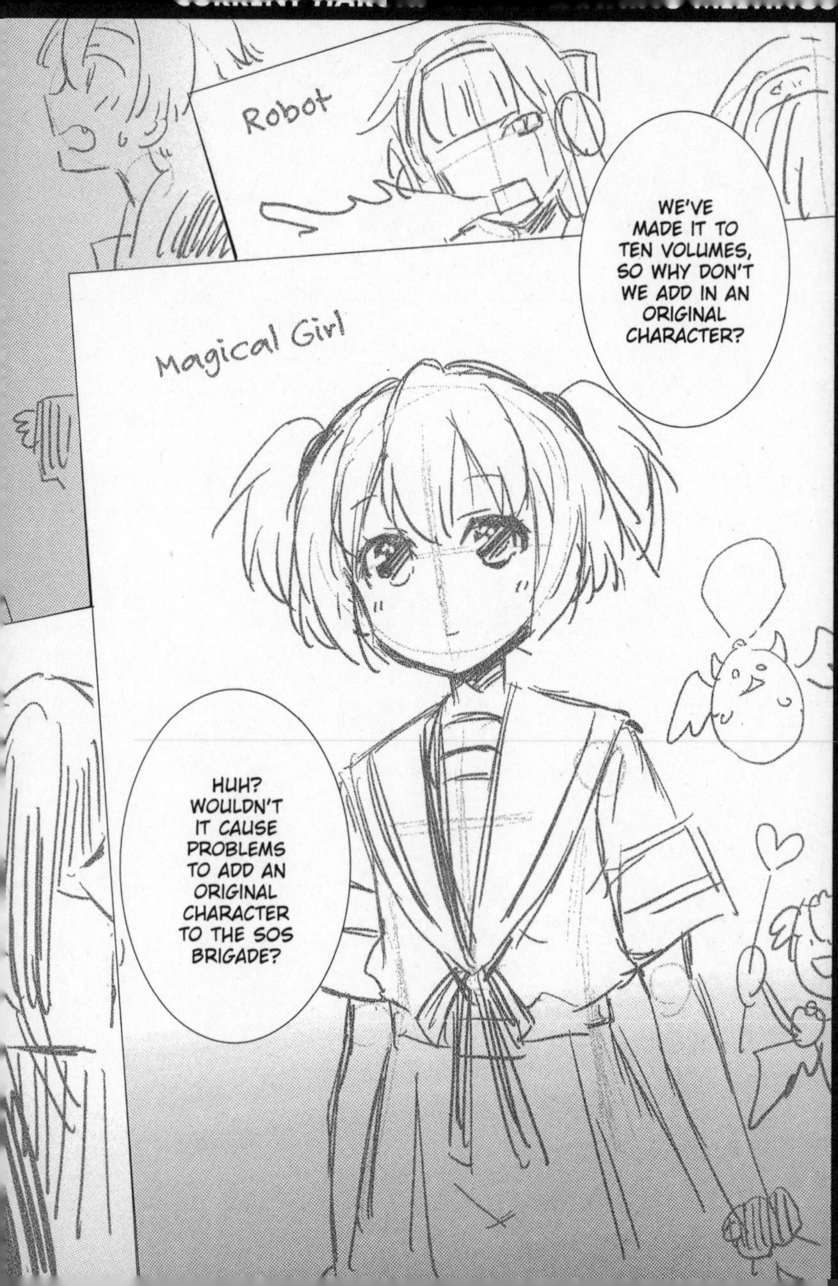
Robot
WE'VE MADE IT TO TEN VOLUMES, SO WHY DON'T WE ADD IN AN ORIGINAL CHARACTER?
Magical Girl
HUH? WOULDN'T IT CAUSE PROBLEMS TO ADD AN ORIGINAL CHARACTER TO THE SOS BRIGADE?

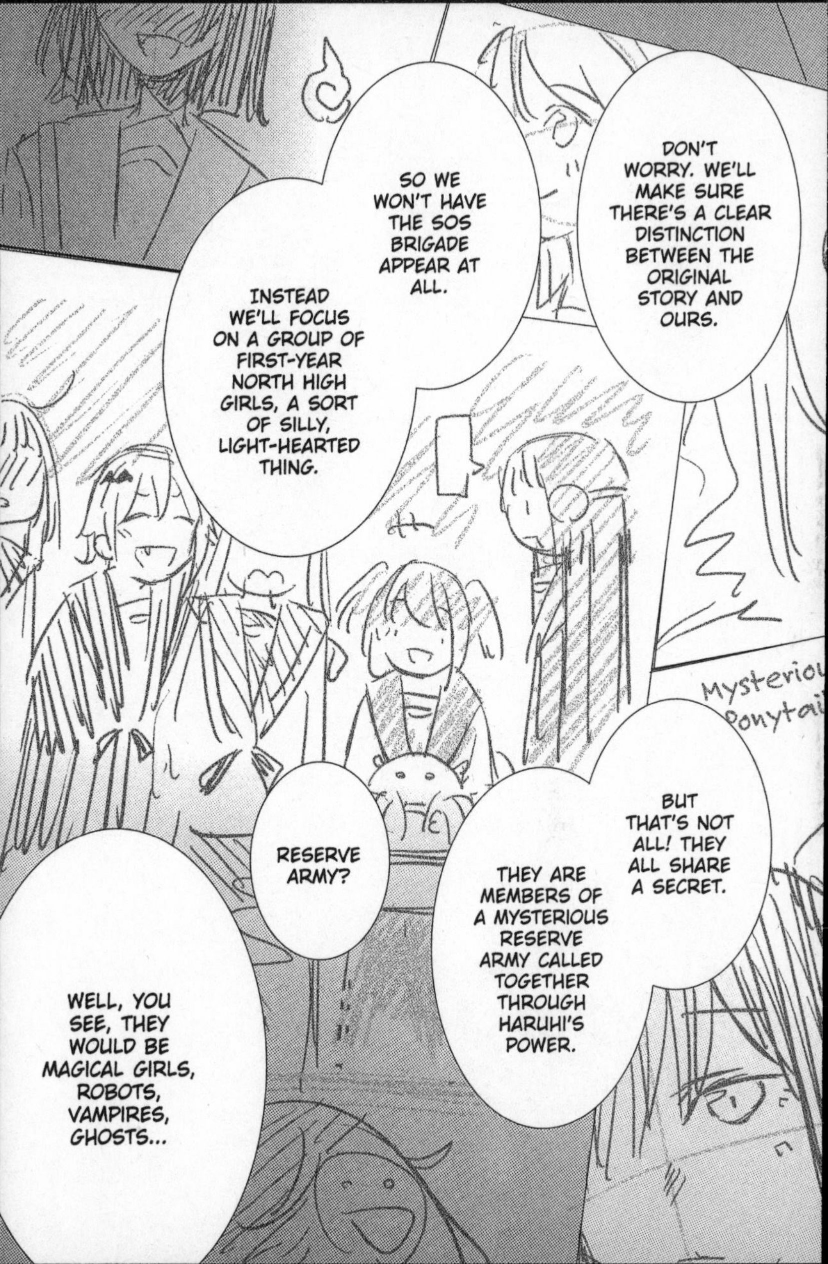
DON'T WORRY. WE'LL MAKE SURE THERE'S A CLEAR DISTINCTION BETWEEN THE ORIGINAL STORY AND OURS.
SO WE WON'T HAVE THE SOS BRIGADE APPEAR AT ALL.
INSTEAD WE'LL FOCUS ON A GROUP OF FIRST-YEAR NORTH HIGH GIRLS, A SORT OF SILLY, LIGHT-HEARTED THING.
Mysteriou
Ponytai
BUT THAT'S NOT ALL! THEY ALL SHARE A SECRET.
THEY ARE MEMBERS OF A MYSTERIOUS RESERVE ARMY CALLED TOGETHER THROUGH HARUHI'S POWER.
RESERVE ARMY?
WELL, YOU SEE, THEY WOULD BE MAGICAL GIRLS, ROBOTS, VAMPIRES, GHOSTS...

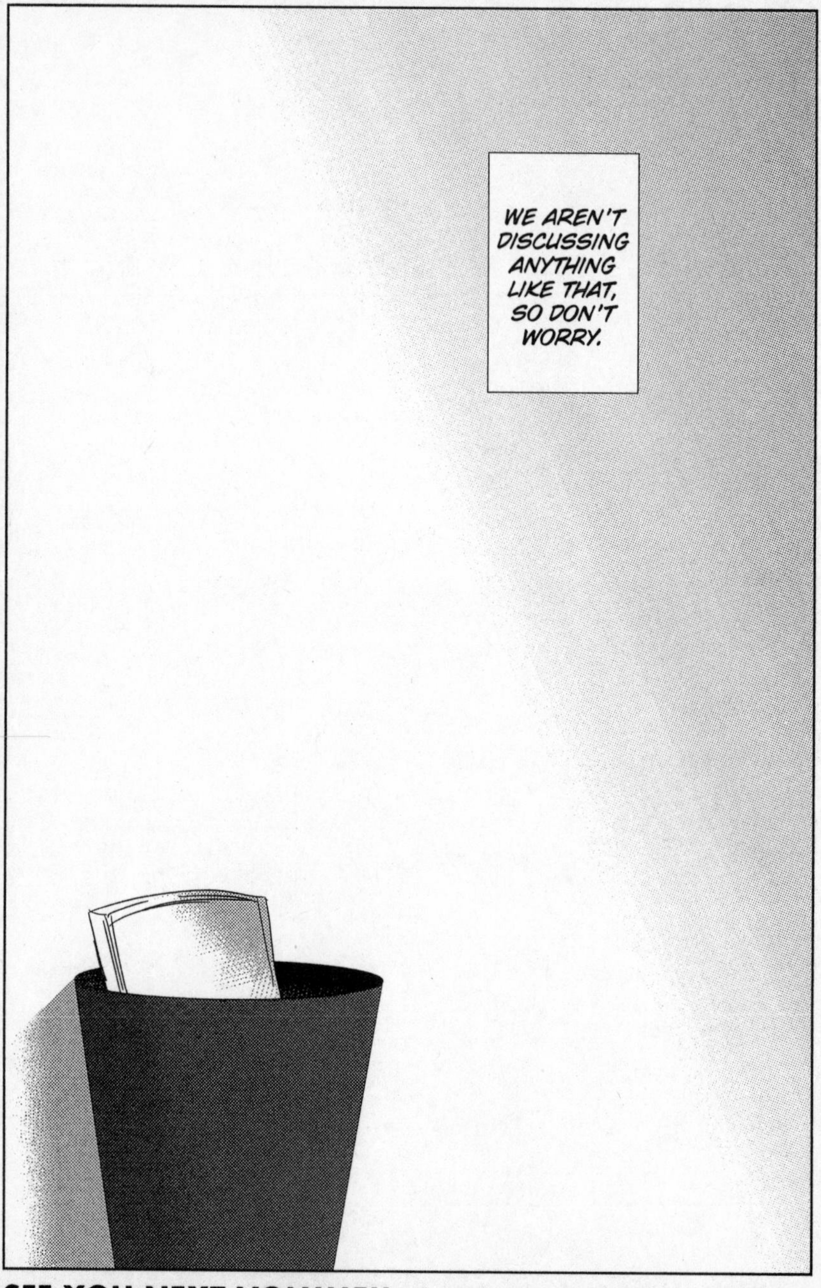
WE AREN'T DISCUSSING ANYTHING LIKE THAT, SO DON'T WORRY.

SEE YOU NEXT VOLUME!!

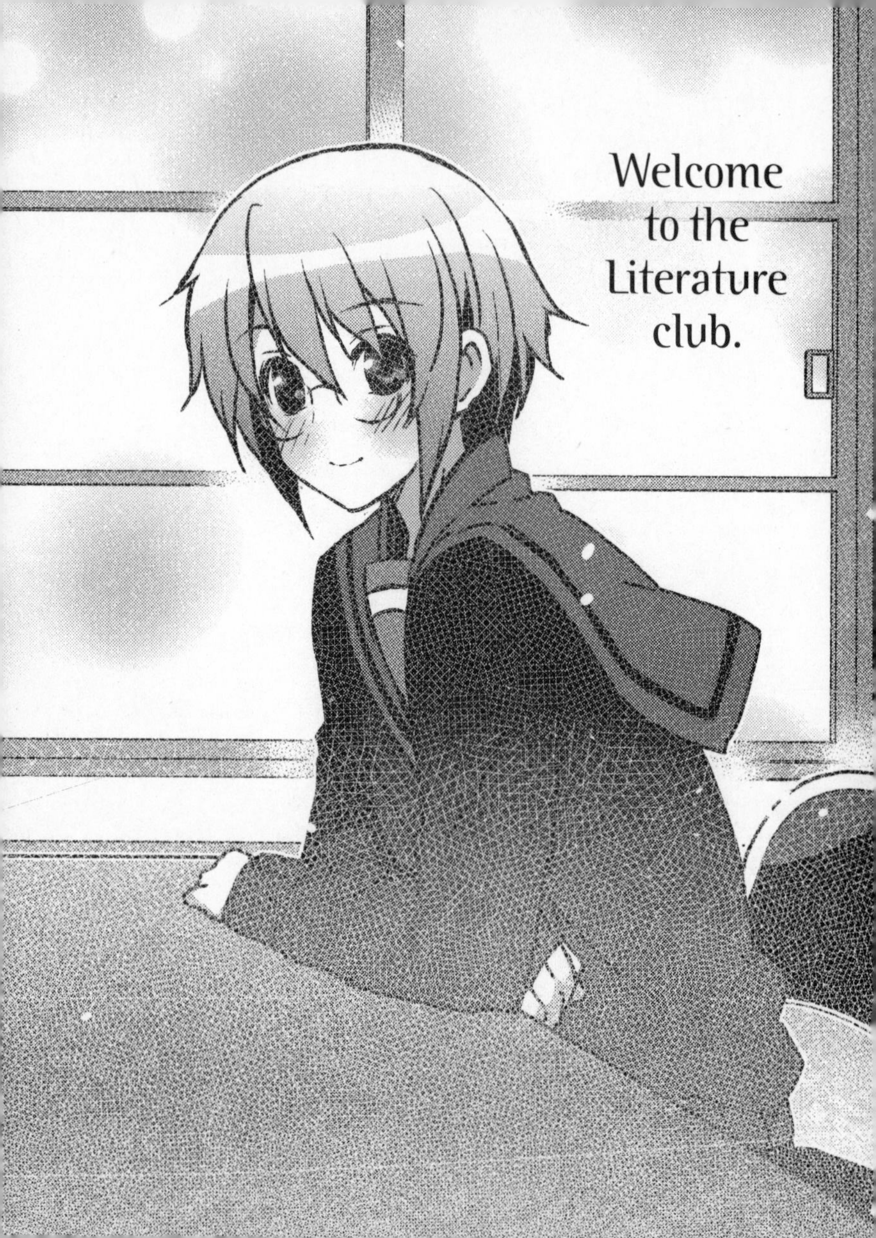
Welcome to the Literature club.

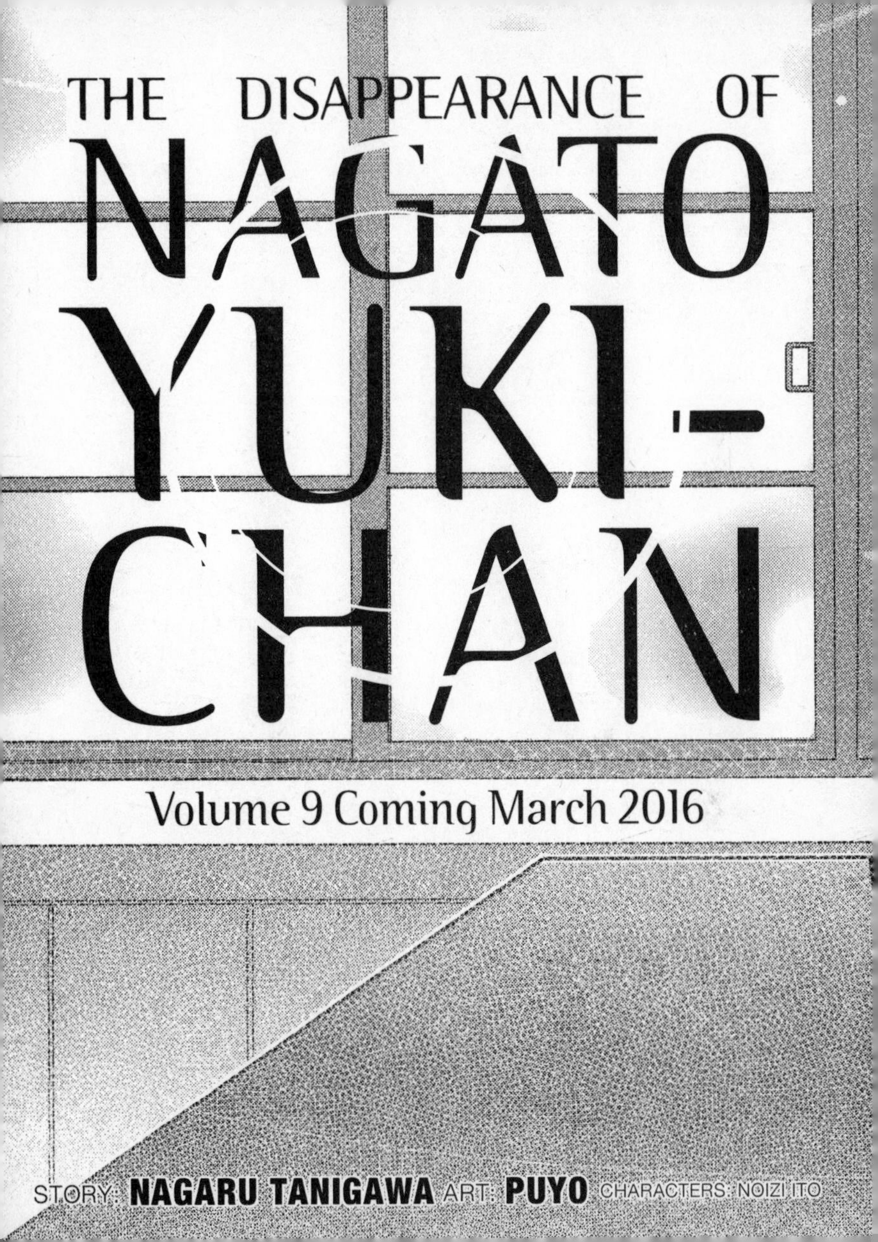
THE DISAPPEARANCE OF NAGATO YUKI-CHAN
Volume 9 Coming March 2016
STORY: NAGARU TANIGAWA ART: PUYO CHARACTERS: NOIZI ITO

HAVE YOU BEEN TURNED ON TO LIGHT NOVELS YET?

IN STORES NOW!

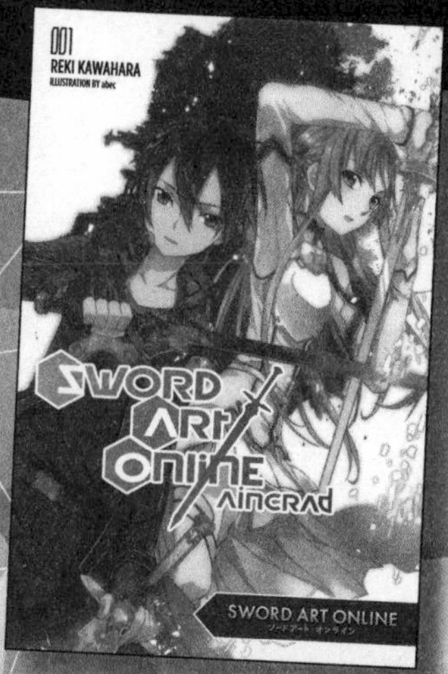
001
REKI KAWAHARA
ILLUSTRATION BY abec
Sword Art Online
Aincrad
SWORD ART ONLINE

SWORD ART ONLINE, VOL. 1–6
SWORD ART ONLINE, PROGRESSIVE 1-3

The chart-topping light novel series that spawned the explosively popular anime and manga adaptations!

MANGA ADAPTATION AVAILABLE NOW!

SWORD ART ONLINE © Reki Kawahara ILLUSTRATION: abec
KADOKAWA CORPORATION ASCII MEDIA WORKS

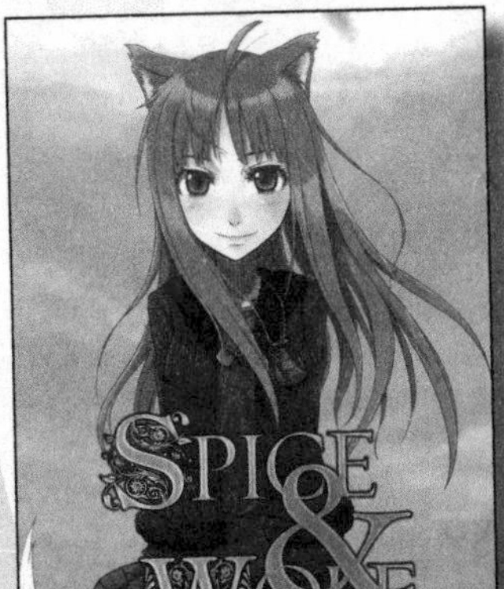
Spice & Wolf
Vol. 1
ISUNA HASEKURA

ACCEL WORLD, VOL. 1–5

Prepare to accelerate with an action-packed cyber-thriller from the bestselling author of *Sword Art Online*.

MANGA ADAPTATION AVAILABLE NOW!

ACCEL WORLD © Reki Kawahara ILLUSTRATION: HIMA
KADOKAWA CORPORATION ASCII MEDIA WORKS

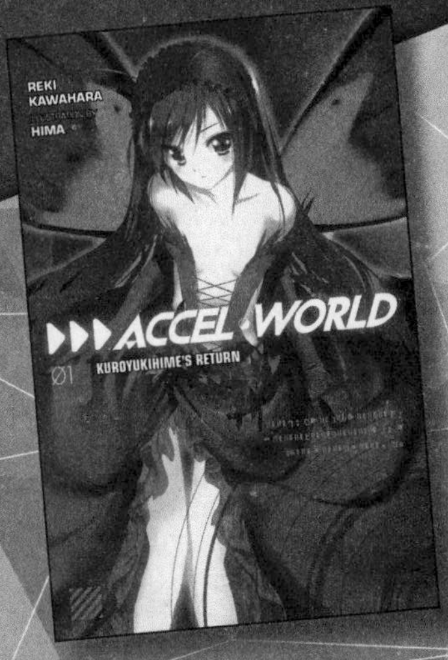
REKI KAWAHARA
HIMA
ACCEL WORLD
01
KUROYUKIHIME'S RETURN

SPICE AND WOLF, VOL. 1–16

A disgruntled goddess joins a traveling merchant in this light novel series that inspired the *New York Times* bestselling manga.

MANGA ADAPTATION AVAILABLE NOW!

SPICE AND WOLF © Isuna Hasekura ILLUSTRATION: Jyuu Ayakura
KADOKAWA CORPORATION ASCII MEDIA WORKS

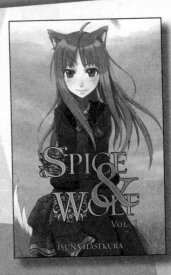

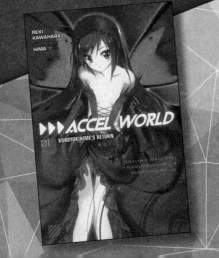

WELCOME TO IKEBUKURO, WHERE TOKYO'S WILDEST CHARACTERS GATHER!!

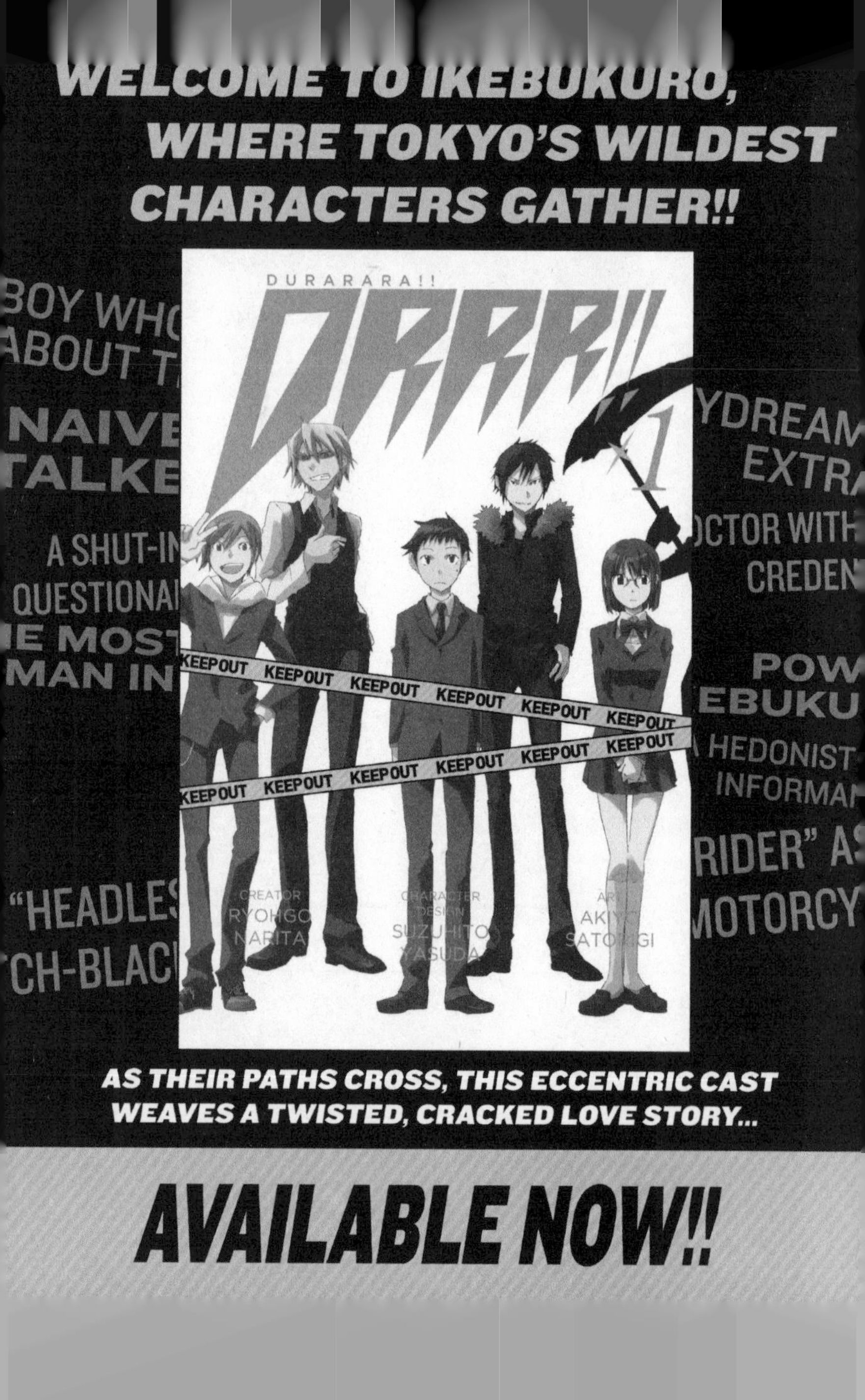
DURARARA!!
DRRR!!
1
KEEPOUT
CREATOR
RYOHGO NARITA
CHARACTER DESIGN
SUZUHITO YASUDA
ART

AS THEIR PATHS CROSS, THIS ECCENTRIC CAST WEAVES A TWISTED, CRACKED LOVE STORY...

AVAILABLE NOW!!

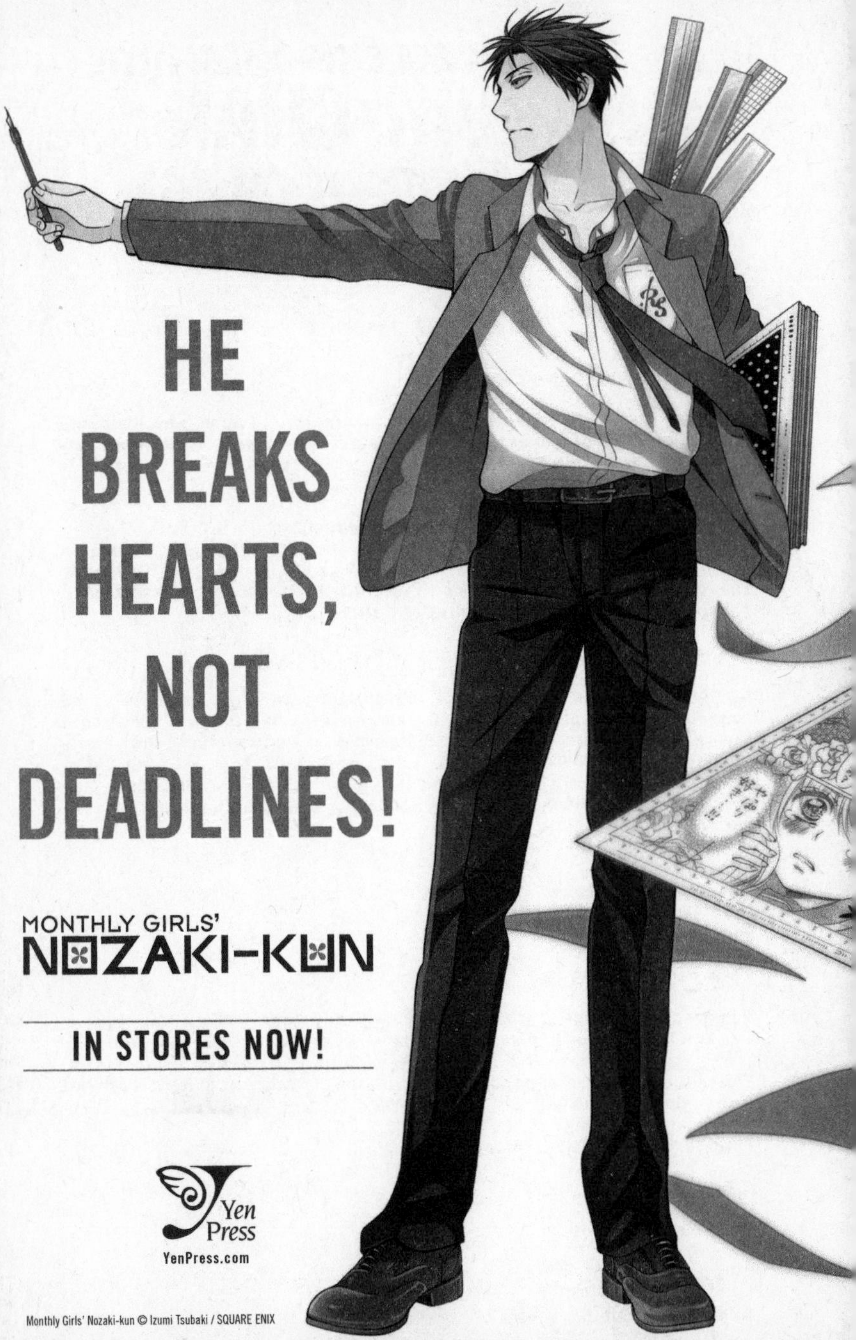
HE BREAKS HEARTS, NOT DEADLINES!
MONTHLY GIRLS' NOZAKI-KUN
IN STORES NOW!
Yen Press
YenPress.com
Monthly Girls' Nozaki-kun © Izumi Tsubaki / SQUARE ENIX

THE MELANCHOLY OF SUZUMIYA
HARUHI-CHAN
⑩

Original Story: Nagaru Tanigawa
Manga: PUYO
Character Design: Noizi Ito

Translation: ZephyrRz
Lettering: Abigail Blackman

The Melancholy of Suzumiya Haruhi-chan Volume 10
© Nagaru TANIGAWA • Noizi ITO 2015 © PUYO 2015. Edited by KADOKAWA SHOTEN. First published in Japan in 2015 by KADOKAWA CORPORATION, Tokyo. English translation rights arranged with KADOKAWA CORPORATION, Tokyo, through TUTTLE-MORI AGENCY, INC., Tokyo.

English translation © 2015 by Hachette Book Group, Inc.

Yen Press
Hachette Book Group
1290 Avenue of the Americas
New York, NY 10104
www.hachettebookgroup.com
www.yenpress.com

Yen Press is an imprint of Hachette Book Group, Inc.
The Yen Press name and logo are trademarks of Hachette Book Group, Inc.

The publisher is not responsible for websites (or their content) that are not owned by the publisher.

First Yen Press Edition: December 2015

ISBN: 978-0-316-35191-1

10 9 8 7 6 5 4 3 2 1

BVG

Printed in the United States of America